ETHNICITY AND THE AMERICAN SHORT STORY

WELLESLEY STUDIES IN CRITICAL THEORY,
LITERARY HISTORY, AND CULTURE
VOLUME 16
GARLAND REFERENCE LIBRARY OF THE HUMANITIES
VOLUME 1940

WELLESLEY STUDIES IN CRITICAL THEORY, LITERARY HISTORY, AND CULTURE

WILLIAM E. CAIN, *General Editor*

ETHNICITY AND THE AMERICAN SHORT STORY

EDITED BY
JULIE BROWN

GARLAND PUBLISHING, INC.
NEW YORK AND LONDON
1997

Library of Congress Cataloging-in-Publication Data

Ethnicity and the American short story / edited by Julie Brown.
       p.   cm. — (Garland reference library of the humanities ; vol. 1940.
Wellesley studies in critical theory, literary history and culture ; vol. 16)
   Includes bibliographical references (p.).
   ISBN 0-8153-2105-8 (alk. paper)
   1. American fiction—Minority authors—History and criticism.
2. Short stories, American—History and criticism.   3. Ethnic groups
in literature. 4. Minorities in literature. 5. Ethnicity in literature.
I. Brown, Julie, 1961– . II. Series: Garland reference library of the humanities ; vol. 1940. III. Series: Garland reference library of the
humanities. Wellesley studies in critical theory, literary history and culture ; vol. 16.
√ PS153.M56E84   1997
   813'.0109920693—dc21   97-25196
                                                   CIP

Printed on acid-free, 250-year-life paper
Manufactured in the United States of America

For My Children, Bobby and Maggie

And for My Grandmother, Cloud-Tipped-Woman, Who
Died Before She Could Tell Them Her Stories

Contents

Contributors

Julie Brown is an English instructor at Clatsop Community College in Astoria, Oregon. A previous work of hers, entitled *American Women Short Story Writers,* was published by Garland Publishing in 1995. She has also written over a dozen children's books, poems, short stories, and critical articles.

Rocío G. Davis has a B.A. in English literature from the Ateneo de Manila University, Philippines, and a Ph.D. from the University of Navarre, Spain, and is currently professor of American and postcolonial literature at the University of Navarre. Her main research interests are Asian American and postcolonial literature, and she has recently edited a volume on ethnic fiction in Canada. Funding for the research for this article has come from the "Literature and History in the Twentieth Century" project sponsored by the Spanish Ministry of Education.

Susan E. Griffin is a graduate student in the doctoral program in English at the State University of New York at Stonybrook. She currently is working on her dissertation, an analysis of the historical narratives of Joan Didion, Susan Sontag, and Jayne Anne Phillips.

Madelyn Jablon is an independent scholar who divides her time between Philadelphia and Rehoboth Beach, Delaware. She is the author of numerous essays on African American literature and theory. Her first book, *Black Metafiction: Self-Consciousness in African American Literature,* was published recently by the University of Iowa Press.

Margot Kelley is an assistant professor at Ursinus College in Pennsylvania, where her teaching emphasis is recent American literature and theory. She is currently exploring ways in which contemporary science, new narrative genres, and multiethnic U.S. literature can be considered together. She is especially interested in ideas of complexity in feminist theory and in both literature and science.

Susan Koppelman lives and works in Tucson, Arizona. She is one of America's leading scholars in the field of the American short story, especially stories by women. She has edited numerous anthologies of short stories, including *Between Mothers and Daughters: Stories Across a Generation*; *Women's Friendships: A Collection of Short Stories*; *Signet Classic Book of Southern Short Stories* and many others. She is currently working on *The History of the Short Story in the United States: 1826–Present.*

Laurie Leach is an associate professor of English at Hawaii Pacific University in Honolulu. Her work has been published in *College English, Biography,* and *The South Central Review.*

Bill Mullen is an associate professor of English at Youngstown State University. He has recently edited a volume of black women's short stories and is working on a study of black short fiction.

Gail Y. Okawa is an assistant professor of English at Youngstown State University. She has published several articles on multi-culturalism in writing and reading, including "Cross-Talk: Talking Cross-Difference," which appeared in *Writing in Multicultural Settings* (MLA Publications).

Linda Palmer is a professor of American literature at California State University, Sacramento, where she has designed and teaches courses in Native American oral myth and contemporary literature. She regularly gives presentations on Native American literature to university, high school, and community groups. She most recently presented a paper on Native American poets Simon Ortiz and Joy Harjo at the Emerging Literature of the Southwest Conference in El Paso, Texas, in September 1996.

Carol Roh-Spaulding is a graduate student at the University of Iowa.

John Streamas, an immigrant Japanese American, is working toward a Ph.D. in American Culture studies and is teaching Asian American studies at Bowling Green State University. He has published stories, poems, and reviews, as well as other studies of Asian American literature and culture. His professional goal is to understand the narratives of non-white Americans in moments of extreme oppression, especially the internment narratives of Japanese Americans.

Qun Wang is an associate professor of English at the California State University, Monterey Bay. He has authored numerous articles on American ethnic literatures and culture as well as on American drama.

He is currently completing a manuscript on August Wilson and a creative writing piece.

Hardy C. Wilcoxon has taught American literature at the Chinese University of Hong Kong for six years. He is currently on a Fulbright scholarship in Damascus with his wife, Kathy.

Chris Wise is currently on Fulbright in Africa. When he returns, he will begin a new position as an assistant professor of English at Western Washington University. He has published several articles on Arab American literature.

GENERAL EDITOR'S PREFACE

The volumes in this series, Wellesley Studies in Critical Theory, Literary History, and Culture, are designed to reflect, develop, and extend important trends and tendencies in contemporary criticism. The careful scrutiny of literary texts in their own right of course remains a crucial part of the work that critics and teachers perform: this traditional task has not been devalued or neglected. But other types of interdisciplinary and contextual work are now being done, in large measure as a result of the emphasis on "theory" that began in the late 1960s and early 1970s and that has accelerated since that time. Critics and teachers now examine texts of all sorts—literary and non-literary alike—and, more generally, have taken the entire complex, multifaceted field of culture as the object for their analytical attention. The discipline of literary studies has radically changed, and the scale and scope of this series is intended to illustrate this challenging fact.

Theory has signified many things, but one of the most crucial has been the insistent questioning of familiar categories and distinctions. As theory has grown in its scope and intensified in importance, it has reoriented the idea of the literary canon: there is no longer a single canon, but many canons. It has also opened up and complicated the meanings of history, and the materials and forms that constitute it. Literary history continues to be vigorously written, but now as a kind of history that intersects with other histories that involve politics, economics, race relations, the role of women in society, and many more. And the breadth of this historical inquiry has impelled many in literary studies to view themselves more as cultural critics and general intellectuals than as literary scholars.

Theory, history, culture: these are the formidable terms around which the volumes in this series have been organized. A number of these volumes will be the product of a single author or editor. But perhaps even more of them will be collaborative ventures, emerging from the joint enterprise of editors, essayists, and respondents or commentators. In each volume, and as a whole, the series will aim to highlight both distinctive contributions to knowledge and a process of exchange, discussion, and debate. It will make available new kinds of work, as well as fresh approaches to criticism's traditional tasks, and indicate new ways through which such work can be done.

William E. Cain
Wellesley College

Acknowledgments

The editor would like to thank Youngstown State University for provision of a student aide to help with research. I would also like to thank Clatsop Community College for providing me with time to complete this project, a helpful computer staff, and an angelic reference librarian.

Editor's Note

Julie Brown

While Washington Irving has historically been credited with "inventing" the short story genre in America, he is only mentioned once in this book. Instead, the genealogy of this difficult-to-define genre is traced back to other ancestors—nameless, faceless people usually overlooked in American literary history. Indeed, the real authors of the genre may well have been those who never owned paper or pencil.

The American short story's history is more than a linear progression from Irving to Hawthorne to Poe to Mark Twain. The American short story has a genealogy as rich and varied as the genealogy of its collective people, embodying many ethnicities. In Gail Okawa's essay, for example, the short stories of many Hawaiian authors may be traced back to "talk story," an important mode of communication in the multiethnic culture of the islands. Madelyn Jablon traces African American short stories by womanist authors such as Alice Walker back to the oral narratives of Africa and the African slaves brought to the United States. Jablon reminds us that such an oral tale was "the nonmaterial artifact that articulate[d] the autobiographical impulse for the enslaved African." Linda Palmer examines contemporary Native American short stories and sees in them the strong influences of Native American poetry and song. Susan Koppelman playfully submits in her essay on Jewish short stories that the short story and the joke are nearly one and the same.

The short story is a fluid and flexible genre that has never been adequately defined. The essays in this collection do not spend time discussing James Joyce's concept of epiphany or Edgar Allan Poe's dictums on length or style. Instead, they explore the possible variations on the short story form. Rocío Davis discusses the "short story cycle," a collection of interconnected short stories, arguing that this hybrid, sometimes marginalized, subversive genre is an appropriate form/forum for writers of African American, Native American, and Asian American cultures. As she states in her essay:

> The between-world writer's situation is the intense reworking of questions that ultimately refer to issues such as oppositionality, marginality, boundaries, displacement, and authenticity: a process rather than a structure, requiring constant variation and review. This process is not different from that involved in the appreciation of a story cycle, in which the evolution and gradual unfolding of the themes, and a discovery of a new kind of unity in disunity, integrate the essence of the form.

Margot Kelley also analyzes the story/novel hybrid, in terms of its importance for Chicana writers like Denise Chavez and Sandra Cisneros. Kelley quotes Cisneros as saying she wanted to write interconnected stories so that "you would understand each story like a little pearl, or you could look at the whole thing like a necklace."

The short story's use as a tool for political change is discussed in several of the essays gathered here. Bill Mullen's insightful essay on African American short stories written in the 1930s and 1940s shows how numerous black editors and publishers came into prominence when a proliferation of black authors wrote stories to challenge the portrayal of blacks in white fiction, noting "the sustaining and controlling role the short story had come to play in the development of mass consciousness about race and ethnicity." John Streamas argues that the short story was an ideal medium for Japanese American writers to discuss the effects of internment camps on those imprisoned there. Chris Wise's essay on Arab American writer Ramzi Salti points out the ways the genre can point up political difficulties that face Arab writers in the western world. For the Native American authors discussed in Linda Palmer's essay, storytelling is a necessity for the author's/community's very survival.

The stories discussed in the essays gathered here have much to say about the role ethnicity plays in American culture. Susan E. Griffin's essay on Sandra Cisneros draws attention to the plight of Hispanic women who feel they have no voice in the dominant white American society—and of the "hollering" that results when they are able to find their voices. Hardy Wilcoxon's essay on Amy Tan and Maxine Hong Kingston demonstrates the intricacies/difficulties of defining "Chinese American" when he shares these short stories with his Chinese students in Hong Kong. Carol Roh-Spaulding analyzes the role of mixed-race identity in her essay on Edith Eaton/Sui Sin Far, concluding that "The short story was the perfect genre in which to illustrate a wavering identity, because Eaton could shift her authorial stance quite often, both from story to story and within stories."

You will find in this book essays about stylistic issues that encompass a richness and polyphonic diversity far beyond the minimalism associated with white authors like Ray Carver or Ann Beattie. Madelyn Jablon, for example, points out the numerous linguistic games and flourishes used in black vernacular. In Gail Okawa's essay, an interview with Hawaiian author Darrell Lum reveals his anxiety—and excitement—about using Hawaiian Pidgen English in his stories. Okawa notes that "Talking story for Lum is a cross-ethnic, multilingual discourse form associated specifically with local culture in Hawaii." Chris Wise notes that Arab American author Ramzi Salti uses aspects of two languages as well—his native Arabic (which cannot precisely convey certain aspects of American culture) and English (which denies him the privilege of writing in his mother tongue).

These essays reflect at length upon what makes each author unique. However, it may be interesting to note four motifs that were found to run through many short stories by minority writers in the United States:

1. The oral nature of ethnic short stories.
2. The challenge of writing in a language that you do not consider to be your own, and that may be the language of your oppressor.
3. The importance of writing about community rather than the individual.
4. The difficulties that writers of color face when writing for white editors, publishers, and readers.

Of course this book cannot speak for all writers of all ethnicities. We must heed the warning of Qun Wang who had this to say about reading Asian American stories as cultural artifacts. For what he so eloquently says here may apply to reading stories by any cultural "other":

> To understand Asian American literature in the postcolonial period is, indeed, to resist the temptation of totalization, to accept the plurality of the Asian American experience, and to appreciate Asian American writers' effort to democratize American literary voice by (re)presenting what has been mis(sing)-represented, by celebrating the cultural diversity of American society, and by calling readers' attention to the peculiarity and uniqueness of the Asian American experience.

There are still so many unanswered questions. It is my hope that this book will be perceived as a challenge for others: just as each essay here contributes to a wealth of existing scholarship in the fields mentioned above, so should each essay here inspire future scholars to explore these issues further. There are many interesting and important challenges still ahead of us. In the words of Linda Palmer, "The point is, of course, that the story is in fact never *completed*, it continues, repeating itself in different manifestations again and again." This book seeks to celebrate, analyze, and reflect upon both the stories and those who tell them.

ETHNICITY AND THE AMERICAN SHORT STORY

1. Identity in Community in Ethnic Short Story Cycles: Amy Tan's *The Joy Luck Club*, Louise Erdrich's *Love Medicine*, Gloria Naylor's *The Women of Brewster Place*

Rocío G. Davis

The powerful images and themes that have emerged with the rise of ethnic literatures have led to a necessary reworking of traditional views of the immigrant and minority situation in the United States. Entrance into what has long been considered the territory of the "other" is made possible by the ever-expanding fiction of writers who repeatedly meditate on the situation of the between-world artist and present us with a search for personal and communal identity through reflections on a homeland and the active responses to the immigrant's "new" world. The complicated process of selfhood and the inescapable doubleness of the between-world subject is the covert theme in much of this ethnic fiction, as the writers question what it is that determines both identity and community, signaling how geographical, ethnic, political, and cultural makeup and differences serve as signifying aspects to this complex self. The recreation of this intricate self in fiction has, interestingly enough, brought about the development and expansion of a literary genre that has proven itself particularly suited to the task of articulating and elaborating its distinctiveness. A survey of ethnic fiction in the United States demonstrates a proliferation of the short story cycle, a hybrid form with roots in the western tradition, which many of the principal ethnic writers have adapted and perfected as a tool through which they enact their dramas. This paper will explore the theory of the short story cycle as a vehicle for the development of ethnic fiction and analyze the cycles of three of the most important ethnic writers in the United States today (Amy Tan, Louise Erdrich, and Gloria Naylor) in an attempt to show how the dramas of identity and community executed by these writers find their fulfillment through a genre that is particularly fitting to the themes they embody.

The dynamics of the short story cycle have converted it into a form that is especially appropriate to the kinds of conflict presented in ethnic fiction. Forrest Ingram, among the first critics to set forth a definition of a cycle, has determined it to be

> ... a set of stories linked to each other in such a way as to maintain a balance between the individuality of each of the stories and the necessities of the larger unit ... (so) that the reader's successive experience in various levels of the pattern of the whole significantly modifies his experience of each of its component parts. (15, 19)

The term "short story cycle" implies, above all, a principle of organization, a structural scheme for the working out of an idea, characters, or themes, even a circular disposition in which the constituent narratives are simultaneously independent and interdependent. A central aspect of the working of the short story cycle is the interaction, the tension that exists between the individual stories and the overall effect of the patterning of the collection. The pivotal challenge of each cycle is twofold: the collection must assert the individuality and independence of each of the component parts while creating a necessary interdependence that emphasizes the wholeness and essential unity of the work. Ingram has further pointed out that consistency of theme and an evolution from one story to the next are among the classic requirements of the form, with recurrence and development as the integrated movements that effect final cohesion (20). As such, short story cycles magnify the relationship among the separate stories to create a larger whole, without destroying the specificities of each individual story.

This genre, though deprived of serious critical attention for a long time, has existed as a basic narrative form since classical times, as collections unified by editor-authors: Homer's *Odyssey*, Ovid's *Metamorphosis*, Boccaccio's *Decameron*, Chaucer's *The Canterbury Tales*, the Indian *Panchatantra*, the Arabian *A Thousand and One Nights*, and Malory's *Le Morte d'Arthur* all demonstrate the principal characteristics of the short story cycle. In this sense, the short story cycle looks back to oral traditions of narrative while embodying signs of modernity. Cycles may be said to emulate the act of storytelling, the effort of a speaker to establish solidarity with an implied audience by recounting a series of tales linked by their content or by the conditions in which they are related. The fact that the original stories arose from folk imagination, from the collective effort of many people, gave each a separate identity, a uniqueness, and an independence which then was subsumed and integrated into a whole by a single author who modified and retold the stories, fitting them into a specific design. The short story cycle has undergone a revival in our century, with such examples as Sherwood Anderson's *Winesburg, Ohio,* Faulkner's *Go Down, Moses,* and Hemingway's *In Our Time,* to name a few. Although it is obvious that the existence of short story cycles is a global phenomenon, still the pragmatic affinity for short stories that shaped the literature of the United States decisively in the nineteenth century seems to persist in the form of a national inclination in the present century for organized short story collections: perhaps the very determination to build a unified republic out of diverse states, regions, and population groups helps to account for this continuing passion for cycles (Kennedy *Modern* viii).

Short story cycles are complex works of art. The fundamental structure emerges from the interaction of the diverse elements in the relatively independent components. While each story has its own static and dynamic structures, connective patterns on all levels draw these together to form a cycle, and the stories are strengthened by varying types of internal cohesion. Furthermore, the title of a volume may indicate an organizing concept that acquires resonance as the collection unfolds: titles that point to a particular locale (such as *The Women of Brewster Place*) or to a unifying element (*The Joy Luck Club*) give immediate focus to the process being unveiled.

The principal approaches to the necessary cohesion may involve, for instance, the process of development of a character, a composite type, or a set of characters; a dominant theme such as a generation gap or search for identity or the delineation of a particular locale or community is often treated symbolically. In general, more than one such pattern rivets story to story. The orchestration of the whole often appears in the ordering of the stories. Kennedy has pointed out that the arrangement can suggest a cyclical process or an incremental action, produce striking juxtapositions of individual texts, or create clusters of closely linked stories within a volume: this organization may range from obvious to subtle, and connections between stories may be patent or covert (*Modern* ix). Since a short story cycle does not usually require the type of ending expected of a traditional novel, its typical concluding section or sections tend to simply round off the themes, symbols, or whatever patterned action the cycle possesses. In this manner, through the drawing together in final stories or series of stories the themes and motifs, symbols, or the characters and their communities that have been developing throughout, the author places the finishing touches on the portrait being created.

Nonetheless, as Ingram has emphasized, the most pervasive unifying pattern of short story cycles appears to be the dynamic pattern of recurrent development. It affects all the elements of the narrative: the themes, leitmotifs, settings, characters, and structures of the individual stories and, in consequence, the entire context of the collection as a unit. The repetition of a theme from different angles, for instance, and its ensuing growth in depth in the mind of the reader may unify a cycle at the same time that it individualizes each story. The shared frustration of the Chinese mothers over their inability to reach their American daughters in Amy Tan's cycle creates a composite portrait of the immigrant's dilemma. This example also demonstrates the development typical of characters in short story cycles as differentiated from the single continuous process one finds most often in novels. Character development in a cycle tends to follow a typically cyclic pattern: those characters who appear in more than one story rarely, if ever, occupy the center of the action in all the stories. While there are cycles unified by a single protagonist, most contain a series of different protagonists or an evolving prototype. Another peculiarity of the cycles is that secondary characters seem to collectively receive as much, if not more, attention than do the protagonists in a novel. Even then, "minor characters" are often delineated through comparison with and contrast to the other characters, some of whom may actively influence their growth or present condition, while others merely serve to deepen the reader's insight by juxtaposition. At any given moment, the action of the cycle is centered in the action of the story which is at that moment being experienced (Ingram 22). As character and setting tend to be determining aspects of the story cycles, orchestration of time patterns acquires almost a secondary place in the structure. Frequently, the individual stories in a collection are organized independently of chronology; the author often demonstrates greater concern with the rhythmic pattern of the telling than in the chronological consistency of the events themselves. Often, no temporal relationship at all exists among the various stories of a cycle, but frequently enough one notices some kind of mythic advance in time or some general reference to historical time: chief concern seems to be reserved for psychological time, symbolic times of seasons, times which recur, and mythic times of legendary events (Ingram 23–24).

The specificities of the form therefore work to make the short story cycle an especially pertinent vehicle for the distinctive characteristics of ethnic fiction in general. The short story cycle itself is a hybrid, occupying an odd, indeterminate place within the field of narrative, resembling the novel in its totality, yet composed of distinct stories evoking different characters and problems. Such a fusion of modes "imposes new strategies of reading in which the movement from one story to the next necessitates reorientation, just as the uneasy reciprocity between part and whole conditions the ongoing determination of meaning" (Kennedy "Towards" 14). Ethnic fiction has also facilitated new strategies of reading and has caused a new awareness through a revisioning of the between-world circumstance. The short story cycle, which hovers between the novel and the short story, is thus a particularly apt medium with which to enact the enigma of ethnicity, the feeling that one falls "between two stools." The ethnic short story cycle may be considered the formal materialization of the trope of doubleness as the between-world condition is presented via a form that itself vacillates between two genres.

The ethnic short story cycle, as a hybrid within a hybrid, ultimately offers diverse levels of reading and understanding and may help further the ethnographic purposes of the writers. On the one hand, there is the patterned closure of the individual stories that enact personal dramas of identity and, on the other, the discovery of larger unifying strategies that bridge the gaps between the stories and construct a larger sphere of action through the creation of communities. Ethnic writers, who may be conscious of a double literary inheritance or, at least, the reality of an insider/outsider point of view, tend to contemplate how binary categories of cultural classification have worked in the production of knowledge and counter-knowledge within the framework of literary and cultural studies, a position from which they redefine and construct alternative identities and communities. Hybridity is an important characteristic of all ethnic literary texts and should therefore be considered a strength rather than a weakness. It does not imply a denial of the traditions from which it springs but rather focuses on a continual and mutual development. In this manner, the text itself becomes the embodiment of the histories, the mechanism for modifying and recreating personal and collective identity.

On different levels, ethnic short story cycles may project a desire to come to terms with a past that is both personal and collective: this type of fiction explores the ethnic character and history of a community as a reflection of a personal odyssey of displacement and as a search for self and community. The between-world writer's situation is the intense reworking of questions that ultimately refer to issues such as oppositionality, marginality, boundaries, displacement, and authenticity: a process rather than a structure, requiring constant variation and review. This process is not different from that involved in the appreciation of a story cycle, in which the evolution and gradual unfolding of the themes and a discovery of a new kind of unity in disunity, integrate the essence of the form. Although there is no limit to the kinds of subjects that are found in cycles, one repeatedly discovers that twentieth-century cycles are preoccupied with certain themes, including isolation, disintegration, indeterminacy, the role of the artist, and the maturation process (Mann 13–14). More specifically, the two principal thematic constituents of the ethnic story cycle are the presentation of identity and community, as separate entities, and the notion of an identity within a community--again, a common theme of ethnic fiction in general.

In the first place, the gradual revelation of character through apparently random glimpses serves to emphasize the idea of a personal and cultural identity as a collective self, shared by people with a common history and ancestry, which provide a consistent frame of reference and meaning. Interestingly enough, ethnic identity is, most often, "a matter of 'becoming' as well as of 'being'. It belongs to the future as much as to the past . . . identities are the names we give to the different ways we are positioned by, and position ourselves within, the narratives of the past" (Hall 227). As such, the act of amalgamation required for the understanding of the short story cycle is the same movement as that needed for the consolidation of the ethnic identity portrayed. The shifting borders of identity, isolation, fragmentation, and indeterminacy find their formal expression in the isolated episodes that make up a cycle. The ethnic self, forced to sift constantly through the assorted influences that mold it, ultimately seems to find completion and coherence in the totality, in uniting within itself the diversity it experiences.

Secondly, there are numerous and varied connective strands that serve to draw the individuals of any short story cycle into a single community, bonds that range from familial relationships to friendship, to belonging to the same town, ethnic group, or sex. However this community may be achieved, it usually can be said to constitute the central character of a cycle (Ingram 22). The passage from appreciation of individual stories to the whole presented in the cycle marks the shift from the individual to community; and it constantly sets the individual against the social group to which he or she belongs. The connections that are established will therefore yield what Kennedy has called the "defining experience" of the short story cycle: a vision of unity or community, accumulated by the reader's discernment of meanings and parallels inherent in the composite scheme (*Modern* 196). But, paradoxically, this vision of wholeness inferred from a cycle may present another side of the coin: the short story cycle may also be viewed as a genre that reflects the struggle between cohesion and fragmentation, between things holding together and things pulling apart. While the fusion of the stories in the reader's imagination may effectively create a vision of community, the actual fact of the stories' independence, their individual closure and completion, may suggest the incapacity to form community. As such, this unique form may also reflect "the *failure* of place and character to unify a work that remains tantalizingly whole yet fundamentally suspicious of completeness" (Lynch 96). In the case of the ethnic story cycle, these two possibilities are clearly evident, as the search for community, specifically for identity within community, is tantamount. Yet, while *The Joy Luck Club* and *The Women of Brewster Place* clearly manifest the generation of a community of women linked by bonds of shared suffering and common understanding, in *Love Medicine* the failure to form and define a community is evident at the close of the final story.

The three story cycles to be analyzed in this essay fulfill the potential of the cycle form as a vehicle for the expression of the particular sensibility and experience of the ethnic subject in diverse ways. Moreover, they share common elements that somehow suggest a link between one specific type of ethnic fiction to another. In each of the cycles, the unifying force of the narratives is a woman who pulls together the diverse elements that make up the collection. Jing-mei Woo, in Amy Tan's *The Joy Luck Club*, speaks in two voices--her own and her dead mother's--and metaphorically embodies the conflicts of the other members of the Joy Luck Club and their daughters. Louise Erdrich's *Love Medicine* unites the different members of the Kashpaw family after June's death. She is the link between the different characters and her death is the impulse that triggers the narrative recounting. Mattie is the central character in Gloria Naylor's *The Women of Brewster Place*. As the community's confidante and its sharpest eye, she is thus well qualified even to express the unconscious urgings of the community and dream a collective dream for the women of Brewster Place. Furthermore, in all three cycles, the problems of race and adapting to the mainstream American life as well as the consciousness of marginality and the inescapable desire to belong are recurrent themes. The multiple narrators of the cycles address over and over again the enigma of their ethnicity, and their conclusions--or the lack thereof-- constitute an essential part of the development of the theme.

Amy Tan's *The Joy Luck Club* (1989) is an attempt to synthesize Asian heritage with American aspirations as it presents a group portrait

of four mother-daughter relationships that have to endure and bridge not
only a generation gap but that created by the waning influence of an
older culture and the overwhelming presence of another. The polyphony
of voices belongs to four Chinese mothers, immigrants to the United
States, and their four daughters, born and raised Americans. The cycle is
divided into four parts, each part further subdivided into four sections,
with each of the characters speaking. The only exception is the late
Suyuan Woo, whose story is told by her daughter Jing-mei. The four-
part division corresponds to the four sides of a mah-jong table, a
linkage between the past and present for the Club aunties. Jing-Mei
Woo takes her mother's seat at the table after Suyuan's death, becoming
the frame narrator. She tells the first and the last stories, linking the
two generations of Chinese Americans. These two stories, ending with
her reunion with her sisters in China, strongly suggest a journey of
maturity and ethnic awakening, not just for her but, metaphorically, for
all the other daughters in the book.

The narrative structure succeeds in manifesting not merely the
individual tragedies of those caught up in the history of Chinese
immigration to America but the difficulties of a culture undergoing
transformation. As a story cycle, *The Joy Luck Club* points to the
loosened family ties and uncertain continuity between generations, a
contrast Tan creates by separating the stories of the mothers and their
daughters. Each person's story demonstrates how her past--the mothers'
painful experiences and the daughters' mother-dominated childhoods--
constantly acts upon the present, modifying her world-view and cultural
sensibility. Interestingly enough, individual personalities within each
generation are not always very clearly defined. Although the eight
characters are divided into four families and given different names, the
collection itself seems to be concerned more with a simple bifurcation
among generational lines: mothers, whose stories took place in China,
and daughters, whose stories are being lived in America; mothers who
are possessively trying to hold fast and daughters who are battling for
autonomy. Marina Heung has pointed out that Tan attempts to
undermine the independence of individual narrative units, to the point
that even the chapter titles, by connecting motifs between disparate
stories, seem interchangeable (611). As a group, these narratives, more
than simply recounting personal stories, dramatize the panorama of a
critical transition in cultural values.

There is nearly always some tension in the exchange between the
mothers and daughters, between old China and the new American
environment. Each of the individual stories is a variation on the theme
of self-identification, ethnic worth, adaptation to circumstances, and

incapacity to comprehend the other. The focus is either on a mother, secure in her ethnicity but unable to understand her daughter's dilemma, or on a daughter, caught in a sophisticated cultural trap, knowing possibilities rather than answers, puzzling over the realities that surround her and trying to find her place in what seems an ambivalent world. Though the mothers and daughters all have different names and individual stories, they seem interchangeable in that the role they play supplants all others and is performed with the utmost seriousness and determination (Ling 138).

The mothers are depicted, in general, as students learning about the cultural realities around them and using their experiences to come to conclusions about essential forms of character strength and weakness. Suyuan Woo's fortitude and will to survive allowed her to overcome the horrors of the Japanese invasion of China by forming the Joy Luck Club as a deliberate defiance of the darkness of current events: "What was worse, we asked among ourselves, to sit and wait for our own deaths with proper somber faces? Or to choose our own happiness?" (11). In this context, the Joy Luck Club itself is, symbolically, the determination to hope in the face of constantly altering social situations and continually shifting rules. An-mei Hsu learns from her mother's suicide how to use the world for her own advantage. She not only traces how her mother makes the Chinese cultural beliefs work for her— "suicide is the way a woman can escape marriage and gain revenge, to come back as a ghost and scatter tea leaves and good fortune"(234)--but she also realizes almost immediately the acute significance of the words of her mother who tells her "she [the mother] would rather kill her own weak spirit so she could give me a stronger one" (240).

The mothers' unerring confidence in the superiority of Chinese ways and the superficiality of American ones causes them to impose, to demand, and to criticize, because they fear their daughters are moving farther and farther away. They do not have, in their experience, anything that could have prepared them for the attitudes they see embodied in their daughters. How Lindo Jong gets out of her hateful first marriage, for example, is a fascinating combination of feminism and fairy tale: using superstition for her own ends, she terrorizes her mother-in-law until she is begged to go. This memory is sacred to her and does not permit her to comprehend her daughter's indifference: "I once sacrificed my life to keep my parent's promise. This means nothing to you, because to you promises mean nothing. A daughter can promise to come to dinner, but if she has a headache, if she has a traffic jam, if she wants to watch a favorite movie on TV, she no longer has a promise" (42). But she blames herself for her daughter's attitude:

> I taught her how American circumstances work . . . but
> I couldn't teach her about Chinese character. How to obey your
> parents and listen to your mother's mind. How not to show
> your own thoughts, to put your feelings behind your face so
> you could take advantage of hidden opportunities. Why easy
> things are not worth pursuing. How to know your own worth
> and polish it, never flashing it around like a cheap ring. Why
> Chinese thinking is best. (289)

Tan's portrayal of the world seen through the American daughters' eyes is harsher, colored less by understanding than by dominance, less by love than by authority. The most important part of the daughters' problems is adjusting to the situation of being a Chinese American, eating different food, and speaking a different language. The absent motherland looms large on the horizon of the immigrant mothers whose "unspeakable tragedies left behind in China" (20) recorded and recounted in vivid detail resonate in their daughters. The childhoods of the daughters of the Joy Luck Club are marked by their mothers' stories, their mothers' mystical and mysterious powers, and by ghosts of the past. They will have to confront this past in order to come to terms with their mothers and the relationships they have built up. Central to these is the novel's title story: "Joy Luck was an idea my mother remembered from the days of her first marriage in Kweilin, before the Japanese came. That's why I think of Joy Luck as her Kweilin story. It was the story she would always tell me. . . . Over the years, she told the same story, except for the ending, which grew darker, casting long shadows into her life, and eventually into mine" (7).

One of the critical contradictions facing the daughters is the relationship between their perceptions of their Chinese heritage and American realities. In this case, the double vantage point appears to have blurred the daughter's vision. This is a feeling common to all the daughters, articulated by Jing-Mei: "My mother and I never understood one another. We translated each other's meanings and I seemed to hear less than what was said, while my mother heard more" (27). The daughters attribute negative aspects of their family and community to Chinese culture and traditions, embodied in the persons of their mothers. But while they were encouraged to seek comfort in the superiority of their cultural heritage, their mental picture of China is only a composite gathered from stories, legends, books, and the movies. The independence of each narrative heightens the sense of the daughters' isolation. They are separate and cannot seem to take comfort, neither from their mothers nor from each other. This fragmentation implies that the arduous task of self-identification confronting them must be taken on alone. But only after personal identity has been determined can bonds of unity be forged.

Throughout the book, Tan contrasts the strong, domineering mothers' stories with the daughters' incapacity for self-definition and the inability to make sense of their lives. The daughters need a tradition to lean on, something they cannot find in their mothers because they are from another world. Jing-mei would often dismiss her mother's advice as "just more of her Chinese superstitions, beliefs that conveniently fit the circumstances" (20). One group of stories concerning the daughters features the struggle for maturity, a rather typical generational tension with the mothers. Generally, the daughters tend to perceive cultural blanks, the absence of clear and definite answers to the problems of family, while the mothers fill in too much, often to provide those kinds of cultural answers and principles that seem to empower them to make strong demands on their daughters. Lindo Jong's comments express a typical attitude: "I wanted my children to have the best combination: American circumstances and Chinese character" (254). This sounds a note of compromise, but in reply to her daughter's declaration, "I'm my own person," she thinks, "How can she be her own person? When did I give her up?" (254).

But the depth of misunderstanding between mothers and daughters is underlined by Jing-mei who, having heard the Joy Luck Club story many times over the years, could still think: "I never thought my mother's Kweilin story was anything but a Chinese fairy tale" (12). Only after her mother's death would she come to realize the painful truth behind it and finish the task her mother could not. As such, *The Joy Luck Club* is not essentially a cycle about divisions; it is the reconciliation between daughters and mothers, the record of the Asian American's struggle to come to terms with all the elements of a Chinese background and the relationship with an American self. The struggle in the book is an essential struggle culminating in affirmation. In the Woos' story, in which the mother/daughter bond is broken by the mother's death, what was once a battle becomes a devastating loss, a loss compensated for by the daughter's taking the place of the mother and finding mother substitutes. The lost mother is entangled with the story of two lost daughters, who, when found and returned to the family, become a means of recovering the mother.

Jing-mei's final story, a paradigm for all the other daughters, leads her to China to fulfill posthumously her mother's deepest longing. Suyuan Woo's death and the unfulfilled hope of finding her twin daughters moves the Joy Luck Club members to encourage Jing-Mei to finish her mother's story for her. "You must see your sisters and tell them about your mother's death," says Auntie Ying. "But most important, you must tell them about her life. The mother they did not know, they must now know. . . . Tell them stories she told you, lessons she taught, what you know about her mind that has become your mind" (30–31). Jing-mei is hesitant at first, uncertain of what is wanted of her and overwhelmed by her impotence.

> And then it occurs to me. They are frightened. In me, they see their own daughters, just as ignorant, just as unmindful of the truths and hopes they have brought to America. They see daughters who grow impatient when their mother talks in Chinese, who think they are stupid when they explain things in fractured English. They see that joy and luck do not mean the same to their daughters, that to these closed American-born minds "joy luck" is not a word, it does not exist. (31)

The Joy Luck Club ends with resolution and reconciliation. The final fusion of the individuals in the stories into a community of women linked by bonds of understanding completes the cycle. The critical tension between cohesion and fragmentation is resolved as Tan's themes parallel the cycle's movement: the women in her stories find fulfillment in the affirmation of their identity and in the consciousness of a community. The principal symbol of the story, the Joy Luck Club, prevails in the renewed relationships between the first and second generation of women who gather around the mah-jong table.

Louise Erdrich's *Love Medicine*, as a Native American short story cycle, reflects the cyclical and recursive nature of stories informed by oral tradition. The storyteller's use of repetition and recurrent development, as well as the image of a communal narrator beyond the limits of time, is reproduced in the cycle's structure. Erdrich's narrative recreates the relationship of individuals with their families, their community, and the land. As with *The Joy Luck Club*, the narrative voices fuse to form what may be considered the actual protagonist of the work. This technique is particularly relevant for many Native American writers for whom such a collective protagonist does not reflect fragmentation, alienation, or deterioration of an individual voice but the traditional importance of the communal over the individual, the polyphonous over the monovocal (Wong 173). The multiple narrators of the stories may exhibit the multiplicity of the ethnic community more than simply the fragmentation of selves.

As a story cycle, *Love Medicine* dramatizes the struggle of a group of Chippewa Indians for survival in the modern world. In its collation of the ways of the old world and that of the new, Erdrich articulates the painful passage of traditional cultural values in favor of a dubious adherence to the mainstream. The first edition of *Love Medicine* consists of 14 stories, apart from June's story in the first section, each narrated by a character in the first person (or, in some cases, several characters) or, less frequently by a third-person omniscient narrator. The work is organized as the juxtaposed stories of eight narrators: Albertine Johnson, Marie (Lazarre Kashpaw), Nector Kashpaw, Lulu Lamartine, Lipsha Morrissey, Lyman Lamartine, Howard Kashpaw, and a third-person narrator. Four new stories were added to the new and expanded 1993 edition, narrated by the characters already mentioned. The relationships between these people, as well as the North Dakota setting, serve to bind the text. The stories are organized associationally, more than chronologically, as the frequent flashbacks demonstrate. Moreover, the title serves to confer harmony: "Love Medicine" becomes an analogy for the odyssey, the search both for love and for healing that all the characters undertake.

The setting is not limited to a single location. In addition to the reservation, we see King's apartment in Minneapolis, Henry Jr.'s hotel room in Fargo, and the frozen fields outside Williston where June walks to her death. The time span is fifty years. The first story is set in 1981, the year of June Kashpaw's death. The next story goes back to 1934 and the chance meeting of Marie Lazarre and Nector Kashpaw on the hill outside the convent. The stories that follow are in chronological order and end two years after the death of Nector by choking. The last story, set in 1984, returns to the subject of June, as Lipsha Morrissey learns she is his mother and Gerry Nanapush his father. This structure symbolically highlights Lipsha's reconciliation with his mother and with the past, for June opens the novel and her son closes it. The prose that describes Lipsha's journey home with the car echoes Erdrich's first description of June. "The snow fell deeper that Easter than it had in forty years, but June walked over it like water and came home" (7) foreshadows Lipsha's "The morning was clear. A good road led on. So there was nothing to do but cross the water, and bring her home" (367). In this manner, the beginning suggests the end as the final story concludes with Lipsha, who like his mother before him, travels across the water to return home.

Apart from these, other connective devices exist on an intratextual level in the narration, such as the repetition of the same event narrated from various perspectives. Patterned after spoken, as well as written, narrative voices, "the characters tell and retell family and community stories from their particular points of view and their own unique idioms, reflecting the polyphony of individual, family, and community voices and the subjectivity of personal and communal history" (Wong 175). In this manner, Erdrich blends stories within stories, as family and community narrative are told and retold from different perspectives throughout the book so that the reader, offered several versions of the same events, is forced to integrate, interpret, and reinterpret the narratives. "There was that time someone tried to hang their little cousin" (21) introduces one of the recurrent stories, how June was almost hanged, a tale told several times by different characters, each one contributing another angle to that childhood incident. Hertha Wong has pointed to other images that create a structural connectivity in the text: several repeated symbols like water (often in the form of rivers or lakes and associated with a series of oppositions: water can join or separate, cleanse or kill, save or erode) and images of edges and boundaries are permeated by a variable repetition of humor (175, 178).

In the first section of Chapter I, a third-person narrator tells a brief story of June Kashpaw's last afternoon, which opens the sequence of narratives to come. June is the cycle's central female character, and her death initiates the actions and memories of the other characters and, to a great degree, unifies the separate stories: she links each of the highly individual characters. She is probably the most tragic character in the collection, a figure more often on the perimeter of others' lives than a center of focus. All the characters are her relatives and they remember her and, to a certain extent, define themselves according to their relationship with her. June is Gordie's ex-wife, Marie's unofficially adopted daughter, Albertine's aunt, King and Lipsha's mother, and Gerry's ex-lover. Even though she never narrates a word, June (or at least her memory) is a palpable absence and the most dominant character in the entire work. Just as readers interpret and reinterpret the linked stories, the characters construct and reconstruct June. Analogically, they define and redefine the world in which June had lived and died, in which the inability to hold fast to a culture because of both intrinsic and extrinsic tension results in fragmentation and division at all levels.

Louise Erdrich's story is, therefore, not one of continuity, relatedness, and harmony with the land and nature, with culture and tradition. Instead, she depicts a cultural milieu where the sacred ceremonies, tribal rituals, and Indian cultural identity have disappeared (Flavin 64). The contrast between the twins Eli and Nector Kashpaw illustrates the divisions. The former is the last man on the reservation who could snare a deer, who knew how to skin a skunk, and was familiar with the ways of the woods; the latter, educated in the schools, loses his mind and cannot remember the history of his tribal battles to tell his granddaughter: "his thoughts swam between us, hidden under rocks, disappearing in weeds, and I was fishing for them, dangling my own words like baits and lures" (19). Much of the reservation land belonging to the Indians has been lost in reparceling and redistribution: "The policy of allotment was a joke. As I was driving toward the land, looking around, I saw as usual how much of the reservation was sold to whites and lost forever" (12). Thus, the connectedness to the land has disappeared; the means to make a living is gone, and the younger generation must find work outside the reservation or stay there and flounder. The story entitled "The Plunge of the Brave" has Nector Kashpaw trying to make a Hollywood living and having to compromise his ethnic pride: "Death was the extent of an Indian acting in the movie theater . . . [and] the only interesting Indian [was] dead, or dying by falling backwards off a horse" (122–4).

One group of stories centers on Nector and Marie Kashpaw and their relationship to Lulu Lamartine and her children. These individual stories highlight the short story cycle's potential for binary revelations as the presentation of these diverse points of view accentuates the theme of the breakdown of relationships, while showing the unique tie the family and reservation life have for these people (Flavin 56). The theme is at once of disintegration and breaking connections and of bonding and restoration. Presenting the story from so many different points of view suggests not tribal or family unity but separation and difference. Characters are seen to be marginalized, not only by society at large but also within the ethnic group or even the family. Family bonds are shown to be tenuous, and a great part of the characters' displacement seems to stem from the lack of security within the family group and from insecurity as to one's origin or parents. Such multiple marginality is reflected structurally in the proliferation and juxtaposition of individual voices (voices often not speaking or listening to each other) positioned between the covers of the book (Wong 177–8).

The idea of fragmentation and the need to unite the shards recurs often in the diverse stories. June, in the first section of the book, " . . . knew that if she lay there any longer she would crack wide open, not in one place but in many pieces that he would crush by moving in his sleep. She thought to pull herself back together" (6). And beauty may even be found in the fragmentation and attempts at unity, as the description of Gordie's scarred face suggests: "There was always a compelling pleasantness about him. In some curious way all the stitches and folds had contributed to, rather than detracted from, his looks. His face was like something valuable that was broken and put carefully back together. And all the more lovable for the care taken" (27). But this implies that what has been broken cannot be truly united again. If the cycle displays a unity of form and content, it is a unity based on a common *disunity*, on a shared failure to achieve wholeness. The discontinuous narratives of the individual survivors of the Kashpaw and Lamartine families, become, ultimately, a portrait of the failure of a community that has succumbed to the tensions that have threatened historically to destroy it. Members who desire survival must flee the community and cannot turn back; those who stay are condemned to languish in oblivion, holding on to the past.

The bleakness of the future and the possession of only a past are themes that weave together the seven stories of Gloria Naylor's *The Women of Brewster Place*. As Karla Holloway suggests:

> the recursive structures of language in literature by contemporary African-American women writers are signaled by what is essentially a "multiplied" text. Recursive structures accomplish a blend between figurative processes that are reflective (like a mirror) and symbolic processes whose depth and resonance make them reflexive. This combination results in texts that are at once emblematic of the culture they describe as well as interpretative of this culture. Literature that strikes this reflective/reflexive posture is characteristically polyphonic. The textual characterizations and events, the settings and symbolic systems are multipled and layered rather than individual and one-dimensional. (618)

The Women of Brewster Place is a short story cycle in which time and place immediately collide. The italicized preface and epilogue constitute the frame that dramatizes the birth and decline of the unifying locale. The first section, "Dawn," is an introduction to the history of Brewster Place, which Naylor characterizes as a "bastard child" that had "no one to fight for [it]. . . . So the wall came up and Brewster Place became a dead-end street" (1–2). In the final section, "Dusk," Brewster Place is abandoned, "only waiting for death, which is a second behind the expiration of its spirit in the minds of its children. But the colored daughters of Brewster, spread over the canvas of time, still wake up with their dreams misted on the edge of a yawn. . . . They ebb and flow, ebb and flow, but never disappear. So Brewster Place still waits to die" (192). The focus in the cycle is on the women of this place, whose own histories are reflected in the bastardization of the locale. For

many of the women who live there, Brewster Place is an anchor as well
as a burden: it is the social network that both sustains and entraps.
Seven stories recount the journeys of a group of African American
women in this particular street, a painful odyssey that did not offer a
solution.

> Brewster Place knew that unlike its other children, the few
> who would leave forever were to be the exception rather than
> the rule, since they came because they had no choice and would
> remain for the same reason . . . Brewster Place became
> especially fond of its colored daughters as they milled like
> determined spirits among its decay, trying to make it a
> home. . . . (4)

The stories in this cycles are linked, perhaps even more than by
locale, by the recurrent themes that are developed individually in each of
the stories. The women of Brewster Place live a shared history: the
weight of African American double consciousness, poverty, dislocation,
separation from family, marginalization from mainstream society
because of what--or how--they are. This panorama, coupled with the
pervasive absence of men in their lives, colors their horizons
fundamentally with the dearth of hope. Mattie's " . . . long, winding
journey to Brewster" (8) is representative of the tales of the other
women who are in Brewster Place simply because they have nowhere
else to go. Isolation from society, symbolized by Brewster Place's brick
wall, forges a spiritual unity between the women. Mattie, Ciel, Etta
Mae, Cora, "The Two," and Kiswana are all women separated from their
familial sources and are left alone to become the communal "daughters"
of the place.

Cyclical development is best appreciated in the echoing of themes
in the different stories. The significant absence of men in the lives of
these women is one of the most repeated themes. The search for the
father figure looms largely in Mattie, Kiswana, and Lorraine's lives,
and, paradoxically, when the latter finds one, she is condemned to
brutally murder him. Mattie, Cora, Ciel, and Etta Mae, for different
reasons, cannot find love nor a steady relationship with a man and are
doomed to live alone. Undesired isolation, together with the
compulsion to escape from something in the past, is, in most cases,
the reason for setting up residence in Brewster Place. Mattie has lost
everything when her beloved son jumps the bail she put up for him,
leaving her without a home, a future, or a family. Lorraine and Theresa
move there hoping for acceptance or at least to escape from prying and
judgmental eyes. Ciel's story reaches its tragic climax in Brewster Place

where, out of a misguided love for Eugene, she has an abortion and later loses her only child. Only Kiswana, in an act of rebellion against her family, is there out of the vacillating conviction that "my place [is] in the streets with my people, fighting for equality and a better community" (83). Her passion for the cause that led her to even change her name blinds her to the fact that values have changed. Yet her dreams remain, symbolically depicted in the flight of a bird she sees out her window:

> A pigeon swept across her window, and she marveled at its liquid movements in the air waves. She placed her dreams on the back of the bird and fantasized that it would glide forever in transparent silver circles until it ascended to the center of the universe and was swallowed up. But the wind died down, and she watched with a sigh as the bird beat its wings in awkward, frantic movements to land on the corroded top of a fire escape on the opposite building. This brought her back to reality. (75)

Mattie Michael is the primary agent of female coalescence in the cycle, the crossroads at which everyone's path meets at some point in the narration. She saves Ciel's life and, through a ritual cleansing, exorcises "the evilness of pain" for her "murdered dreams" (103–4). She also supports the other women, providing Etta Mae Johnson "light and the love and the comfort" (74) after her ill-fated encounter with Reverend Woods to allow her to transcend her desolation. Further, she gently chides Cora Lee about her "full load" of children and, along with Etta Mae, defends Lorraine against Sophie's bitterness.

The individual stories of this collection are perhaps the most clearly independent of the three story cycles analyzed. Although there are occasional cross-references from one story to another, as with Mattie's knowing Ciel as a child and her long friendship with Etta Mae or Kiswana'a inviting Cora Lee to the Shakespeare production, the stories are clearly separate, individual character portrayals. Significantly, most of the chapter titles consist simply of the full name of the protagonist of that specific story. The only exceptions to this rule are "The Two" and "The Block Party." In the former, Lorraine and Theresa's individual identities are fused into one in a story that centers on the effects of critical gaze on the lives of these marginalized women. The latter does not contain individual names but rather incorporates a suggestion of cohesion of all the women presented earlier in a dream that metaphorically synthesizes all of their dreams. This apparent emphasis on narrative disconnectedness may suggest the story cycle's capacity to present, once again, an inherent disunity, a failure to create community, and the dramatic isolation of the protagonists. But the book's subtitle, "a novel in seven stories," also provides additional clues as to the text's essential narrative strategy as it insinuates a simultaneous and necessary independence and integration.

African American culture's insistence on unity, even in the face of powerfully divisive opposition, is at the heart of the cohesion of the stories. More specifically, the unity of form and content in the book is essentially related to its exploration of the redemptive possibilities of female coalescence (Awkward 37). The climax of the cycle process in this text is the actual moment of unity, of assertion of the imperative unity that seems to have been threatened by the presentation of narratively disjointed stories. The recurrent themes and dramas enacted by the diverse women demonstrate the essential psychological and circumstantial affinities between them and offer significant evidence of these women's recognition of such affinities, the first major step in creating and sustaining the community the wall of Brewster Place built. The dramatic scene of the destruction of the wall that separates Brewster Place from the rest of the city, albeit in a dream, is an embodiment of the imperative solidarity that makes this group of women more than just neighbors. As such, "The Block Party" suggests that a new order results from the utter chaos surrounding the brutal rape of Lorraine: an order based on the female protagonists' comprehension of their interconnectedness and need for each other.

It is Mattie's vision and voice that control the final section of the novel and provide the work with the final hopeful note: the fulfillment of her dream of a supportive female community. The protagonists of the individual sections of *The Women of Brewster Place,* in response to Cora's assertion that a week of rain has failed to wash Lorraine's blood from the wall, work hysterically to tear down the structure. These women

> . . . flung themselves against the wall, chipping away at it with knives, plastic forks, spiked show heels, and even bare hands; the water [from a thunderstorm] pouring under their chins, and plastering their blouses and dresses against their breasts and into the cracks of their hips. The bricks piled up behind them and were snatched and relayed out of Brewster Place past overturned tables, scattered coins, and crushed wads of dollar bills. They came back with chairs and barbecue grills and smashed them into the wall. (186)

The fact that this vision is presented as a dream may be interpreted, as Michael Awkward suggests, as "an illusion that serves to perpetuate the text's content and formal disjunctions in much the same way that the self-deceptive dreams of Naylor's characters prolong their personally injurious self-divisions" (62). Nonetheless, it can also serve as the subconscious articulation of an ideal for which the women of Brewster Place strive, an analogy for the ethnic situation in general. The fact that the cycle actually ends with Mattie waking up the morning of the party and that the reader never finds out what truly happens at that crucial gathering may be an affirmation of quiet, sustaining, personal dreams as opposed to the violence of the cathartic dream of resistance.

These short story cycles, as discourses of ethnic self-definition and creation of community, demonstrate the strong collective impulse that has characterized much of minority fiction. Using oral narratives and the paradigms of storytelling, these writers weave together the sources of meaning to ensure the survival of the group, through the affirmation of the individual. The questions about self-representation are answered through narratives that articulate stories of survivors in a world full of questions and doubts. The manner in which various ethnic writers have appropriated the short story cycle as a metaphor for the fragmentation and multiplicity of ethnic lives is itself an articulation of the between-culture position and the complex process towards self-identification. As such, the multiple impressionistic perspectives and fragmentation of simple linear history emphasize the subjectivity of experience and understanding. The subsequent narratives, a reflection of a tendency towards a hybrid form, provide enriching glimpses of societies in the process of transformation and growth.

REFERENCES

Awkward, Michael. "Authorial Dreams of Wholeness: (Dis)Unity, (Literary) Parentage, and *The Women of Brewster Place.*" Eds. Henry Louis Gates, Jr., and K. A. Appiah. *Gloria Naylor: Critical Perspectives Past and Present.* New York: Amistad, 1993. 37–69.
Erdrich, Louise. *Love Medicine* (New and Expanded Edition). New York: HarperCollins, 1993.
Flavin, Louise. "Louise Erdrich's *Love Medicine*: Loving over Time and Distance." *Critique* (Fall 1989): 55–64.
Hall, Stuart. "Cultural Identity and Diaspora." Ed. J. Rutherford. *Identity: Community, Culture, Difference.* London: Lawrence and Wishart, 1990. 222–237.
Heung, Marina. "Daughter-Text/Mother-Text: Matrilineage in Amy Tan's *The Joy Luck Club.*" *Feminist Studies* 19. 3 (Fall 1993): 597–615.

Holloway, Karla F.C. "Revision and (Re)membrance: A Theory of Literary Structures in Literature by African-American Women Writers." *Black American Literature Forum* 24.4 (Winter 1990): 617–631.

Ingram, Forrest L. *Representative Short Story Cycles of the Twentieth Century: Studies in a Literary Genre.* The Hague: Mouton, 1971.

Kennedy, J. Gerald. *Modern American Short Story Sequences: Composite Fictions and Fictive Communities.* New York: Cambridge University Press, 1995.

Kennedy, J. Gerald. "Towards a Poetics of the Short Story Cycle." *Journal of the Short Story in English* 11 (1988): 9–24.

Ling, Amy. *Between Worlds: Women Writers of Chinese Ancestry.* New York: Pergamon Press, 1990.

Luscher, Robert M. "The Short Story Sequence: An Open Book." Eds. Susan Lohafer and Jo Ellyn Clarey. *Short Story Theory at a Crossroads.* Baton Rouge: Louisiana State University Press, 1989. 148–167.

Lynch, Gerald. "The One and the Many: English-Canadian Short Story Cycles." *Canadian Literature.* 130 (Autumn 1990): 91–104.

Mann, Susan Garland. *The Short Story Cycle: A Genre Companion and Reference Guide.* New York: Greenwood Press, 1989.

Shear, Walter. "Generational Differences and the Diaspora in *The Joy Luck Club*." *Critique* XXXIV. 3 (Spring 1993): 195.

Tan, Amy. *The Joy Luck Club.* New York: Ivy Books, 1989.

Wong, Hertha D. "Louise Erdrich's *Love Medicine*: Narrative Communities and the Short Story Sequence." Ed. Kennedy, J. Gerald. *Modern American Short Story Sequences: Composite Fictions and Fictive Communities.* New York: Cambridge University Press, 1995. 170–193.

2. Marking Race/Marketing Race: African American Short Fiction and the Politics of Genre, 1933–1946

Bill Mullen

On January 11, 1945, the Writers' War Board issued a pamphlet titled "How Writers Perpetuate Stereotypes." Chaired by Rex Stout, a white man, the Board had come together at the urging of blacks and white liberals concerned with the wartime perpetuation of derogatory images of blacks in the arts and mass media, from literature and the stage to film and radio. Surveying numerous examples from each medium, the board issued a sweeping report and ranking of racial stereotypes perpetuated by white American writers. It found that the American theater, in part on the strength of the 1944 Broadway all-black cast play *Anna Lucasta*,[1] (Hughes 53) was the "most liberal of all the media in presenting minority characters sympathetically and honestly" (Murray 259). Next most progressive was the novel, followed by the motion picture, which though it "continued to make disparaging presentations of minorities," had shown "some improvement" (Murray 259) through stereotypical yet novel all-black films like MGM's 1943 *Cabin in the Sky*. Further down the list was radio, followed by the comics, the northern press, and the advertising industry. Last, and most heinous of race offenders, was the short story. This genre, in the board's scathing estimate, "uses the most stereotypes, and is the worst offender" (260) of black and non-white sensibility.

The board supported its findings with a survey of 185 short stories published in popular magazines. In these, it noted, only 16 characters were Negroes, 10 were Jews, "and subtle disparagement of minority characters was noted throughout the 185 stories read" (Murray 259). Specifically, 42 percent of the Anglo-Saxon housewives in the stories had maids and other servants, while only 13 percent of non-Anglo-Saxons did; "'heart' motivations such as love, marriage, affection, patriotism, idealism and justice were attributed to Anglo-Saxon

characters" (259), while "head" motives such as interest in money, self-
advancement, power, and dominance were attributed to non-Anglo-
Saxon ones. In summary, the board concluded, "In magazine stories,
Anglo-Saxons received better treatment than minority and foreign
groups: in frequency of appearance, importance in story, approval and
disapproval, status and occupation, and in traits" (Murray 258).[2]
    The Writers' War Board survey came at a propitious moment. Only
one year earlier, in the September 2, 1944, *Saturday Review of
Literature*, a professor Harry A. Overstreet chided the magazine's readers
and writers to examine anew representations of race and ethnicity in all
fictional genres, specifically the short story. "The time is more than
ripe for fiction writers to examine the whole program of image-making"
wrote Overstreet. "By the turn of a phrase, or by a simple description of
a Negro character, they can sharpen the racial conflict or lessen it. They
have in large measure been responsible for many of the false and
misleading images that persist in the white man's mind. For the most
part they have used him (the Negro) either as material for the white
man's entertainment or as evidence to prove the white man's
superiority" (Ford and Faggett 10).
    Like the War Board's report, Overstreet's complaint was broadly
directed at what had become by 1944 an untenable problem for black
writers and readers: namely the control by and replication of white
dominated images of themselves—and of other non-whites—in both
commercial and literary fiction. That both complaints targeted
magazines and magazine audiences—specific purveyors of short
fiction—indicates a clear recognition at mid-century by both progressive
whites and African Americans of the sustaining and controlling role the
short story had come to play in the development of mass consciousness
about race and ethnicity. This essay will explore how and why race and
ethnicity came to matter so much in the short story by the end of World
War II. It is a long story about the short story, one with roots reaching
all the way back to World War I of the role of both American literary
and mass culture in the construction of American racial identity. One
aspect of the story is how a handful of writers, editors, and publishers
of American fiction recognized, canonized, and deployed the short story
as a cottage industry to create a hegemonic commercial order to which a
conventional and reactionary portrait of race in America was central.[3]
The other, foreshadowed by the anecdotes above, is how African
American writers began to deconstruct this hegemonic narrative in the
form of both individual acts of race rebellion within the short story
genre and a sophisticated, commercially-based assault on the production
and distribution of mass market periodicals in the United States. The

net result was the reversal, by the end of World War II, of more than three decades of reactionary race politics in the production and consumption of the American short story and the foreshadowing of emerging black autonomy in the genre in the post-war period.

* * * * * *

In 1934, *Esquire* magazine published the short story "To What Red Hell." The story, about a fire and riot in a state prison, was the magazine's first appearance by a novice writer named Chester Himes. Written from an Ohio prison, where he was doing 20 years for armed robbery, the story was based on the Easter 1931 fire and riot at the state penitentiary. A jarring, visceral, frenetic account of conflagration and violence, the story appeared with Himes' prison number next to his byline.

Only one year before, Chester Himes had published his first short story, also written in jail, on a typewriter purchased after he was inspired by reading Dashiell Hammett's stories in *Black Mask*, a pulp detective magazine (Oakes, *Conversations* 20). Himes' "His Last Day" appeared in Robert Abbott's black periodical *Abbott's Monthly* in 1933 as did "Prison Mass," another prison tale. In 1933 Himes also published "The Meanest Cop in the World" and "A Modern Marriage" in the newspaper *Atlanta Daily World*. Like the *Baltimore Afro-American*, it was one of a number of prominent black newspapers publishing short stories in the 1930s because of an absence of other viable venues for black writers.[4]

Chester Himes' early stories were, like his pulp fiction influences, tough and slick yet marked by a radically new black perspective on American life. "His Last Day," for example, is a stark account of a twice-convicted killer named Spats' last days in prison before his execution. Written in a brilliantly original hybrid of black vernacular and hardboiled magazine verse, the story juxtaposed two worlds typical to Himes' early tales: one white, free, and prosperous, the other black, poor, and confined.

Between 1934 and 1937 Chester Himes published no less than four short stories using this formula in *Esquire*, a magazine that, in its time, virtually never published African American short fiction: "To What Red Hell"; "The Visiting Hour" (1936); "Every Opportunity" (1937); and "The Night's for Cryin'" (1937). This was no mean feat. In the "Magazine Averages" appendix for *Best American Short Stories of 1938*, Whit Burnett and Edward O'Brien's annual review of American short fiction, *Esquire* was listed first—above *Story, Atlantic Monthly, Harper's Magazine, Frontier and Midland, Prairie Schooner*—in number of distinctive stories and first in number of stories earning "asterisks" for special distinction (453). While these numbers varied from year to year throughout the 1930s, *Esquire* was perennially "rated" by O'Brien and Burnett as one of the top fiction magazines in the country. These ratings signified not only *Esquire's* official standing as a lightning rod of commercial taste and literary "quality" but the near total dominion exerted by O'Brien and Burnett over short fiction in the 1930s. In addition to his collaboration with Burnett on one of the most influential short stories magazines of the decade, *Story*, founded by Burnett in 1931, O'Brien's annual *Best American Short Stories* was a bellwether of the genre, an instant attempt at canon-making and a highly regarded stock index to the fortunes of individual short story writers and stories in a given year.

Yet despite his quadruple appearance in *Esquire*, Chester Himes was never anthologized in these same *Best American Short Stories* collections throughout the 1930s or 1940s. Despite his success in cracking the top short fiction markets, Himes remained, as a short story writer, obscure: his numerous published short stories were never even collected until 1990, six years after his death. This despite the fact that Himes can easily lay claim to being, by any standard, not only the most prolific and successful black short story writer of mid-century but the first after Charles Chesnutt's placement of his turn of the century *Conjure Woman* stories in *Atlantic Monthly* to gain what is fashionably called today "crossover" appeal to a white readership.

The story of Chester Himes' short stories provides an apt starting point for reconsideration of the marks and marketing of race between 1933, his breakthrough publishing year, and 1946, the year after publication of Himes' first novel, *If He Hollers Let Him Go*. Himes' short stories complicate a narrative of 1930s proletarian literature, for example, by providing examples of how a black prison and underclass survived the Depression; they also challenge accounts of the African American canon of the decade, which tend to pay Langston Hughes, Zora Neale Hurston, Marita Bonner, and Richard Wright the largest (and sometimes exclusive) debts for short fiction writing. Indeed, in addition to *The Ways of White Folks* and the occasional publication by Hurston, most accounts of black short fiction of the 1930s single out only Wright's stories in *Uncle Tom's Children* (1938) as the lone 1930s example of black inroads in the genre. Finally, Himes' accomplishments in reaching the heights of the (white) commercial and literary market beg the question of why, and how, a black writer could do so while constructing a vision of black underclass life dominant culture readers in such markets would have little firsthand exposure or access to.

Using Himes as a starting point, a more complete account of black short fiction published from 1933 until the end of World War II would apprehend that it helped to initiate an African American cultural politics that combined at least two strategies represented by the cumulative and intersecting successes of Himes, Hughes, Bonner, Hurston, and Wright: on one hand, this strategy included an engagement with the mechanisms and standards of the white-dominated commercial publishing world eager to add to the stock of the short story, regardless of the author's color (Burnett and O'Brien's market control here being the most prominent example); on the other, a strategy for a racially rebellious and in most cases Left-influenced fiction that would assault the very standards by which both black life and black writing were "indexed" in American life. These contrary yet complementary literary strategies, one of slick mass appeal, one of calculated racial resistance, can be tracked through examining the substance, form, and marketing of black short stories in this period. Combined, these strategies produced a radically revised place for the short story in African American literature in the post-war period.

* * * * * *

In 1937 Richard Wright's "Fire and Cloud" was awarded first prize of $500 in *Story Magazine*'s annual short story competition. It was a stunning moment both for Wright—who had previously published mostly in the Left press—and for black fiction. No black author had ever won such a prestigious commercial literary prize for a short story. Only one year earlier, Wright had published "Big Boy Leaves Home" in *The New Caravan*, a momentous anthology of African American writing, but the *Story* award clearly indicated big things for a writer essentially known only to a small, restricted group of Chicago radicals, activists, and intellectuals.

Wright's commercial success in the genre was, in retrospect, no surprise. In *Black Boy*, the first part of his autobiography, he describes the hypnotic influence pulp and gothic fiction held over his earliest literary creations, including his first published work—a short story, "The Voodoo of Hell's Half-Acre," published as "Hell's Half-Acre" in the Jackson *Southern Register* newspaper in either 1923 or 1924, when Wright was still in eighth grade.[5] Wright also recalls in *Black Boy* devouring short fiction in *Harper's, The Atlantic Monthly,* and *The American Mercury* while working as a bellboy in Memphis in 1926.[6] For the sake of this essay's argument, it is worth noting that the influences of commercial mainstream short story venues predate

Wright's connections with and writing for *The Masses, Anvil,* and *Left Front,* Left-wing little magazines he discovered upon his arrival in Chicago in 1927. Indeed, Wright's celebrated early efforts at writing revolutionary poetry, beginning with publication of "I Have Seen Black Hands" and "A Red Love Note" in *Left Front* in 1933 are predated by a more politically benign (even bourgeois, according to some critics) effort in short fiction: "Superstition," published in the April 1931 *Abbott's Monthly Magazine.*

That both Richard Wright and Chester Himes acknowledge "pulp" and commercial literary fiction as early influence on their own short stories and begin publishing short fiction in the black press only to move into the (white) commercial limelight indicates one trajectory black short fiction took throughout the 1930s. Yet as with Himes, by the mid-30s Wright's popular fiction leanings had also undergone excruciating tests in the forge of black proletariat and underclass experience: Himes' in prison, Wright's in the post office of Depression-era Chicago. From these two vantage points, under influences as disparate as Raymond Chandler and Sherwood Anderson, emerged a style of short story (and eventually the novel) that would dominate African American fiction until publication of Ralph Ellison's *Invisible Man.* It is characterized by a rigorous scrutiny of social and economic conditions under the extremities of racial oppression that has much in common with larger proletarian aesthetics to which Wright, and to a lesser extent Himes, was a debating contributor.[7] Yet equally characteristic of the stories are a highly conscious, constructed language, style, and narrative form equal to and replicative of the standards of the mass market magazine literature of the day. What I want to argue here is that Wright's and Himes' mastery of pulp and mass fiction form made the radical views on race and class (if not gender) they each in different ways intoned in their short fiction "salable." The revolution might not be televised in their short stories, but it would at least win prizes.

Let's examine for a moment, for example, the awarding of first prize to Wright for "Fire and Cloud" in 1937 from *Story Magazine,* a publication that heretofore had published some of the most stereotypically racist fiction of its era.[8] Wright's famous tale about a southern black preacher named Taylor caught in a race and class war between Communist organizers and a racist southern cabal deployed in more sophisticated form all the markings of less-nuanced potboiler fiction of his era: the Reverend is an heroic martyr, bordered by Manichean forces of good and evil; poor, dispossessed African Americans in the town are monumental underdogs to the stark

Machiavellian brutality of the town's racist whites. Finally, there is the story's famous melodramatic ending, achieved after a brutal round of beating, suffering, and trial by fire of the protagonist at the hands of white racists:

> A baptism of clean joy swept over Taylor. He kept his eyes on the sea of black and white faces. The song swelled louder and vibrated through him. This is the way! he thought. Gawd ain no lie! He ain no lie! His eyes grew wet with tears, blurring his vision: the sky trembled; the buildings wavered as if about to topple; and the earth shook. . . . He mumbled out loud, exultingly: "Freedom belong t the strong!" (220)

Wright's brilliant interweaving of the apocalyptic fervor of the black Pentecostal church and Communist dialectics into a melodramatic "big finish" oddly foreshadows their exploitation in more vulgar hands of, for example, the special effects rapture that concluded MGM's all-black 1943 musical extravaganza *Cabin in the Sky*. Indeed it was this hyperdramatic tendency in Wright's early work that opened him up to the much later criticism by James Baldwin that Wright was merely a nineteenth-century melodramatist in social realist guise, a Harriet Beecher Stowe from the hood. In fact it was Wright's deployment of popular convention in the short story that is a key to understanding his often-quoted but seldom-examined complaint in "How Bigger Was Born" that reviews of *Uncle Tom's Children*—into which "Fire and Cloud" was collected in 1938—made him realize "that I had made an awfully naive mistake. I found that I had written a book which even bankers' daughters could read and weep over and feel good about" (Introduction to *Uncle Tom's* xxvii). Richard Yarborough has thoughtfully argued that Wright's reaction was "less to particular flaws in *Uncle Tom's Children* and more to mainstream American culture's capacity to defuse the potency of harsh critique through the very act of commercial consumption and subsequent emotional release" (xxvii). Yet as Wright himself pointed out, his "naivete" had been in part his unconscious eliciting and replication of the tendencies of "commercial consumption" by, in effect, adopting the conventions of sentimental fiction and melodrama to his own page-turning brand of Marxist social realism.

It was these recognizably commercial elements, deployed in most of the stories in *Uncle Tom's Children*, that helped make the book a landmark in both black political *and* commercial publishing. In addition to its *Story* prize, "Fire and Cloud" also won second prize in the prestigious O. Henry Memorial Award contest of 1938, a competition that heretofore had avoided fiction heavily marked by racial or political themes. The revised 1940 edition of the book also included "Bright and Morning Star," previously published in *New Masses* (1938). That story spawned a mini-industry of acclaim and self-replication unprecedented in black short fiction history: Wright's friend Ted Ward dramatized it in 1939; it was included in O'Brien's *Best American Short Stories* of that year and was eventually included in his larger anthology *Fifty Best American Short Stories* (1914–1939). Finally, it is worth noting that the original edition of *Uncle Tom's Children* was issued by Harper and Brothers in 1938 as a Story Press Book, the press initiated by the, by and large, racially and politically conservative (though commercially ingenious) white writer and editor Whit Burnett in the 1930s as a means of controlling, directing, and popularizing the shape of the short story canon.

By 1938 then, comfortably straddling *New Masses* and *Story* as the first African American writer sanctioned by mass white commercial acceptance, Wright had in effect shown a new way to black short story writers: make it down, make it real, but make it sell. "Irish writers learn your trade/sing whatever is well made," Yeats had warned his contemporaries in "Under Ben Bulben." Similarly, Wright's example was a clarion to black writers of short fiction who came after. His prizes and sudden acclaim were to alter not just the market but the standards by which both black and white writers were to evaluate black short fiction, standards over which there would be increasing definition and debate in ensuing years, as I will show.

For Chester Himes, similarly, the short story was in part a chance to measure himself against white commercial literary standards while testing the limits of racial and political dissent within those standards. Recalling his earliest reading experiences of the early 1930s, Himes cited "cheap American fiction, that is, fiction published by slick paper magazines . . . I read the early stories of Dashiell Hammett and Raymond Chandler before they became known to the world. *The Maltese Falcon* by Hammett was one that appeared in serial form in *Black Mask* before it became a book" (Bandler, *Conversations* 108). Himes specifies that it was the "verisimilitude" of Chandler—"his imagery and phraseology," that inspired his earliest efforts. In addition, Himes cited "early William Faulkner," particularly *Mosquitoes,* one of Faulkner's most commercial books—and the influence of early white magazine writers as predating his contact with black writers. Among these, Wright's *Black Boy* and Hughes' *The Big Sea* are named, both appearing after 1940.

Himes' reading patterns suggest that, as with Wright, he was able in part to "package" a radically critical black urban underclass experience into the always already constructed conventions of a commercially viable pulp fiction realism. This is the formula for nearly all of Himes' early stories up to and including his 1940 story "Marihuana and a Pistol," a surreal but hardboiled account of a gunman's dope-induced attempt at a clumsy hold-up. These terse proletarian vignettes revealed Himes' increasing frustration and rage based on his own experience as an itinerant laborer—bus boy, factory worker, shipyard fitter—during and after the Depression. Alternating with this angry literary persona was still another Himes, one who could costume or ventriloquize voices appropriate to more stereotypical popular conceptions of his subject. In "Headwaiter," first published in 1937 in *Opportunity* as "Salute to the Passing," Himes writes with ironic bemusement about Dick, black headwaiter at the prestigious white Park Manor Hotel:

> He could find no suitable words for the moment. He pitied her in a sincere, personal way, for he knew that the countess was the one person in all the world whom she considered as a friend. But he could not express his pity. He was only a headwaiter. He thought there was something sublime in her gallantry which would not let her grief prostrate her; and he knew the countess would have wished it so. (10)

More than just a means of parodying black class pretensions, or enforcing irony, Himes is simply voicing here: taking style where style would take him—into commercial magazines. Indeed, since Himes published stories with regularity in both all-black periodicals like *Opportunity* and white ones like *Esquire*, stories like these were likely composed with more than one potential readership in mind. Himes was, in effect, signifying,[9] improvising on the style, structure and even marketing conventions of the short story genre to transform everyday black experience into pulp fiction or an ironic black sensibility into commercial sense.

Either way, all ways, it worked. Together with Wright, Himes was to transform the form and status of black fiction by the end of the 1930s. Between 1933 and 1940, Himes published 17 stories in mainstream black and white commercial magazines—far more than any other black writer. In 1940 Richard Wright, fast on the heels of his immensely popular *Uncle Tom's Children,* published *Native Son,* a best seller and Book of the Month Club Selection funded by a Guggenheim that Wright was awarded in part through his success in the short story genre. Into *Native Son* Wright distilled, as many scholars have noted, a decade's worth of political and intellectual growth and writing experiment. Simultaneously, and no less importantly, *Native Son* was a virtual pastiche of literary and commercial influences, ranging from popular detective fiction to Dostoyevsky, the black press to *King Kong*.[10] Black literature, the story goes, was never the same. But examination of the period immediately following publication of *Native Son* suggests that it was perhaps Wright's (and Himes') accomplishments in short fiction that more significantly altered the landscape of black letters or at least gave it new direction in the marking and marketing of race in fiction in the 1940s and beyond. For example, of the group of writers commonly associated with Wright's leadership of the South Side Writers' Group, where he wrote and shared the stories that would become *Uncle Tom's Children*, none produced a significant novel during the 1940s. Most—Margaret Walker, Fenton Johnson, Frank Marshall Davis, for example—became poets. Others like Ted Ward became dramatists. Still others like Arna Bontemps chose the sociological essay.[11]

But a largely forgotten member of the South Side Writers Group took a different tact, one that would have lasting impact on the course of black letters in the 1940s. Fern Gayden spent the early years of the decade balancing a social work career with fledgling attempts in the short story genre. In early 1944, Gayden allied with her friend and South Side neighbor, Alice C. Browning, herself experimenting in the short story form after studying for a Masters in literature at Columbia. Gayden and Browning simultaneously hit upon the idea of starting a magazine.

> What should be in it? The answer for both was easy: For a long time, we, the editors, have been attempting to improve our writing techniques and to express ourselves through the short story. The other day, the idea struck us that among thirteen million Negroes in America, there must be many who were eager to write creatively if they had a market. At this point *Negro Story* was conceived and quickly the machinery was started which would bring it to you. There must be thousands of you hungering for stories about Negroes who are real people rather than the types usually seen in print. (*Negro Story*, I, 1)

Gayden and Browning's idea to devote a new black literary magazine to the short story was, as this passage suggests, no accident. The title itself, *Negro Story*, was a race play on *Story*, Whit Burnett's exceedingly successful commercial venture. In an interview with Horace

Cayton, Browning also said that it was Wright's winning of the 1937 first prize from *Story* for "Fire and Cloud" that had first fired her own imagination about the possibilities for creating a "market" for black short fiction. Gayden, too, was in Wright's circle of influence in unique ways, having been his case worker when he first arrived in Chicago and an early reader of his first short stories; Browning, meanwhile, lived merely doors down from the home on Vincennes Avenue Wright had purchased for his family before leaving for New York in 1937. The two decided to pay Wright a visit. Knowing that a Wright story could provide real and cultural capital for a new publishing venture, they asked for and received permission to reprint "Almos' a Man," a Wright story that they had seen collected in the *O. Henry Award Prize Stories of 1940*. Wright agreed.[12]

In the spring of 1944, *Negro Story*'s first 63-page issue appeared. In a "Letter to Our Readers" on its first page, Browning and Gayden began to describe their cultural and political agenda. "We feel that, with few exceptions, the Negro creative writer has not achieved the same degree of maturity as say the Negro artist in the field of music or the fine arts or the Negro in other phases of life" (1). Specifically, they targeted the potential of the short story:

> We believe good writing may be entertaining as well as socially enlightening. To agree with this, one needs only to look back at many of the best sellers which have molded public opinion and focused attention on social evils. We hope that accumulated copies of *Negro Story* will serve as a valuable record of present day writing. (1).

Browning and Gayden's simultaneous stress on the commercial and political potential of the short story was obviously an indirect reference to the success of *Uncle Tom's Children*. This editorial call for a consumer-oriented protest fiction would become a significant editorial refrain in *Negro Story*. In the second issue of the magazine, published in June of 1944, Browning and Gayden elaborated. Because of its centrality to the magazine's philosophy and mission I quote at length:

> That the Negro writer should propagandize and reflect bitterness of attitude is understandable, but he must try to study the techniques of writing and portray his material as artistically as possible. We feel that we can say, with justification, that the theme of the virtuous Negro victim and the savage white tyrant may be overworked, when the Eleanor Roosevelts, Lillian Smiths, and other courageous leaders are

destroying their "demons" in America, and many whites and
blacks are striving to solve their common problem. These
stories have their place, but we do not intend to show only the
"rosy" side of Negro life with the sentimentalized heroine and
hero. We want to present real live characters. If writers can
present these characters in various phases of Negro life . . .
the stories will help to eradicate the stereotypes in American
thinking, concerning the Negro. . . . Our main desire is for a
good story. It may be realism, romanticism, naturalism or
phantasy, *as long as* it is good. We are urging young writers
to study story techniques in order to present effectively the
wealth of dramatic material at hand. There is a wide change in
conditions. The Negro is achieving status and consciousness in
all phases of life.

Summing it up, we are trying to say that the writer who
chooses Negro life for his theme is confronted by a huge task.
It is his responsibility to widen his horizon, examine the facts
and to give truthful and honest interpretations of life. We
would like to have humor and entertainment. We want some
exciting love stories, stories of psychological conflicts—
anything that lends itself to a good plot. The writers should
carry these stories to the climax with adequate suspense and
then effect the denouement without an anti-climax. (*Negro
Story*, I, 2, p.1)

Part foreshadowing of the angry language and substance of the
1945 Writers' War Board survey of representations of race, part fiction
workshop teacher's instruction, and part compromise with wartime
white liberalism of the day, Browning and Gayden's editorial "Letter"
was a peculiar manifesto. Synthesizing more than a decade's study of
the marks and marketings of race in American fiction, their plea for a
"well-wrought" short story that could destroy race prejudice was a
racialized revision of the rhetoric—and accomplishments—of O'Brien's
and Burnett's longstanding deployment of the short story as a form of
cultural—and financial—capital. Indeed the echoes of and diversions
from Martha Foley's own introduction to *Best American Short Stories
of 1942* could hardly be accidental. In 1943, one year before the
appearance of *Negro Story*, Foley, succeeding the recently deceased
editor, had for the first time in a *Best Short Stories* volume addressed
the preponderance of racial and ethnic themes in ways strikingly
similar: "The number of stories about Negro life . . . has been so
large as to appear phenomenal," wrote Foley. "These stories are not the

deliberate, propagandizing type which featured the depression years of the early thirties, nor are they stories written simply out of pity; instead, they are told for the human values in them" (Introduction x).[13]

Negro Story then was truly to be, at least in part, the Negro *Story*. To do so, it would need to demonstrate what Richard Wright and Chester Himes had already proved: that black short fiction could be a high-fidelity recording of black life while falling well within the conventions of salable magazine literature. To this end Gayden and Browning published bi-monthly on average a dozen short stories in *Negro Story* between the spring of 1944 and the spring of 1946.

A portion of the work came from the magazine's acknowledged inspirations and stars, Chester Himes and Wright—Himes, for example, published six stories during its two-year tenure, more than any other writer. Another early contributor was Ralph Ellison, whose first *Negro Story* story, "Mister Toussan," published in the magazine's second issue, came after Ellison's stint as managing editor of *Negro Quarterly*, another war-time journal devoted in part to short fiction. Ellison's appearance in *Negro Story* was a commercial and literary imperative for Gayden and Browning; his work had already appeared in *Common Ground, New Masses, American Stuff*, and *Negro Digest*, the latter considered by the editors as an important but less literary local competitor.[14] Ellison's stories in *Negro Story* also show him choosing, as had Wright and Himes, between literary modes: "Mister Toussan" deploys complex symbolism of flight and allegory foreshadowing the modernist ambitions of *Invisible Man*; other stories, like "The Birthmark" were thirties-style realistic vignettes on racism, this one about a man and woman who identify their murdered friend after he is brutally beaten by a white highway patrolman. Indeed the Ellison short stories in *Negro Story*, like a jazz player's early years, were conservatory pieces to test out various modes of generic virtuosity—precisely as Gayden and Browning had called for.

But it is also true that all of *Negro Story*'s stories shared a risk taking in subject and style that deliberately altered the markings and marketings of race in the short story genre, and more largely in African American literature and popular culture. The breadth of Browning and Gayden's vision of the story as both literary experiment and commercial product provided writers both black and white with infinite ways of addressing and shaping the story of black life during the war. This dazzling variety journalist and part-time *Negro Story* Editorial Adviser Earl Conrad characterized as central to a war-time renaissance in black writing. Conrad dubbed this renaissance the "blues school" and put *Negro Story* at its center. The magazine, he noted, "frankly presents all

of the issues of segregation and protest, the complexities of Negro-
white labor relationships, intermarriage, and all matters of color, 'race,'
caste, class and sex" (*Jim Crow*, 60). This variety was central to a
"flow of Negro writing comparable to the upsurge of socially
enlightening literature that brightened and finally dominated the thirties.
It has taken the form of a belated but decisive reply to *Gone with the
Wind*" (*Jim Crow* 53). Conrad again hit the decisive note: *Negro Story*
would counter white America with a critical, racialized version of mass
popular fiction. This work would be fired and modified by a thirties'
legacy of literary radicalism to which African American writers like
Wright, Gayden, Himes, and Ellison were central and by the urgent
understanding that an effectively marketed mass culture could at last
combat centuries of racist, oppressive mass culture iconography that
Wright, speaking plainly in "The Man Who Went to Chicago," called
"trash."

It was in order to target and effect this change that Gayden and
Browning devoted the majority of space in *Negro Story* to writers who
were amateurs. Roughly 75 percent of the fiction and poetry published
in its pages was by previously unpublished writers, many friends or
acquaintances of the editors, whose work reflected precisely the mass
cultural influences of what Browning and Gayden called pejoratively,
but without denying their sway, "the slicks." These stories, written by
soldiers, postal clerks, schoolteachers, social workers, newspaper
reporters, "housewives" and dozens of fledgling, aspiring writers could
not help but emblematize the issues Conrad identified as "blues
school"— ones of gender, race, class. Nor could they avoid reiterating
the conventions, cliches, and even stereotypes of the mainstream white
and black magazines that had helped to transform these lifelong readers
into writers.

Thus "I Had a Colored Maid," by Margaret Rodriguez, the first
story to appear in Volume I of *Negro Story*, blends melodrama
seemingly derived from Hollywood movies or hackneyed magazine
fiction with a powerfully direct expose of racism. Connie, a black
domestic, is unjustly accused by her racist white mistress, Miss
Merryweather, of stealing—a scene so fraught as to be almost an
archetype in black women's experience. The story's resolution
intertwines outrage at this social injustice with an overwrought but
poignant epiphany: "Miss Merrywether was suddenly assailed by a
thousand emotions, too baffling and too tremendous for her austere self
to grasp at one time. And so she sat down at her desk, Miss
Merrywether did, and stared at Connie. And while she stared, Lily, the
war, Connie, Connie's dead brother in the South Pacific, and poor Mrs.

Martin's dead twins paraded solemnly before her eyes" (I, 1, 8).
Rodriguez' calculated denouement deploys within a novice writers' flair
for melodrama an essential and heretofore unexpressed African American
point of view on domestic servitude within a larger ironic cultural
critique of a racist war.

In "Viney Taylor" by Lila Marshall, a hardworking domestic with a
cheating defense industry husband puts aside his overt sins until she
catches the girl on the side. After they fight violently, Viney is hidden
from police by sympathetic neighbors. Too indifferent to search for the
culprit, the cops walk away: "'Fightin' over some old no-good man,' I
guess. 'C'mon les have a drink' said one. 'And laughing heartily, the
two big officers strode down the street, forgetting that there had been
two women fighting and that they had come to uphold the laws'" (I, 2,
27).

In addition to anticipating concerns that would dominate post-war
black women's literature, stories like this one functioned in *Negro
Story* as generic equivalents to blues songs or folk ballads, reiterating
everyday truths about institutional American racism and neglect in the
guise of salable magazine fiction. Put another way, the commercial
short story "formula" was inflected with a blues holler spirit from the
black side of town.

Thus many stories in *Negro Story*—like blues and ballads—were
on the same theme: told and re-told in different issues, by different
writers as a way of turning the short story into something like the
political bullhorn poetry had been for an earlier generation of Left
poets.[15]

"Rest Stop" by Davis Grubb in the Oct.–Nov., 1944 issue and
"Private Jeff Johnson" by Margaret T. Goss (Burroughs) in the July–
August, 1944 issue and "Let Me at the Enemy—an George Brown" by
Chester Himes in the Dec.–Jan., 1944–45 issue, for example, all dealt
with black soldiers brutalized physically or emotionally by a Jim Crow
Army. Docu-fictions like these, based on real-life harassments and
persecutions of black troops widely reported in the black press, in turn
became in the hands of a master metaphorist like Hughes "high culture"
artifacts like Langston Hughes' "Private Jim Crow," published in the
sixth issue of *Negro Story*. A haunting imaginary drama, Hughes'
surreal play depicts a black soldier riding a Jim Crow train, ridiculed all
the while by a white conductor and the mocking cries of crows offstage:
"You may be an officer, but you're still black. Them bars don't mean a
thing to us" (*Negro* I, 6, 8). If Hughes' work is the better-known and
more accomplished "figure" of African American cultural politics of the
1940s, the short stories of writers like Himes, Grubb, and Goss became

in *Negro Story* its lesser known but no less significant "ground." Such
synthesis and symbiosis bore out, as Hughes and other thirties' radicals
had hoped, some dialectical relationship between folk culture, literary
production, and a black generation's revolutionary aspirations for racial
and social change. In this way, African American mass culture as it
began to evolve during World War II was a belated manifestation of the
1930s American Left's desire for a means of seizing and revising mass
consciousness and its tools for the attempted elimination of race, class,
and gender prejudice. It is this development among others that Manning
Marable alludes to when he calls the 1940s—rather than the radical New
Deal thirties or civil rights era 1950s—the "watershed" era in African
American cultural politics.

* * * * * *

Before it ceased publishing in the spring of 1946, having expended
its meager operating resources, *Negro Story* had altered not only the
status of the short story in America but the stature of the African
American writer. Gwendolyn Brooks' first significant literary prize was
for poetry published in the magazine; Frank Marshall Davis and
Margaret Walker each published some of their very first poems there;
Chester Himes earned a Rosenwald Fund Scholarship for stories
published in the magazine that allowed him to complete his first novel,
If He Hollers Let Him Go. The magazine's circulation crested at 1,000
according to Earl Conrad, reaching black-owned bookstores and
newsstands in New York, Washington, and Pittsburgh; college
campuses like Howard and Tuskegee; military bases abroad; soldier
subscribers overseas. For this reason Robert Bone has called the
magazine "the focal point in black writing in America" during its
publication tenure.

Bone is right, but I would delineate his claim more precisely as
follows: *Negro Story* infused black cultural politics of the 1940s with a
much-needed reexamination of the markings and marketings of race
partly by choosing the right genre to reexamine. The mass appeal,
commercial potential, and relative ease of appropriation endemic to the
short story genre made its reevaluation an essential step in the
reconsideration of race and racial representation for African American
writers and intellectuals in the late 1930s and early 1940s. Evidence that
the genre was partly "turned around" in these decades is, in retrospect,
staggering: during and after the immediate post-war period, Hughes,
Himes, Wright, Ralph Ellison, John Henrik Clarke, Sterling Brown,
John Caswell Smith, Frank Yerby, Albert Murray, John Oliver
Killens, Mary Elizabeth Vroman, Ann Petry, Alice Childress, and

James Baldwin all used the genre to dramatize a score of race and civil rights concerns. These same stories radically revised the landscape of the literary marketplace for African American writers, breaking open previously closed all-white doors (like *The New Yorker*) and pushing and sustaining all-black publications (like *Negro Digest*) committed to publishing black short fiction. The genre was also crucial to the 60s Black Arts Movement: Nikki Giovanni, Hoyt Fuller, Frank London Brown, Lerone Bennett, Jr., LeRoi Jones, Martin Hamer, Ernest Gaines, Anita Cornwell, Diane Oliver, Toni Cade Bambara, Alice Walker, Gayl Jones, Paule Marshall, Ann Allen Shockley, and Julia Fields all used the genre to articulate black nationalist, womanist, and feminist concerns that launched not only a social revolution but a permanent alteration in the status of African American fiction.

Yet even this post-war refinement of wartime resistance strategies was foretold by *Negro Story* in ways laden with irony appropriate to the long story of the short story in black literary history and cultural politics. One anecdote will have to suffice. In Martha Foley's *Best Short Stories of 1946*, no fewer than seven stories from the 1945 editions of *Negro Story* were listed in the book's "Distinctive Short Stories in American Magazines, 1945"—the only stories by African American writers so designated for that year. They included Ellison's "The Birthmark," Himes' "The Song Says 'Keep on Smilin'" and "My but the Rats Are Terrible," Random House editor Bucklin Moon's "Slack's Blues," and Charles Neider's "The Outcast." The last two stories, by "Richard Bentley," were "The Slave," and "Tomorrow," a story about an attempted date rape by a soldier on leave. Richard Bentley, I learned in 1995 from Barbara Browning Cordell, Alice Browning's only child, was in fact a pseudonym for Alice Browning. Writing under a false name to protect her job as a Chicago public schoolteacher, Alice had slipped the yoke and changed the joke, as Ralph Ellison says. Frustrated at having been rejected too many times by the white commercial "slicks," Alice had not only invented a magazine to edit but invented a name to write under. Markings of race/marketings of race in the short story genre were also about markings and marketings of gender for Browning, a member of a generation of African American women whose popular front strategies necessarily extended to insuring the preservation of minimal but hard-won social and personal gains.

Alice Browning's sly turn might be a footnote to the history of American short fiction, but it is a crucial one for reinvestigation of the role of the short story—and the periodical—in the construction of black cultural politics before and after World War II. It is at least clear that

Browning and Gayden's leadership of *Negro Story* continued a project to revolutionize the form, substance, and placement of the short story Himes and Wright had begun, giving it a decidedly feminist and mass market twist. Though they themselves faded from literary view after the war, Browning and Gayden demand reclamation as cultural workers of a significant order in mid-century, race rebels with a cause, literally and symbolically paving the way for a future post-war generation of black female writers, editors, and intellectuals. Returning to the formation of African American cultural politics of the 1940s is thus one way to excavate the road taken by these and other black woman warriors. It is an enterprise Terry McMillan, who knows a thing or two about race and gender markings and marketings, might today refer to as *Breaking Ice*.[16]

NOTES

1. In the September 23, 1944, *Chicago Defender*, Langston Hughes' column described attending a performance of "Broadway's newest smash hit with an all-Negro cast, *Anna Lucasta*" (53). The play was a significant hit whose success was widely reported in the black press, including *Negro Story*. See *Langston Hughes and the Chicago Defender: Essays on Race, Politics, and Culture, 1942–1962*. Ed. Christopher C. De Santis. (Champagne: University of Illinois Press, 1995).

2. For more statistical information on black life and representations of black life during the war, see Florence Murray, ed., *The Negro Handbook 1944–1945* (New York: Current Books, 1946).

3. In a longer version of this essay, I describe the way that white writers and editors, beginning in 1915, began to create a canon of American short fiction through annual collections such as *Best Short Stories*, edited annually by Edward O'Brien from 1915 to his death in 1942. O'Brien, along with the white editor Whit Burnett, founder of *Story* magazine, exerted tremendous control and influence over the canonization of virtually all of the "modern masters" of the American short story, including Sherwood Anderson, Hemingway, Willa Cather, and others. Rarely was a non-white or black writer recognized by O'Brien in his *Best Short Stories* collection, in part because of neglect of the black press where many stories by black writers appeared throughout the 1920s and 1930s. Only *Opportunity* was listed by O'Brien as a magazine worthy of distinction in regard to publication of short stories. *Crisis, Abbot's Monthly*, and black newspapers such as the *Baltimore Afro-American*, which routinely published short stories by black writers in these years, were either not read or ignored by *Best Short Stories*.

4. The *Afro-American* was a leader and innovator in black short fiction, publishing hundreds of stories from the 1920s until 1950, when Nick Aaron Ford and H.L. Faggett published *Best Afro-American Short Stories 1925–1950* (Boston: Meador Publishing Co., 1950, reprint ed. Kraus Reprint Co., 1969). The collection featured mostly novice, amateur writers borrowing heavily from mass and pulp fiction conventions and reflected a generally conservative, middle-class orientation characteristic of the newspaper's readership and editorial point of view. Stories were meant primarily as diversions or light entertainment. "Everybody has his own daily problems, and the newspaper which must carry the news, can, through the means of fiction, turn its readers' minds away from the real to the imaginative," wrote Carl Murphy, President of Afro-American Newspapers in the introduction to *Best Afro-American Short Stories* (6).

5. According to Arnold Rampersad, no copies of the story or the newspaper edition in which it appeared are extant.

6. *The American Mercury* is more famously cited in Wright scholarship for its editor H.L. Mencken's influence on Wright; Mencken's scathing editorial about southern racism which convinced Wright that words could be "weapons." Also, for more on Wright's early reading pulp and mass fiction, see Kenneth Kinnamon, *The Emergence of Richard Wright* (Urbana: Univ. of Illinois Press, 1972). See also Ross Pudaloff's "Celebrity as Identity: Richard Wright, *Native Son*, and Mass Culture" in *Studies in American Fiction* 11 (1983): 3–18.

7. Wright's "Blueprint for Negro Writing," published in 1937 in *New Challenge*, is still an excellent source for understanding Wright's synthesis of proletarian aesthetics with his formative experiences in and among the Chicago poor and working-class during the Great Depression. His essays and articles for *New Masses* published while he was in Chicago and later New York are also valuable for understanding Wright's contribution to the ongoing debate about the political efficacy of literature. Himes, while never a member of the Communist Party and frequently a satirist of its aims and methods, was nevertheless in alliance with Communist organizers in Los Angeles' shipyards during the war, and oftentimes during the 1940s a militant essayist on the need for black writers, intellectuals, and activists to combat racism and classism. See, for example, "Negro Martyrs Are Needed" in the May 1994 *Crisis*; "Now Is the Time! Here Is the Place!" in the September 1942 *Opportunity*; and "Zoot Riots Are Race Riots" in the July 1943 *Crisis*.

8. Some of these racist stories, by fledgling white writers, were even collected into O'Brien's *Best Short Story* collections. One example is "Niggers Are Such Liars" by Richard Paulett Creyke, first published in the July 1937 *Story* and collected in *Best Short Stories of 1938*. Several young boys who suspect that the black cook at their summer camp is illicitly swimming in the lake row him out in the middle and

dump him in. He drowns. The story is intended to be an ironic morality tale but features heinous representation—and lack of consideration for—the character of the cook.

9. I am referring to the West African and African American tradition of rhyming, punning, and otherwise altering linguistic usage and convention to invert or improvise on conventional standards of meaning and representation. See Henry Louis Gates, Jr., *The Signifying Monkey* (New York: Oxford, 1988). Himes, I would argue, is signifying as well on a whole genre, even a market for short story writing.

10. A good book on the popular culture references in and influences on Richard Wright's novel still waits to be written.

11. Bontemps did, of course, publish novels, including the brilliant *Black Thunder*. But his best-known 1940's work was his landmark sociological *They Seek a City*, written with the white proletarian novelist Jack Conroy and first published in 1945. It has been republished in a revised and expanded edition as *Anyplace but Here*.

12. Robert Bone's essay "Richard Wright and the Chicago Renaissance," *Callaloo*. Vol. 9, n.3 (1986): 446–468 provides a very good account of the inception of the magazine and a brief, less satisfying analysis of its intentions and impact. Though he is one of the few scholars to have recognized *Negro Story*'s existence and importance, he makes no attempt to read closely the contents of the magazine or to identify the political positions, overt or hidden, taken by its writers and editors.

13. More evidence of the bizarre and prejudiced standards used by mainstream white editors and publishers to evaluate short fiction is apparent in that same 1943 volume of *Best American Short Stories*. Included in the selections for that year is "The Little Black Boys" by an unknown graduate student named Clara Laidlaw. The story, about a white schoolteacher's affection for twin black boys, is an embarrassingly regressive and sentimental portrait of race. By contrast, Richard Wright's now-classic short story "The Man Who Lived Underground," published in the spring 1942 *Accent*, was merely one of many stories named but not reprinted in the "Roll of Honor" section of the book.

14. In fact *Negro Digest* was far more successful and widely read and distributed than *Negro Story* ever was. The support of the Johnson Publishing Company dwarfed the resources of Browning and Gayden, who published their first issue, according to Bone, with $200 borrowed from Charles Browning, Alice's husband and public relations assistant for the *Chicago Defender*. Browning later admitted that she had overextended herself and her resources by also trying to publish books, children's magazines, and a Lionel Hampton *Swingbook*, which, in fact, appeared in 1946 in a limited edition. Never did either editor, from all evidence, turn a profit from the

magazine, which was funded out of pocket and through contributions
from Chicago organizations like local CIO chapters.
15. I am indebted to Cary Nelson for this connection between political
    change and genre revision in his wonderful book *Repression and
    Recovery: Modern Poetry and the Politics of Cultural Memory*
    (Madison: University of Wisconsin Press, 1990).
16. I am referring to the title of Terry McMillan's anthology *Breaking
    Ice: An Anthology of African-American Fiction* (New York: Penguin,
    1990).

REFERENCES

Baldwin, James. "Everybody's Protest Novel." *Notes of a Native Son.*
Boston: Beacon Press, 1955. 13–23.
Bandler, Michael J. "Portrait of a Man Reading" in *Conversations with
Chester Himes.* Ed. Michel Fabre and Robert E. Skinner. Jackson:
University of Mississippi Press, 1995. 108–111.
Bone, Robert. "Richard Wright and the Chicago Renaissance." *Callaloo.*
Vol. 9, n. 3 (1986): 446–468.
Conrad, Earl. *Jim Crow America.* New York: Duell, Sloan and Pearce, 1947.
Foley, Martha. "Introduction." *Best Short Stories of 1943.* Ed. Martha
Foley. Boston: Houghton Mifflin Company, 1943.
___. *Best American Short Stories of 1946.* Boston: Houghton Mifflin
Company, 1946.
Ford, Nick Aaron, and H.L. Faggett, eds. *Best Short Stories by Afro-
American Writers, 1925–1950.* Boston: Meador Publishing Co., 1950,
reprint ed. Kraus Reprint Co., 1969.
Himes, Chester. *The Collected Stories of Chester Himes.* New York:
Thunder's Mouth Press, 1990.
Hughes, Langston. *Langston Hughes and the Chicago Defender: Essays on
Race, Politics, and Culture, 1942–1962.* Ed. Christopher C. De Santis.
Champagne: University of Illinois Press, 1995.
Marable, Manning. *Race, Reform and Rebellion: The Second
Reconstruction in Black America, 1945–1982.* Jackson: University Press
of Mississippi, 1984.
Murray, Florence, ed. *The Negro Handbook 1946–1947.* New York: Current
Books, 1947.
Negro Story. Ed. Alice C. Browning and Fern Gayden. Vol. 1, n. 1–6; Vol.
II, n. 7–9. Westport, CT: Negro Universities Press, 1970.
Nelson, Carey. *Repression and Recovery: Modern American Poetry and the
Politics of Cultural Memory.* Madison: University of Wisconsin Press,
1990.
Oakes, Philip. "The Man Who Goes Too Fast" in *Conversations with
Chester Himes.* Ed. Michel Fabre and Robert E. Skinner. Jackson:
University of Mississippi Press, 1995. 17–22.

O'Brien, Edward, ed. *Best American Short Stories of 1938.* Boston: Houghton Mifflin Company, 1938.

Wright, Richard. *Black Boy.* New York: HarperCollins, 1993.

___. "The Man Who Went to Chicago." *Eight Men.* New York: Thunder's Mouth Press, 1987. 210–250.

___. *Uncle Tom's Children.* New York: Harper Collins, 1936. Reprinted 1993.

Yarborough, Richard. "Introduction." *Uncle Tom's Children.* New York: HarperCollins, 1993. ix–xxviiii.

3. Womanist[1] Storytelling: The Voice of the Vernacular

Madelyn Jablon

Today. My simple passion is to write our names in history
and walk in the light that is woman.

—Sonia Sanchez, *Poem*

Feminists equate voice with power and silence with passivity.
Scholars of African American women's writing share this understanding
of speech and silence as made evident by readings of Zora Neale
Hurston's *Their Eyes Were Watching God.* Critics interpret Janie's
acquisition of voice as a sign of her autonomy. They perceive her
telling her own story as the culmination of empowerment. Critics note
that when Janie shares her story with Phoebe, she relies on the
vernacular tradition of call-and-response, the antiphonal interaction
between artist and audience. The privileging of speech and "speakerly"
writing also reveals the influence of vernacular tradition and the
celebration of spontaneity and improvisation in artistic invention.
Experiments with narration such as the introduction of free indirect
discourse and shifts in point of view suggest vernacular social
constructions of transubjectivity, the indeterminate nature of identity,
and the communal nature of narrative. These discussions of Hurston's
novel are evidence of the centrality of black expressive cultural
traditions in womanist fiction.

One consequence of these readings of Hurston's novel has been the
formulation of a canon of womanist texts debuting protagonists who
are empowered by speech. Barbara Christian's landmark study
"Trajectories of Self-Definition: Placing Contemporary Afro-American
Women's Fiction" chronicles this movement. Like similar studies of
white women writers, her analyses rely on character studies that
presuppose an understanding of the text as a mimetic document.[2]

Influenced by developments in communication and discourse analysis, subsequent scholars of black women's writing have redefined their subject and method. Deborah McDowell and Mae Henderson have developed alternative approaches to the study of womanist fiction. McDowell does so by redefining character as a process and identity as "a transient event."[3] Henderson's paradigm rests on defining voice as a polyphonic constituency of voices "borrowed from the outside" (119). These scholars share recognition of the social nature of language and identity. They see black expressive traditions through the lenses of dialogism and communication theory.

Regardless of their particular theoretical perspectives, scholars of womanist fiction recognize its debt to African traditions. This debt is explained by theorists such as Amiri Baraka (formerly LeRoi Jones) and Houston Baker, Jr., who observe that the Africanisms most likely to survive relocation were those that could not be destroyed. Baraka suggests that music, dance, religion, and the arts survived because they produced no visible or tangible artifacts: "these nonmaterial aspects of the African's culture were almost impossible to eradicate . . . and are the most apparent legacies of the African past" (Jones 16). Baker calls these surviving Africanisms "nonmaterial counterintelligence" (38). Voice and the autobiographical impulse are foremost among these:

> The generative conditions of diasporic African life that privilege spiritual negotiation and the work of consciousness also make autobiography the premier genre of Afro-American discourse. Bereft of material, geographical or political inscriptions of a state and a common mind, diasporic Africans were compelled to seek a personal, spiritual assurance of worth. Their quest was analogous to Puritan religious meditations, such as Jonathan Edward's *Personal Narrative*, in the mainland British colonies of North America. For, like their Puritan fellow in deracination and forced immigration, Africans were compelled to verify a self's being. They were forced to construct and inscribe unique personhood in what appeared to be a blank and uncertain environment. Our intellectual history privileges the unseen and the intangibly personal. (39)

Voice is the nonmaterial artifact which articulates the autobiographical impulse for the enslaved African. In his discussion of the evolution of African music in the "new world," Baraka depicts the autobiographical vernacular voice in its musical context. First he describes the emphasis on rhythmic, rather than melodic or harmonic qualities and the use of "polyphonic or contrapuntal rhythmic effects" (27). Then he explains that the African drum reproduces the sound of the human voice and how sensitivity to changes in rhythm, timbre, stress, and pitch are also necessary to understanding African music and languages. His hypothesis was that sensitivity to "significant tone" was "passed on to the new world" (26). Lastly, Baraka describes the antiphonal and improvisational qualities of African music and its functionality. Whereas Western musicians play "classically," aiming to sound as if they have rehearsed, African and African American musicians aim to recreate the sound of the human voice in a spontaneous outburst of expression. Baraka says, "the Western concept of the cultivation of the voice is foreign to African or Afro-American music" (30).

These attributes of African music and language are present in womanist fiction. Their presence reflects the womanist agenda of celebrating traditions and recognizing affinities among the diverse peoples of the African Diaspora. The following examination of first-person homodiegetic narrators in womanist short stories adds to our understanding of voice and the vernacular traditions that inform it.[4]

In her study of the oral tradition in African American literature, Gayle Jones observes how the privileging of the third-person point of view in the study of Western literature has led to the de-valuing of African American literature. According to Jones, applying this preference for third-person narration to African American literature is "something like judging English drama by Racine's dramatic method" (132). Jones' study of African American writers who engage the vernacular by privileging the first-person point of view responds to this bias by developing a theory endemic to black expressive traditions. Like Robert Stepto, Barbara Christian, and Houston Baker, Jones argues that first-person narrative plays a central role in the history of African American literature. Consistent with this understanding of first-person narrative, womanist writers engage first-person point of view to demonstrate self-authentification and self-definition.[5] Voice serves as a vehicle of self-expression and a synecdoche of identity for womanist storytellers whose experiments with first-person point of view negate the constructs on which the precedence of third-person narrative rests.[6] As a synthesis of the triad of vernacular voices, that of the preacher, musician, and griot, the first-person voice of the womanist storyteller posits alternative definitions of identity and a recasting of relationships among writer, narrator, and audience.

J. California Cooper is an award-winning playwright, novelist and short story writer. Her short fiction records the voices of everyday

people. Unlike any writer since Hurston, her work demands to be read
aloud. Her short story "The Big Day" is narrated by a homodiegetic
narrator who fills the dual roles of narrating agent and focalizer.[7]
Biggun's story recalls the funeral of her friend, whose "big day"
commemorates ninety years of living including a forty-five year
marriage that survives the trials of childrearing, age, and infirmity. The
funeral includes a repertoire of church traditions: the oratory of three
preachers, the reading of Scripture, the antiphonal responses of the
congregation, the stirring contributions of vocalist and pianist, and a
meal of chicken, roast ham, and corn following the church service.

   Among Biggun's descriptions of the day's events are stories about
her own life, for in Cooper's fiction, womanist storytelling issues from
the tension between the narrator and the various stories she tells. The
narrator of "The Big Day" is also ninety years old. The juxtaposition of
stories about herself with commentary about the funeral and the life of
the deceased reveals the narrative's ideological underpinnings.
Following a description of her friend's long marriage, Biggun "talks"
about her own romantic life, including a passing thought about the
deceased:

> Just think, if I'd a married him, I'd a had somebody to keep
> these old bones warm all these years my bed been empty.
> But . . . he wasn't the man for me . . . I wasn't the girl for
> him. I picked my own man, he died. Another one, I left that
> trifflin fool and he was the best lover. Another one, we was
> together a long while, he wasn't no real good lover, but was a
> good man. He died. I was tired then. Nuff, enough. (4)

Additional contrasts between the narrator and her friend present the
narrator's way of life as preferable. Whereas he is remembered for his
smiles and laughter, she will be remembered for the orneriness best
epitomized by her favorite saying: "I ain't ready." She isn't ready to
leave her home, to leave the church, or the widow's house. When she
gets into bed at the end of the day, she tells God: "You can call on me
do You get ready to. But I'm gonna tell you right now, just like I been
tellin you for years now . . . I AIN'T READY" (13). Her
stubbornness suggests a possible explanation of why she is alive and
her friend is not.

   Although the funeral is the ostensible subject of the story, the
narrator's digressions upstage it. The deceased friend, mute and passive,
is unable to object to his role as minor character. His story is at the
disposal of his friend, for he exists only as long as she remembers him.

Although she feigns reluctance—"I ain't ready for all this talkin. Cause I'm sad" (4)—his funeral is an opportunity to tell her stories. Biggun uses language to negotiate experience. Harnessing the power of the word, she controls reality. Her insistence on naming herself illustrates how she creates reality through language, particularly sound. Her grandchildren call her "Mama," then "Big Mama," but when there are "too many mamas in between," she has them call her just "Biggun" (5). She "don't 'low no 'granmaw' stuf cause it sounds like somethin you snatch off a hog" (5). This placing of priority is with good cause because the name she chooses for herself minimizes her maternal role and her relation to the speaker and emphasizes an omnipotence akin to God's.

Biggun's is an aural world where sound takes precedence over meaning. She speaks a womanist language that subverts semantics. The importance of sound is evident in Biggun's description of the church service, which reads as if told by a blind person recalling a scene by the sound it produces. She recalls the foot stomping of the congregation: "the pattin of the feet some people is playin out their feelings with" (9). This passage moves toward the reproduction of sound, and Biggun's diegetic narrative metamorphosizes into a mimetic reproduction of sound. Musical notes punctuate the passage, illustrating the rhythmic exchange of piano and patting feet. This transcription of sound captures the spirit of the mourners. The "significant tone" which Baraka identifies as characteristic of African language and music is reproduced in the rhythm of the feet. Time is calibrated in eighth notes, quarter notes, and whole notes that suggest the sound extending into the sentence and serving as a muted backdrop for the percussion of patting feet. The piano "talks" and the audience responds with feet and voice.

The introduction of musical notation, repetition, and the unconventional punctuation and typography demonstrate what Michael Awkward identifies as the "black expressive cultural precedence for technical experimentation."[8] More specifically, the musical notes that punctuate the passage exemplify "denigration." Awkward defines this term as "appropriative acts by Afro-Americans which have successfully transformed, by the addition of black expressive cultural features, Western cultural and expressive systems . . ." (9). Cooper's "denigration" of Western forms is a weapon in her arsenal of womanist tactics. In addition to her "denigration" of musical notation, she "denigrates" the conventions of spelling by repeating a letter in the middle of a word to emphasize the oral quality of speech and the primacy of sound: "the preacher steps up slowwwly" (9).

From sound, Biggun constructs the world. Listening to the voice
of the soloist, she distills the details of the singer's life not by *what* she
sings but by *how* she sings:

> Had a good, strong deep voice full of sorghum syrup,
> blackberry juice, collard greens and plenty of pain. That
> woman sent me somewhere! That she was holdin on to God
> and her man was all in the cracks of her voice. I hear it! I
> know the sound! Of a woman who loves her God, and her man
> and who thinks she is ugly, big and awkward cept with one
> thing, a beautiful voice. She use it every time she can, so her
> man can hear it . . . and forget that other pretty woman who
> won't let him lone. (9)

Biggun uncovers the soloist's story in her voice. Her story moves
Biggun because it is a chapter in the storyteller's own romantic life.
Consistent with black expressive cultural traditions, Biggun's words
testify to the singer's talents and her skillful improvisation of "classical
blues" themes. Hazel Carby defines "classic blues" as "a discourse that
articulates a cultural and political struggle over sexual relations: a
struggle that is directed against objectification of female sexuality
within a patriarchal order but which also tries to reclaim women's
bodies as the sexual and sensuous subject of women's songs" (749).
This womanist blues tradition is evoked in the soloist's song. It is also
present in this final excerpt, where many of the womanist narrative
strategies converge: juxtaposition, denigration, the superimposition of
the diegetic through the transcription of an oral text, and the
undermining of Western phallocentric systems of signification. Here the
conventions of women's fashion are "denigrated" by the bodies of
strong, active women:

> I look at all the fine, bright clothes on some of the young and
> old strong bodies. Some don't look just right cause the
> woman's arms are muscled and strong from pullin and hoein
> cotton, pullin corn, washin by hand and wringin them big
> heavy sheets and quilts out. Reachin for distant berries, pullin
> greens, and workin in the cabbage patch. Strong arms, strong
> backs, muscles in legs strong from pushin and pullin not only
> things, but life. Sweat already under some arms, I see. Some
> of these clothes was meant to be for little frail weak, stylish,
> lady-like bodies. I see a ruffle on a strong corded neck, a
> crocheted collar coverin the shoulder of a woman who plows
> for herself. She probably crocheted that collar too. (7)

This digression is an affirmation of the black woman's strength, beauty, and abilities. The object of the first sentence is "strong bodies." Subsequent sentences refer only to body parts—"arms," "legs," "neck," and "shoulder." Rather than incapacitate, the dismemberment of the black woman's body produces an explosion of energy. Her anonymity enhances her power. Whereas Biggun controls her destiny by choosing her own name, this "nameless" woman, referred to only as "woman" or "she," is empowered by African tradition, which invests authority in those who remained unnamed and who cannot be summoned or controlled.

The subject of "The Big Day" is subverted by a narrator whose digressions shift attention from the man in the casket to the woman who is speaking. Her appreciation of cultural traditions—the church, music, women, and their traditions—make her a womanist. Her assertion of power through the naming of herself, and through the subordination of meaning to sound, identify her as a radical feminist engaged in rebuilding society. Her subtle commendation of sexual liberation (rather than marriage), non-traditional relationships, and her praise of strong women who plant, harvest, wash, and crochet locate this story squarely in the tradition Alice Walker defines as womanist.

Central to most discussions of point of view is the controversy concerning the identification of similarities observed in the author and the narrating agent or focalizer. This is especially relevant to the analysis of fiction narrated from the first-person point of view. Instructors of introduction to literature courses are continually reminded that readers often assume that the voice of the narrator is the voice of the author. New critics and their descendants argue that such assumptions violate the autonomy of the work and commit an injustice toward a writer who may have nothing in common with the characters she creates. By distinguishing between extradiegetic and diegetic narrative voices, narratologists suggest a compromise. These theorists recognize the potential presence of an authorial voice in extradiegetic material such as forewords, addresses to the reader, introductions, and afterwords. Affinities between extradiegetic and diegetic narrative voices increase the perceived validity of the narrative voice.[9] For example, the author's note that appears on the page preceding "The Big Day" is an extradiegetic narrative that suggests an affinity between author and narrator. The note's grammar and syntax resemble that used in the short story. Paragraphing, the use of ellipses, sentence fragments, and tmesis are additional devices which appear in the words of both "author" and narrator.[10] The author's note also expresses the strong spirituality that informs the fiction, for it says the author stays as close to God and His wisdom as possible. This affinity and the fact that the narrator is consistent throughout the stories in the collection suggest that readers who recognize author and narrator as synonymous are justified. However, in her discussion of point of view and author-character relationships, Susan Lanser argues otherwise. She suggests that "the narrator who does not take part in the story world is most closely associated with the narrative voice" and that "the authorial voice is not conventionally equated with the private narrator, the named narrator-character or the focalizer" (154).

According to Lanser, the more complex the first-person narrator-character, the less likely he or she will be "mistaken" for the author. Lanser says, "I also suspect that the more frequently a writer uses first-person narration—the greater the number and variety of I-narrators he or she creates—the smaller the likelihood that autobiographical connections will continue to be presumed" (154). Examples from British and Anglo-American literature are used to support Lanser's hypothesis, but her theory is challenged by works that issue from the African American vernacular tradition. First-person narration is characteristic of much African American literature. Subsumed by this first-person voice is a tradition that places paramount importance on subjectivity. The voice that speaks is more important than the story it tells. When art is the process and not the product, the autobiographical subject is paramount to artistic experience.

Cooper's spirituality is central to her fiction and her feminism. Its presence in "The Big Day" can be seen in church rituals including a sermon, the citing of Scripture, and the call-and-response of preacher and congregation. Religious traditions also inform the style and purpose of the story, which reads as a sermon addressed to the reader. Its theme might be advertised on a billboard: "ARE YOU READY?" The narrator's digressive commentary is reminiscent of the personal anecdotes provided by the preacher in an effort to make the text relevant to the contemporary audience. Cooper's short story channels the didacticism of the sermon to recognition of women, their work, music, and pleasures.

Womanist storytellers often rely on folktales as a source for the creation of characters, stories, and storytelling technique. Many characters resemble Brer Rabbit, who outsmarts opponents who are bigger and more powerful. Bett, the protagonist of A. Yemisi Jimoh's short story "Peace Be Still," recalls this folk character. However, Jimoh gives Bett three voices that represent distinct levels of socialization. An emphasis on the spoken word is made evident by the contrasting of two documents or literary texts which must be "spoken of" or presented in the context of a conversation to be meaningful and relevant. Bett is evidence of Mae Henderson's theory that black women speak in a "plurality of voices as well as a multiplicity of discourses" (122). "Peace Be Still" contains a repertoire of first-person narrative voices. The italicized words used to set off an interior monologue reveal the death of Bett's daughter by drugs. Quotation marks are used to indicate the words Bett speaks to herself as when she tells herself to "hurry up" in order to catch the bus. These voices take turns speaking, but the result is a dialogue in which the speakers neither hear nor respond to each other. This conversation is interrupted by John, the newspaper vendor who engages Bett in discussion of the recent murder of the Davisons. The three voices introduced in the opening passage of the short story represent the levels of Bett's psyche. The narrative commences with the voice from her inner self recorded in stream-of-consciousness narration and concludes with the voice she uses to speak to others, presented in the dialogue with John. These voices are contrasted with two printed documents: the first is a letter in Bett's purse recommending her services to prospective employers and the second is a newspaper article reporting the death of the Davisons. By synthesizing these narratives, the reader constructs a narrative that explains what has occurred. Enacting revenge for her daughter's death, Bett has murdered her employer, a physician who profited from the drug addictions of people like her daughter through the sale and distribution of illegal drugs. Before Bett murdered the doctor, however, she had the foresight to procure a letter of reference from him. The final monologue suggests that she will seek employment with the police officer assigned to investigate the case. If employed, she will do what is necessary to confound the investigation and deter discovery of her crime.

Writing and speech are also contrasted in Viki Radden's short story "Riding the Wheel of Fortune." Radden, recipient of a Hawthornden International Fellowship for Writers, creates a protagonist who is also a master of subterfuge. She also uses her voice to contextualize the writing of others. "Riding the Wheel of Fortune" is narrated by a high school student, the leader of The Association of Lonely Black Girls (A. L. B. G.). As "secret agents extraordinare," they do "sly things girls aren't suppose to do" (34). When Brad Holliman crosses out the name that identifies her brother's parking space, replacing it with the word "JIGABOO," the girls sip Jolt cola, munch on potato chips, and develop a plan. That evening, the narrator pours powdered sugar into the radiator of the Volvo that Brad loves: "a few grains for each time he called us niggers, but most of all . . . for the spray paint on her brother's parking space" (34). She has built a "wheel of fortune," thereby proving her mother's favorite saying: "what goes around comes around."

Although one narrator is young and the other old, both Bett and the protagonist of "Riding the Wheel of Fortune" engage in acts of subterfuge by telling stories that usurp the power of the written word. The "speakerly" quality of their stories contrasts with the formal language of the literary world. Ultimately, their voices wrestle control over the writing and how it is to be received. In this way, womanist storytelling deconstructs literature, a signifying structure of the dominant culture, "to formulate a critique and transformation of the hegemonic white male symbolic order" (Henderson 135).

Many theorists of African American literature suggest that culture is paramount in determining who speaks and how. Reading voice as a reflection of social forces aimed at a specific audience has impacted the study of voice in African American literature. Borrowing from Hans-Georg Gadamer and M. M. Bakhtin, Henderson suggests both intersubjective and intrasubjective characteristics of the black female subject:

> As gendered and racial subjects, black women speak/write in multiple voices—not all simultaneously or with equal weight but with various and changing degrees of intensity, privileging one *parole* and then another. One discovers in these writers a kind of internal dialogue reflecting an *intrasubjective* engagement with the *intersubjective* aspects of self, a dialectic neither repressing difference nor, for that matter, privileging identity, but rather expressing engagement with the social aspects of self ("the other[s] in ourselves"). It is this subjective plurality (rather than the notion of the cohesive or fractured subject) that, finally, allows the black woman to become an expressive site for a dialectics/dialogics of identity and difference. (137)

Henderson's postulation of the speaking subject suggests that womanist storytelling can be understood as a dramatization of an internal dialogue of social voices.

Like "The Big Day," Cooper's short story "Femme Fatale" is narrated by a homodiegetic narrator. The story begins with Roscoe introducing herself and stating the story's moral. This introduction reveals that she is a "griot-historian-shaman-seer-wise woman."[11] She describes her childhood and what it was like to grow up in an indulgent, loving family: "I was spoiled, chile, spoiled. Anything I wanted, I got. Within reason. Mostly food. Cakes, pies, candy, cookies, cobblers, ice cream" (2). This light hearted-tone ceases, however, when Roscoe recalls the tragic death of her parents (loggers who drown) and the loneliness that followed. Although she is raised by her old-fashioned grandmother, she develops an obsession with television romances. During her teens she comes to believe that, like the starlets who appear on her screen, she too is a *femme fatale*:

> I saw pretty women, handsome men and love stories. I loooooved the love stories. One of the programs talked about this Femme Fatale and that's when I realized that one of them Femme Fatales was in me. Couldn't nobody else see her, but I knew she was there. I felt her deep down inside of me. See? Yes, indeedy! (4–5)

Because she is not sought by high school football players, she courts Wyndel, whose two-hundred pounds is "mostly in his waist, thighs and arms" (6). Initially, she is disappointed because he doesn't bring flowers, and he wears his "regular clothes" instead of something "special" on dates (9). After mild rebuke, she finds his behavior considerably improved. When he takes her to a hotel, orders "wine and a light repast," and confesses that he is "a fool for love," Roscoe agrees to marry him (10). Although she believes she has made this decision for herself, it is her grandmother who has really made it for her. Roscoe agrees to marry a man she doesn't love because her grandmother has warned her about sex before marriage and the commodity value of sexual inexperience: "You better not let everybody know what's up under your clothes. Your future husband might not like it and it'll go bad for you if you love him and he finds out" (10). Before she dies, her grandmother gives her more advice, which is also accepted wholeheartedly. Speaking metaphorically, she tells Roscoe to "go down the road of life," and she gives her $17,000 to pay some of "the tolls." Roscoe takes this advice along with her grandmother's shoes: "told them shoes they were grandma going with me to see something" (13).

Wyndel dies before they can be wed, however, so Roscoe moves into an apartment in the city where her life is alternately controlled by the internalized voices of her grandmother and the *femme fatale*. When she locates an apartment, she says, "I don't know how I knew to do all this so it had to be the Femme Fatale" (15). She decorates her apartment with plastic flowers, a "shiny satinese glamour bedspread"— "all for the Femme Fatale part of her" (15). She gets a job, a new hairstyle, false eyelashes, and fingernails and is not deterred from her plan by a manicurist who laughs at her request for gold flecks in her toenail polish. Roscoe retorts: "A Femme Fatale can do whatever she wants to" (16). She changes her name to Darlin, "a sweet-talkin name" and begins her search for a mate with the men who reside in her apartment building (17). She selects Hudson in Apartment #6 and pursues her plan. The appetizing smell of salt, pepper, onion, and garlic boiling in a pot of water on the stove inspires Hudson to praise her good cooking when he walks by her door. After accepting a date and an invitation to visit his apartment, she realizes she has made a mistake. Her grandmother had "talked to her about love" explaining that "it ain't everything but it's well mixed in the foundation of love and marriage" (22). Hudson didn't fit the prescription. Roscoe explains:

> Well, he flexed his big muscles and did all kinds of exercise in the bed. You could sure tell he was athletic. But the one muscle that would have made a difference was the one he didn't know what to do with it. See? All that body and, far as I could tell, it was only good for show and running and eatin. I'm not talkin about "how much" of it either. I wanted to tell him, "Listen, it ain't no lance. Don't throw it! We ain't in the Olympic. We in bed tryin to make love. Win a heart. Not a medal" (21)

Depressed over her failure to find a man, she prays to God. Like a fairy godmother, Miss Mimi, the landlady, appears at the door of her apartment to advise her and assume the role left vacant by the death of her grandmother. Miss Mimi convinces Roscoe to use less makeup and to redecorate her apartment in more subtle hues. She reads verses from Second Timothy about selfish, godless men like Hudson. Finally she teaches Roscoe that a "real Femme Fatale is not false and gaudy . . . she has class" (28). At Miss Mimi's urging, Roscoe begins a relationship with Roland in Apartment #4 and gets him to propose. After their marriage, they return to Roscoe's home in the country to reopen the store where Roscoe's parents and grandmother worked. Roscoe has accomplished her objective and the Femme Fatale who resides within her appears content with her husband and their marriage. Unhappiness is suggested in this description of her days, however:

> On Monday, Wednesday, Friday and Saturday, I am a wife and do all the things that keep my house runnin smooth and clean. I pamper him every day. I have no set rules for him because I like the rules he set for himself.
> Tuesday, Thursday and Sunday, I bathe pamper myself, go to the beauty shop if I want to, whatever. He cooks. I lounge

around in lounging clothes. I take care of my own nails and things now. (I kept breakin the other kind off.) I am a Femme Fatale every day, but especially on those days.

But . . . on any day, I can be a Femme Fatale if I feel like it. Roland put a bell out here by the window so I can ring for him when I need him. So, see? I'm just gonna lean out the window and ring this bell. He closes up and comes right on in.

Look, here he comes now.

See? (40)

Unlike Janie who works beside Tea Cake in the fields, or Roscoe's parents who work side by side at logging sites, Roscoe lounges while Roland tends to the store. She has found someone to take over her grandmother's business so that she can enjoy her leisure. Submitting to the demands made by the internalized voices of grandmother and Femme Fatale provides Roscoe with a marriage that works according to rules and conventions: Roscoe's husband is a houseboy trained to respond to the sound of her bell. An adolescent obsession with glamorous movie stars and Hollywood romances leads to a life of garish imitation and self-indulgence. While Bett's internal voices reveal the different social dimensions of her personality—public and private selves—Roscoe's internal voices belong to others, "outsiders," who advise and instruct her. Following their advice results in Roscoe living the life of a woman on a pedestal. For better or for worse, Bett and Roscoe are masters of the plurality of discourses Henderson observes in her study of black women.

According to Steven Cohan and Linda M. Shires, "the telling of a story exceeds not only the story but the stable personification of the storyteller as well" (112). As characters "in process," womanist storytellers are inherently unstable. The short stories discussed here are appropriate vehicles for womanist writing, for in each short story the protagonist moves toward self-definition: her identity is constructed as a transient event; her voice is privileged, and her point of view is central to the story. Taken as a group, the voices in these short stories form a chorus: Biggun, Brett, Roscoe, and the others sing loud and proud.

NOTES

1. Alice Walker defines womanist as "a black feminist or feminist of color . . . a woman who loves other women, sexually and/or nonsexually and appreciates and prefers women's culture." The

term originates from the folk expression, "you're acting womanish" (xi).

2. In "Trajectories of Self-Definition: Placing Contemporary Afro-American Women's Fiction," Barbara Christian describes the history of African American women's writing as a movement toward independence and self-definition. In a later essay, "But What Do We Think We're Doing Anyway: The State of Black Feminist Criticism(s) or My Version of a Little Bit of History," Christian acknowledges some of the problems resulting from her efforts to establish a canon of black women writers. In "Toward a Feminist Narratology," Susan Lanser makes this assessment of the shortcomings of feminist theory and suggests ways to remedy it.

3. Deborah McDowell discusses character as process in "Boundaries: Or Distant Relations and Close Kin" (61). Donald Wesling and Tadeusz Slawek discuss voice as a "transient event" in *Literary Voice: The Calling of Jonah* (39).

4. Lanser attributes this term to *Narrative Discourse* by Gérard Genette. According to Lanser, Genette distinguishes between narrators who are not part of the story world and narrators who are; the term *heterodiegetic* is given to narrators who are not a part of the story and the word *homodiegetic* to narrators who are characters in the fictional world (37). This study will examine first-person narrators who are also characters in the stories they narrate.

5. The premise of Robert Stepto's study *From Behind the Veil: A Study of Afro-American Narrative* is that the African American literary tradition is a movement toward self-authentification. Self-definition is the term Barbara Christian's employs in "Trajectories of Self-Definition" where she suggests that the history of black women's fiction is a movement toward self-definition.

6. Discussion of voice as a synecdoche occurs in the introductory chapter of Wesling and Slawek's *Literary Voice*.

7. Cohan and Shires define these terms: *"Focalization"* consists of a triadic relation formed by the *narrating agent* (who narrates), the *focalizer* (who sees), and the *focalized* (what is being seen and, thus, narrated) . . . (95).

8. Quoted from Michael Awkward's response to McDowell's essay, "Boundaries: Or Distant Relations and Close Kin" (76).

9. Lanser explains this corollary as follows:

> The extrafictional voice is the most immediate vehicle available to the author, and although most novelistic

communication does not take place on the extrafictional level, the extrafictional voice carries more than its quantitative proportion of impact. Because much of the extrafictional material is encountered before the fiction begins, and because the extrafictional voice carries the ontological status of history, it conventionally serves as the ultimate textual authority (*The Narrative Act* 129).

10. Tmesis is an alien phoneme inserted in the middle of a word to create a new word. Cooper's "slowwwwly" exemplifies this technique. I do not use this term as Roland Barthes does in *The Pleasure of the Text* where he identifies tmesis as a characteristic of reader response: a "source or figure of pleasure . . . a seam or flaw resulting from a simple principle of functuality" which occurs at the moment literature is consumed by the reader (11). It is, in short, the reader's selection of what will and will not be read.

11. I am indebted to Charlotte Watson Sherman for coining this term in the introduction to the anthology she edited, *Sisterfire: Black Womanist Fiction and Poetry* (xviii).

REFERENCES

Awkward, Michael. *Inspiring Influences: Tradition, Revision, and Afro-American Women's Novels.* New York: Columbia University Press, 1989.

Baker, Houston, Jr. *Workings of the Spirit: The Poetics of Afro-American Women's Writing.* Chicago: University of Chicago Press, 1991.

Barthes, Roland. *The Pleasure of the Text.* New York: Hill & Wang, 1975.

Carby, Hazel. "It Jus Be's Dat Way Sometime: The Sexual Politics of Women's Blues." *Feminisims: An Anthology of Literary Theory and Criticism.* Eds. Robyn R. Warhol and Diane Price Herndl. New Brunswick: Rutgers University Press, 1991. 746–758.

Christian, Barbara. "But What Do We Think We're Doing Anyway: The State of Black Feminist Criticism(s) or My Version of a Little Bit of History." *Changing Our Own Words: Essays on Criticism, Theory, and Writing by Black Women.* Ed. Cheryl A. Wall. New Brunswick: Rutgers University Press, 1989. 58–74.

___. "Trajectories of Self-Definition: Placing Contemporary Afro-American Women's Fiction." *Black Feminist Criticism: Perspectives on Black Women Writers.* New York: Pergamon, 1985. 171–86.

Cohan, Steven, and Linda M. Shires. *Telling Stories: A Theoretical Analysis of Narrative Fiction.* New York: Routledge, 1988.

Cooper, J. California. "The Big Day." *The Matter Is Life.* New York: Anchor/Doubleday, 1991. 1–13.

___. "Femme Fatale." *Some Love, Some Pain, Sometime.* New York: Doubleday, 1995. 1–40.

Henderson, Mae Gwendolyn. "Speaking in Tongues: Dialogics, Dialectics, and the Black Woman Writer's Literary Tradition." *Reading Black, Reading Feminist: A Critical Anthology*. Ed. Henry Louis Gates, Jr. New York: Meridian, 1990. 116–42.

Jimoh, A. Yemisi. "Peace Be Still." *Sisterfire: Black Womanist Fiction and Poetry*. Ed. Charlotte Watson Sherman. New York: HarperCollins, 1994. 54–56.

Jones, Gayl. *Liberating Voices: Oral Tradition in African American Literature*. Cambridge: Harvard University Press, 1991.

Jones, LeRoi. *Blues People: Negro Music in White America*. New York: Morrow Quill Paperbacks, 1963.

Lanser, Susan. *The Narrative Act: Point of View in Prose Fiction*. Princeton: Princeton University Press, 1981.

___. "Toward a Feminist Narratology." *Feminisms: An Anthology of Literary Theory and Criticism*. Eds. Robyn R. Warhol and Diane Price Herndl. New Brunswick, Rutgers University Press, 1991. 613–629.

McDowell, Deborah. "Boundaries: Or Distant Relations and Close Kin." *Afro-American Literary Study in the 1990s*. Eds. Houston Baker, Jr. and Patricia Redmond. Chicago: University of Chicago Press, 1992. 51–70.

Radden, Viki. "Riding the Wheel of Fortune." *Sisterfire: Black Womanist Fiction and Poetry*. Ed. Charlotte Watson Sherman. New York: HarperCollins, 1994. 32–35.

Sanchez, Sonia. *Wounded in the House of a Friend*. Boston: Beacon Press, 1995.

Sherman, Charlotte Watson. *Sisterfire: Black Womanist Fiction and Poetry*. New York: HarperCollins, 1994.

Stepto, Robert. *From Behind the Veil: A Study of Afro-American Narrative*. Chicago: U of Illinois Press, 1979.

Walker, Alice. *In Search of Our Mothers' Gardens*. New York: Harcourt, Brace, Jovanovich, 1983.

Wesling, Donald, and Tadeusz Slawek. *Literary Voice: The Calling of Jonah*. Albany: SUNY Press, 1995.

4. A Minor Revolution: Chicano/a Composite Novels and the Limits of Genre

Margot Kelley

> Where do genres come from? Quite simply from other genres.
> A new genre is always the transformation of an earlier one, or
> of several: by inversion, by displacement, by
> combination . . . it is a system in constant transformation.
>
> —Tzvetan Todorov

The composite novel, an apparent hybrid of the novel and the short story, seems to exemplify Todorov's claim that new genres are formed "by combination." While it is closely aligned with the short story cycle, which has quite a long history, the composite novel is "new" both insofar as it is a melding of two prior forms and in that it has gained widespread popularity in the United States only recently. As Ann Morris and Maggie Dunn note in *The Composite Novel: The Short Story Cycle in Transition*, "only in the twentieth century did the composite novel become a mature genre" (1). Moreover, while Morris and Dunn's list of composite novels published between 1820 and 1993 in the United States, Europe, and England includes nearly 400 titles, more than half were published since 1966, and most of this latter group by American authors. This timing may lead one to presume that their prominence now is part of the contemporary efforts to "replenish" the "exhausted" genre of the novel and/or to capitalize on the so-called renaissance of the short story during the 1970s. And while both claims probably have some truth, neither helps to account for the fact that— during the last fifteen years—the authorship of composite novels has disproportionately included women who live in positions of "double marginality" as members of visible minorities and/or as lesbians. In particular, one group of female authors who have used the composite novel form often and to interesting ends are Latinas, especially Mexican

American women. Such a connection between genre and authorial
identity leads me to add a small nuance to Todorov's concerns and to
consider not only where a new genre comes from but also why it comes
to be used by particular subsets of writers at a given time.

Some critical attention to the correlation between the use of this
genre and authorial identity has been pursued, linking the form to
region and to gender. I have written elsewhere about some of the
reasons that female writers may regard the composite novel as a
particularly useful form (see Kelley), and Mary Louise Pratt has
discussed its link to geographical regions. Commenting specifically on
the short story cycle (rather than the composite novel), she notes that
"on the regional periphery . . . the short story cycle has been most
likely to make its appearance" and adds that "such cycles do a kind of
groundbreaking, establishing a basic literary identity for a region or
group, laying out descriptive parameters, character types, social and
economic settings, principal points of conflict for an audience
unfamiliar either with the region itself or with seeing that region in
print" (187–188).

Pratt asserts that the cycle is a "minor" form, the "marked" or
"lesser" relative of the "major" form of the conventional novel (175).
This claim prompted me to consider the notion that the composite
novel ought also to be regarded as a "minor" relative and to consider the
implications of that formal relationship. Here, the theoretical discussion
of minor literature offered by Gilles Deleuze and Felix Guattari has been
helpful; to them, "minor literature" refers both to the secondary status
accorded to the work and to the author as a member of a minority. But
they are quick to add that those two attributes are necessary but not
sufficient conditions for considering a literature "minor." In *Kafka:
Toward a Minor Literature*, Deleuze and Guattari contend that a
"deterritorialized" author can create a literature "capable of disorganizing
its own forms, and of disorganizing its forms of content" (7, 28). The
"deterritorialized" author is one who—as part of a cultural and linguistic
minority—faces "the impossibility of writing, the impossibility of
writing in [the majority language], the impossibility of writing
otherwise" (16). Given this relationship to language, the
deterritorialized author has the capacity, in this minor literature, to say
what cannot be articulated in a major literature, and Deleuze and
Guattari's discussion emphasizes the differences in language, form, and
content between the two. These differences cannot be enumerated once
for all minor literatures because "a minor, or revolutionary, literature
begins by expressing itself and doesn't conceptualize until
afterward. . . . Expression must break forms, encourage ruptures and

new sproutings" (28). Nevertheless, they assert that minor literatures do have several shared characteristics; specifically, a minor literature is "that which a minority constructs within a major language. But the first characteristic of a minor literature in any case is that in it language is affected with a high coefficient of deterritorialization . . . the second characteristic of minor literatures is that everything in them is political . . . [finally] the third characteristic of minor literature is that in it everything takes on a collective value" (16–17). Abdul JanMohamed and David Lloyd ascribe this collective value to the authors' desires to present a "collective subjectivity," an aim that can be linked to

> cultural and political factors. In those societies that are caught in the transition from oral, mythic, and collective cultures to the literate, "rational," and individualistic values and characteristics of Western cultures, the writer more often than not manifests the collective nature of social formation in forms such as the novel, thus transforming what were once efficacious vehicles for the representation of individually, atomistically oriented experiences into collective modes of articulation. (9–10)

Among composite novels, the Chicano/a *Bildungsroman* is particularly overt in emphasizing the negotiations of characters and a culture "caught in the transition" between the collective and the individual orientation. The *Bildungsroman* is an ideal genre for writers interested in making literary texts that disorganize the form and content of a predominant genre for revolutionary purposes. Because it has a long, well-documented history, employs unidirectional time and strong causality, and is routinely used to present "individually, atomistically oriented experiences," the *Bildungsroman* conveys especially clearly ideological assumptions prevailing in Western culture; therefore, the challenges proffered by Chicano/a writers are readily discernible.

If we consider Chicana composite novels as an instance of minor literature, we can contextualize both the attributes frequently ascribed to these works and the ideological imperatives behind their transformations of the novel and short story in the making of a new type of *Bildungsroman*. However, since many Chicana writers assert that they are working in relation to their Chicano predecessors of the 1960s and '70s, we need to briefly investigate possible connections between the men's and the women's textual strategies. As Ramón Saldívar aptly puts it, "Chicano narratives carry out a counterhegemonic resistance to the dominant ideology at the level of various symbolic languages, attempting to figure what we might call, echoing Goran Therborn, an 'alter-ideology'"(17). However, these Chicano narratives do not enact as fully the revolutionary transformations as do the works of the female successors. In their composite novels, Chicanas, on the one hand, write themselves out of the silence imposed by their male precursors and, on the other hand, contribute to the Chicano tradition of sustained critique of the dominant/majority canon. The need to do both, according to Roberta Fernández, comes from the sense that the Chicano literary movement of the 1970s "had left the women out," an exclusion that led her to want to create a more complete representation of Latino/a identity: "what these Latino writers have done for the males," Fernández added, "which is reconstruct the life of the male in his circumstances, I am going to do for the women" (Interview). In doing so, Chicanas develop a cannily inflected "minor" form, one that is simultaneously complicitous with and a critique of the Chicano tradition and contestatory of the major American tradition. This complex relation that Chicana texts have to their different textual environments requires that we attend to their work as "minor," but that we acknowledge that it is minor in a different sense than was the work of Kafka, for example. The works themselves, and the postmodern/post-structuralist context in which their writing has emerged, require us to regard the distinction between major and minor, between center and margin, differently than we would have even a few decades ago.

I. The Chicano Tradition of Revision

While critics date the beginnings of a Mexican American literary tradition back to the United States' annexing of the southwestern region in 1848, most cite its flourishing as taking place in the 1960s and '70s (Paredes 806; Rebolledo and Rivero 21). With the formation of the Teatro Campesino in 1965 and the opening of Quinto Sol Publications in 1967, forums dedicated to disseminating Mexican-American drama and literature became available, and Chicano writers began to reach wider audiences in the United States. Among the best known of the fiction writers whose work was published through Quinto Sol are Rudolfo Anaya, Rolando Hinojosa-Smith, and Tomás Rivera.

Anaya's work has been especially influential in making Chicano/as and others aware of Chicano writing. Indeed, describing her discovery of Anaya's best-known work, *Bless Me, Ultima*, Denise Chavez said it "was an incredible revelation . . . there are people like me who are writing books" (Interview). Both the fact of his writing and the writing itself have been important to recent Chicano/a writers who share

Anaya's concerns with borders, with negotiating between competing cultural identities, with living and speaking in two languages, and with developing literary techniques to convey the efforts of a protagonist who is an indigenous person. Anaya maintains that the kind of protagonist who will be able to become free is "a person of synthesis, a person who is able to draw, in our case, on our Spanish roots and our native indigenous roots and become a new person, become that Mestizo with a unique perspective" (247). In *Bless Me, Ultima* (1972), Anaya presents a Mestizo consciousness in the person of young Antonio and stylistically replicates that consciousness through the careful interplay of numerous binary oppositions and through the mixing of English and Spanish.

If we think about Anaya's work in relation to Guillermo Gómez-Peña's description of the attributes of much Chicano writing, its centrality to critical discussions of Chicano literature becomes even clearer. Gómez-Peña explains that

> our artistic product presents hybrid realities and colliding visions within coalition. We practice the epistemology of multiplicity and a border semiotics. We share certain thematic interests, like the continual clash with cultural otherness, the crisis of identity, or, better said, access to trans- or multiculturalism, and the destruction of borders therefrom; the creation of alternative cartographies, a ferocious critique of the dominant culture of both countries, and, lastly, a proposal for new creative languages. (130)

He goes on to say that these characteristics have become important because of a "'deterritorialization' of vast human sectors" which enables "cultures and languages [to] mutually invade one another" (130). Within literary texts, this interpenetration has led to a need for "syncretism, interdisciplinarianism, and multi-ethnicity" as well as a "greater and more diverse" set of "artistic options in terms of the medium, methodology, systems of communication, and channels of distribution for our ideas and images" (131). Anaya's novel certainly displays these characteristics at the thematic and linguistic levels; however, it does not do so equally at the formal level. *Bless Me, Ultima* is a conventionally organized *Bildungsroman*, with traditional chronology, full causal links between episodes, and chapters that cannot be read independently.

Like Anaya, Rolando Hinjosa and Tomás Rivera have written fictions which enact the "border semiotics" and "ferocious critique" Gómez-Peña described. However, they experiment more with form, largely by recovering the oral tradition that had been important in

Mexican American border culture. Tomás Rivera's . . . *y no se lo trago la tierra* (*And the Earth Did Not Devour Him*, 1971) is arguably a composite novel, a series of vignettes interspersed with very short— usually a paragraph or two—impressionistic pieces which together offer a picture of Mexican-American migrant workers' lives at mid-century. But as it is written entirely in Spanish, it is not—properly speaking— an instance of minor literature in a U.S. context. Still, Rivera's work is significant in this context because he extends the narrative revisions that are crucial to the Chicano tradition; in this text, he employs multiple voices, thereby developing a multi-perspectival approach. Through the stream of consciousness presentations of the varied narrators and the briefness of the pieces, Rivera captures the sense of the told tale, of the oral form. In doing so, he hearkens back to the *corrido* (the Texas-Mexican border ballad). Like the hero in a *corrido*, the boy protagonist in *Tierra* is on an epic journey characterized by an effort to develop a sense of identity, both as an individual and within a community.

As well as invoking the *corrido* tradition, Rivera's manipulations of form alert us to his effort to challenge the conventions of the *Bildungsroman*. He shifts between short stories and impressionistic paragraphs, giving the reader the sense that each short paragraph is the kernel of something more; these "underwritten" sections force the reader to sense that the language is both incredibly rich and also impoverished. Deleuze and Guattari note that deterritorialized writers have the options either to "artificially enrich" their impoverished language by "swell[ing] it up through all the resources of symbolism, of oneirism, of esoteric sense, of a hidden signifier" or to "choose the other way, or, rather . . . invent another way"(19). This "other way," the route that Kafka and Rivera select, involves

> go[ing] always farther in the direction of deterritorialization, to the point of sobriety. Since the language is arid, [they] make it vibrate with a new intensity. [They] oppose a purely intensive usage of the language to all symbolic or even significant or simply signifying usages of it. Arrive at a perfect and unformed expression, a materially intense expression. (19)

This use of an arid, deterritorialized language, in turn, leads to a corresponding "dessication" of form; conventional connectors, markers of cause and effect, and indicators of specific relationships among sections are reduced or eliminated, and they must be filled in by the reader. As José David Saldívar has argued, "the most significant [semiotic forces] in Rivera's *Tierra* are its negation of a fixed, coherent narrative sequence and structural breakdown of conventional cause-and-effect. His new narrative . . . offers a disordered and fragmented story line but succeeds in creating a view of the Chicano migrant world from the protagonist's consciousness" (57).

Some of Rolando Hinojosa's late texts combine Anaya's linguistic experiments with Rivera's formal ones. Hinojosa switched from writing in Spanish to writing in English, because English is currently "the majority language," and therefore he deems it appropriate to write texts in which "English will predominate, but [in which] Spanish will never completely disappear" (in Jussawalla and Dassenbrock 261). The combination he uses helps to convey a sense of the Border region, since language is a "unifier and as strong an element as there is in fixing one's sense of place" ("Sense" 21). This concern for place and for representing place through an appropriate language fueled Hinojosa's experiments with form. In "The Sense of Place," Hinojosa explains that because place is "essential" to him, his "stories are not held together by the *peripeteia* or the plot as much as by *what* the people who populate the stories say and *how* they say it" (21). Such an approach leads him to create something that is not "the formula novel"(22). In an interview with Saldívar, he explained that he is "very interested in genre," that part of his impetus to experiment is to ensure that "if other Mexicanos in the U.S. want to write," they will be "free to write in any mode that they want" ("Our Southwest" 186, 187). Perhaps the two experiments for which Hinojosa is most well known are his formulation of Belken County, a border area developed and elaborated in several of his texts, and his "estampas" format, a use of sketches that work together to form a novel. To combine the individual elements into a coherent whole, Hinojosa—like Rivera—relies upon a logic of accretion, an elaborate parataxis which may lead one to regard his work as similar to that of some modernists and postmodernists. However, Hinojosa is quite explicit in distinguishing his efforts from those of "mainstream" experimentalists; he asserts that he used these vignettes for "different reasons" than do "European modernist" authors. "I wanted to produce not one character in the nineteenth-century novel mode with redemption at the end for the man or woman," he explained; instead, "I want to present, say, the whole Texas-Mexican people as the protagonist" and wanted to do so using a form in which "the reader has to collaborate with the writer" (in Jussawalla and Dassenbrock 274). In short, Hinojosa's linguistic efforts, his communal subject, his formal experiments, and his political intentions situate his English-predominate texts firmly within the framework of minor literature that Deleuze and Guattari, as well as JanMohamed, delineate.

II. Chicana Visions and Re-visions

Seeing the Chicano tradition as one of linguistic and formal experimentation that includes a deliberate and increasing incorporation of orality into literature, an attention to border places and border subjectivities, and a concerted revision of the short story and the novel to transform the *Bildungsroman* genre is particularly important to allowing us to critically regard the efforts of their female successors. Indeed, we see it is but a tiny step narratologically and ideologically from Hinojosa's estampas that amalgamate into a novel to Sandra Cisneros' vignettes which do the same thing in *The House on Mango Street*. This connection is important, for while Cisneros' 1995 receipt of a MacArthur Fellowship publicly confirms her significance as a writer, her works have received relatively little critical attention. In 1989, Ellen McCracken argued that its curious genre was one reason that *The House on Mango Street* (1984) had not been the subject of more critical commentary (64), adding that the situation was exacerbated because Cisneros "transgresses the dominant discourse of canonical standards ideologically and linguistically. In bold contrast to the individualistic introspection of many canonical texts, Cisneros writes a modified autobiographical novel, or *Bildungsroman*, that roots the individual self in the broader socio-political reality of the Chicano community"; she deviates from linguistic expectations, "recuperating the simplicity of children's speech . . . [even though] such simple and well-crafted prose is not currently in canonical vogue" (63–64); and finally, she "demystif[ies] . . . women's issues, especially the problems [of] low income Chicana women" (66). McCracken's points suggest to me that the reasons for the delay in attention to Cisneros' work are precisely the reasons one would regard her text as "minor."

Eliana Ortega and Nancy Saporta Sternbach argue that it is not Cisneros alone but Latinas generally who are ignored or under-represented in the canon. In "At the Threshold of the Unnamed: Latina Literary Discourse in the Eighties," they observe that although Latinas have been recording their "experience through a wide range of literary and artistic expressions" since 1848, the first "book-length works of criticism concerning Latinas" did not appear until 1985, and that even "the most progressive anthologies and criticisms in the last five years [as of 1989] reveal a failure to include a Latina perspective" (3–4). This failure is all the more obvious now because it is concurrent with "a virtual explosion of Latina writing in the eighties" (10), writings that provide a discourse that "confronts, questions, and denies the regulatory norms and values of U.S. society" (4). Within this Latina writing, Chicana writings form a body of work that is "culturally unified," exhibiting several features endemic to a minor literature and consistent with Chicano writings. For example, Rebollado and Rivero observe that Chicanas write simultaneously of politics and collectivity; they note that "the Chicanas' concerns for and about political and social [oppression arise] from long years of communal experience" (23). These concerns are conjoined with a concern with identity; Gloria Anzaldúa argues that Chicana art is "about identity, among other things and her creativity is politics. Creative acts are forms of political activism employing definite aesthetic strategies for resisting dominant cultural norms" (Rebolledo and Rivero 23). Again like their male predecessors, Chicanas write of identity in terms of myriad negotiations—between the Anglo privileging of the individual and the Hispanic valorization of the collective, between the dominant English of public culture and the "Spanish mothertongue" (Ortega 14), between the emphasis on the oral and that on the written.

These negotiations make Chicanas—who are (in Anzaldúa's words) "'speaking from cracked spaces'"—especially likely to create a literature "seen as being a literature 'between'"(Rebolledo and Rivero 25). The space that Chicanas write from—crack, margin, or border—demarcates a zone that is properly understood as not entirely a part of either culture, as a deterritorialized region. By not being entirely either, though, Chicanas potentially gain access to both. Rebolledo and Rivero emphasize the notion of Chicanas writing in a borderland (both geographically and in terms of identity or subjectivity) that incorporates both cultures:

> Chicanas have always had [a concern] about borders. Fluidity, translation, multiplicities, limits, complications, alienations, the other, the outsider, the insider, the center, the margin. And, although the concern has always been there, it has become more clearly articulated, more explicit, more prevalent [in the 1980s]. It is a concern that derives from the triple and more cultures that must be explained, understood, constantly translated. Chicanas are Malinches all. It was Malinche, after all, who is understood symbolically to be the first indigenous woman to speak in tongues, that is, she spoke more than one indigenous language. (Rebolledo and Rivero 30–31)

While this Malinche status enables Chicanas to speak more than one indigenous language, Ortega and Sternbach suggest that this capability is not unequivocally advantageous. They argue that it may be a reason the literature is overlooked (belonging neither in the English department nor in the Spanish department) and that it may prompt the Chicana to "turn against herself internally" (14). In making the latter point, Ortega and Sternbach observe that the construction of the self always involves language as the vehicle of ideological interpellation into the dominant culture. As a bilingual person, the Latina "must be inscribed into two symbolic orders: English, the language of the hegemonic culture, and Spanish, the mothertongue. The positioning of this speaking-I into two symbolic orders signifies that she will constantly be negotiating her alliances with one or both of these orders" (14). In doing so, she will develop multiple identities. While Chicano writers share this situation, it is exacerbated for Chicanas by gender, by the need to negotiate the conflicting gender roles afforded her within her local community and her larger, national community.

Rebolledo and Rivero smoothly transform what Ortega and Sternbach have identified as a source of conflict into an opportunity for creativity, observing that this multiplicity need not adversely affect the Chicana or the representations of self and reality in Chicana texts. She maintains that the long-standing exercise of "living in contradictory and multiple realities has required the negotiation of many survival techniques" and that Chicanas "find themselves richer for it. So, the translations, the slipping and sliding continue" (31). At the level of literal "translation, " this slipping and sliding may take the form of true bilingualism within texts; however, more often the texts are "fully accessible to monolingual English speakers" and are more accurately described as "informed by a Spanish mothertongue" (Ortega and Sternbach 15). At the level of identity formation, the concern with translation among multiple realities often involves the protagonist becoming a wordworker, like Malinche (an indigenous woman who not only can speak but can speak more than one language), and often is reinforced through spatial metaphors.

The sense of Cisneros' language being "informed by a Spanish mothertongue" was one of the reasons McCracken cites for *Mango Street's* neglect. In just the few years since her essay was published in 1989, however, an increasing attention to multicultural American literature has contributed to making Cisneros' composite novel well-known, at least on college and university campuses. In that context, it is often read as both a literary and an ethnographic text—as are many Chicana writings. In fact, describing Chicana writing, Alvina E. Quintana said that "women writers like ethnographers focus on microcosms within a culture, unpacking rituals in the context of inherited symbolic and social structures of subjugation. Women writers are acting as their own ethnographers, using the word for self-representation" (209–210). Chicanas write with the intention of chronicling their world, a world that is bilingual and bicultural, a world in which the "I" must continually negotiate the border terrain. This is the task that Cisneros seems to have embraced in *The House on Mango Street*, and her success in achieving this helps us begin to situate this text within the "minor revolution" that Chicanas are encouraging and redefining.

The *House on Mango Street* is a *Bildungsroman*— a *Kunstlerroman,* to be more precise—about Esperanza Cordero. Because Esperanza is coming of age as a teller of stories, language figures overtly in the novel. The narrative voice is cunning; although one initially assumes that the narrator is a child, Shannon Sikes has pointed out a variety of disruptions in the narrator's tone and knowledge level, which suggests that the narrator is "perhaps a fully grown but definitely at least an older Esperanza" (Sikes, 4). This childlike voice is particularly important for it can be understood as concertedly bilingual and as a trait of the "minor" quality of the text. Describing her own language practices, Sandra Cisneros explained that when she wrote *Mango Street*, she "thought [she] was only a product of [her] English. But," she continued, "now I know how much of a role Spanish plays, even when I write in English. If you take *Mango Street* and translate it, it's Spanish. The syntax, the sensibility, the diminutives, the way of looking at inanimate objects—that's not a child's voice as is sometimes said. That's Spanish!" (in Jussawalla and Dassenbrock 288). Not only is it a Spanish-influenced discourse, it is also one that deterritorializes language in relation to the majority structures. Like Kafka, who heightened the intensity of the language by writing "like a child," by "mimic[ing] this [major] language . . . produc[ing] stories by reducing them to elemental verbal elements, verbal 'desiring machines'" (Renza 33), Cisneros creates desiring machines that employ a seemingly simplistic language, phrasings seared clean of all excess.

And she creates a narrative structure equally loosed of encumbrances. She shares Rivera's and Hinojosa's reliance on parataxis and their attenuation of cause and effect markers; however, whereas Rivera juxtaposed impressionistic paragraphs with lengthier pieces, Cisneros follows Hinojosa, weaving her entire text of tiny short stories, each only one to three pages long. The absence of causal connections and the brevity and independence of each vignette challenge our expectation that a *Bildungsroman* will employ clear links to combine episodes to indicate development. Cisneros ascribes this formal choice to her disinterest in "the linear form." She told interviewer Reed W. Dassenbrock:

I didn't know what I was writing when I wrote *House on Mango Street,* but I knew what I wanted. I didn't know what to call it, but I knew what I was after . . . I wanted to write a series of stories that you could open up at any point. You didn't have to know anything before or after and you would understand each story like a little pearl, or you could look at the whole thing like a necklace. That's what I always knew from the day that I wrote the first one. I said, "I'm going to do a whole series of these, and it's going to be like this, and it'll all be connected." I didn't know the order they were going to come, but I wasn't trying to write a linear novel. (in Jussawalla and Dassenbrock 305)

What she does write is—impossibly—an exemplary "desiring machine," a text in which desire "constantly couples continuous flows and partial objects that are by nature fragmentary and fragmented" (in Renza 30). She does so by presenting and then immediately whisking away a huge variety of images whose intensity makes Esperanza's experiences appear to crystallize, to take on paradigmatic and, therefore, collective value. In doing so, she presents the social systems that adversely affect Esperanza and her neighbors—including the system of gender identity in "Hair" and "Boys and Girls," of class structure in *The House on Mango Street,* of economics aligned with patriarchy in "Alicia Who Sees Mice," of sexual subjugation in the Sally stories, etc. And to clarify the difficult task Esperanza undertakes in trying to evade the strictures of these systems, she presents images of women who do not challenge the systems (like Rafaela) and images of women who unsuccessfully challenge them (like Sally). Finally, Esperanza—"a girl who didn't want to belong"(109)—maintains that she will exit this world of poor housing, of racial and sexual disempowerment, of economic inequity in order to have "a house all my own" from which she can return "for the ones who cannot get out" (108, 110). She promises to take care of "bums" (whom she'll let live in her attic), and to never forget "how it is to be without a house" (87).

The focus on houses is thematically important and consistent with still another attribute of minor literature that Deleuze and Guattari noted in Kafka's work. They point out that he employed many spatial metaphors and that at the formal level those metaphors were complemented by his use of "blocks" and "segments" of text, joined together to form "assemblages" which work as "writing-machines" (53–88). Cisneros' text—and indeed Chicana writing in general—is also replete with spatial metaphors that contribute to their revisions of the genres of the novel and the short story. From the description of houses in the first vignette, "The House on Mango Street," to that of Meme Ortiz's house and the basement room he rents to Louie, to that of the Earl of Tennessee's apartment (in Edna's basement), to that of the Mamacita who does not leave (across the street) and that of Rafaela who may not leave, descriptions of rooms and their inhabitants create a sense of the neighborhood as world. Like the stories which together form a novel, the dwellings combine to form a world that is clearly marked by racial, ethnic, gendered, and economic concerns. It is Esperanza's—but it is also that of urban Latinas more generally: as Julian Olivares argues, Cisneros here inverts Gaston Bachelard's notion of the house as a space of "comfort, security, tranquility, esteem," presenting the apartments instead as sites that "constrain"(162) in order to indicate that the "inside, the *here*, can be confinement and a source of anguish and alienation . . . [for the economically] downtrodden but, primarily, [for] . . . the Hispanic woman" (161).

While the rooms that form apartment houses are regarded by Esperanza as less appealing than the houses which the Corderos drive by on Sundays, Cisneros suggests the reverse is—in literary terms—true for her. Talking to Cisneros about her effort to combine stories into a novel, Dassenbrock noted that "many Chicano writers seem to . . . have worked with a group of short stories rather than a continuous narrative" (in Jussawalla and Dassenbrock 304–5), and asked her why they were taking that tack. She pointed out that many were young writers, interested in honing their craft by building "rooms" before they tried "building a house," but quickly added "maybe we don't want the house—" (in Jussawalla and Dassenbrock 305). The "house" she doesn't want overlaps, ideologically, with the one that Esperanza yearns for. The extended linear narrative—the conventional novel—is the canonical house that Cisneros is "just not taken by" (in Jussawalla and Dassenbrock 304). Overtly rejecting this form, Cisneros's composite novel "attacks what it itself could have become . . . [it] exists in the process of becoming 'the third linguistic world,' a literature that *de facto* sabotages whatever social or systematic code happens to control the means of major literary production at the moment" (Renza 33).

Among the social forces controlling the means of major literary production at this moment is the system of publishing houses, and these play a significant role in the reception that Cisneros' text has earned. First published in 1984 by Arte Publico Press, a small press committed to publishing Chicano/a materials, *The House on Mango Street* was re-released in 1989 by Vintage Books. Since then, as I noted above, the text has become a college mainstay—has become "canonical." To a lesser degree, *The Last of the Menu Girls* by Denise Chavez dances on the border of remaining transgressive and becoming canonical. While the full text is still published by Arte Publico, the title story is now the penultimate fiction selection in the canon-defining, *The Norton Anthology of American Literature* (4th ed., vol. 2). Placed between a story by Leslie Silko and one by Louise Erdrich, it seems rather clearly to be part of the editors' effort to "widen the canon." Still, the story and the composite novel of which it is a part retain their minor status and their ability to challenge some of the assumptions of more-conventional canonical writings.

Rocío Esquibel is the protagonist of the seven stories which comprise the full text. And like Esperanza, she comes of age as a writer, asserting that identity for the first time in the concluding story (188). Whereas Esperanza wants to leave her neighborhood and find a house in which to write, Rocío's mother urges her to "write about 325 and that will take the rest of your life . . . you don't have to go anywhere. Not down the street, not even out of this house. There's stories, plenty of them all around" (190). And her mother is clearly right, for the novel itself takes place largely in the house and the neighborhood.

While *Mango Street* enacts a narrative strategy of *assemblage* and employs room and house metaphors, *Menu Girls* extends both of those efforts. Chavez requires that the reader participate in connecting the stories to create a unified whole but also requires that she work to make the stories cohere in and of themselves. Further, *Menu Girls* demands that readers explore sundry real and imaginary spaces, moving eventually to an exploration of the idea of space itself. Rocío's stories are told from several narrative perspectives—disrupting the continuity that could be afforded by a single narrative stance. And the stories are further defamiliarized by Chavez's use of a wide variety of strategies which fracture and fragment the narrative. For instance, the title story is organized as a series of reveries or responses to the questions on a job application. "Space Is a Solid" requires the reader to integrate sections narrated by different characters, while "The Closet" demands that the reader make the connections between the various closets and their functions in Rocío's identity formation. Through such disjunctive strategies, Chavez highlights the nonlinear character of the narrative as a whole. In her essay "Heat and Rain," Chavez explained that her "readers should stop looking for traditional stories . . . Writing, to me, is an assemblage of parts, a phrase here, an image there" (31–32). The remainder of *Menu Girls* confirms this emphasis on assemblage.

One of the most striking ways in which Chavez defies our expectation that assemblage will involve a fairly simple "filling in" of the absent cause-and-effect markers is through not arranging the stories chronologically. The stories are of two sorts—very impressionistic, short pieces like "Evening in Paris" and longer, more overtly complicated and experimental ones like "The Closet." Rejecting either chronological order or an ordering by increasing or decreasing narrative complexity, Chavez requires the reader to suspend the—usually unquestioned—expectation that a *Bildungsroman* will employ unidirectional time (even if devices like flashbacks are embedded). "Time, to me," she explained, "is a very fluid element. And I move back and forth in memory and actuality" (Interview). This fluidity helps the reader to recognize that Rocío's "lifeline" is not unidirectional, that she must be reborn; her coming of age requires the breakdown that allows her to leave her compartmentalizing impulses behind and to become more fully integrated and interested in synthesis.

Furthermore, like Cisneros, who was "just not taken by" extended linear narrative, Chavez sees herself as "not a writer of plot." And describing *Menu Girls*, she speaks in terms that closely echo Cisneros: "to me," she explained,

> they begin as short stories, then it [*Menu Girls*] became somewhat novelistic in the sense that you follow the same characters throughout. However, to me, they have a life of their own and I began to see them as scenes. As some kind of theatrical presentation of some type that was maybe not short stories, maybe not a novel, maybe not even scenes—in some reality that exists on its own. (Interview)

Later, she added that the text also has "a different kind of a structure . . . there is an internal structure that I tried to adhere to or that I tried to be aware of. But it's not your A, B, C, moving to D [structure]" (Interview).

While Cisneros wrote in an English infused with the tones and rhythms of Spanish, Chavez incorporates Spanish words and phrases directly into the text. Indeed, as Rocío gradually comes to terms with her own bicultural identity, she thinks and speaks more often in Spanish. In the early stories, all Spanish is quoted or part of a title. The final line of "Compadre," though, is half English, half Spanish—and fully comprehensible to a monolingual English reader. Chavez, a bilingual native of New Mexico, explained that the balancing between languages was intended to convey Rocío's efforts at "finding herself within her world and her culture and her skin" (Interview).

Several of the earlier stories, particularly "Shooting Stars" (in which Rocío considers several models for womanhood) and "The Closet" (which provides her with insights into the "secret lives" of women in her own household), demonstrate Rocío looking for ways to connect to the world. Not surprisingly, these efforts are most fully realized in the final story; there, as Chavez explains, the reader is able to see Rocío as "a person who is connecting with her culture. And she had negated language, culture, all of those kinds of things," but is slowly coming to value them. By the end, this revaluing is clear not only in her bilingualism but also in her cooking of tacos and tamales and her ability to finally spend comfortable time with Regino, the handyman who is Nieves' compadre. Both by having Rocío eat with Regino and by having her use Spanish, Chavez says she tried "to make it known that she has, somehow, a connection to her roots." Still, like other writers who are creating minor literatures, Chavez maintains that the text ought not to exclude monolingual English readers and that while "we're becoming a global society, and I say it's now time to learn Spanish," we are still in a culture in which "English is the language that we need to speak. However you want to give a little bit of flavor to it" (Interview).

In arriving at this sense of connectedness to her family and her heritage, Rocío is also able to participate in the "ethnographic" imperative of her real-life counterparts. In agreeing to write the stories of the house and the neighborhood, Rocío becomes the keeper of the tales, a task that involves a degree of cultural and ethical responsibility. Chavez maintains that Rocío "becomes responsible for the stories that she has heard . . . because she takes them onto herself as part of her mythology or history. And that is how she perpetuates or incorporates whatever it is that is sacred to her in those stories" (Interview). Seeing the local stories as sacred, as of personal and collective value, Rocío is able to mend her own internal fractures and begin to organize experience in order to convey it to others.

Chavez's series of stories form an unusual *Bildungsroman*, one in which the narrator does not get older in successive stories (although she is probably oldest on the last page of the book) and in which both the structure and the sorts of characters depicted require the reader to rethink the conventional focus on major events and socially noteworthy individuals as central to one's coming of age. This approach simultaneously enacts an exploration of the revolutionary potential of minor literature and allows readers to hear from and about marginalized peoples, to hear the "unspoken voices of women" (Interview). Such a possibility is quite important, for—as Debra Castillo points out—"the vast majority of Latin American women [and she includes Chicanas], unless they have the great good luck to have . . . the advantages of birth, education, and affluence—do not write at all. Period" (27).

Perhaps more so than even Cisneros and Chavez, Roberta Fernández seeks to give voice to such women; her explicit aim in *Intaglio: A Novel in Six Stories* is to convey the ways women "expressed themselves, creatively, in a preliterate society" (Interview). Indeed, *Intaglio* seems ready-made for analysis by Ortega and Sternbach, who assert that "literature by Latina women will depict, but not limit itself to, the reality, experiences, and everyday life of a people whose working-class origin serves as a springboard to understanding cultural contexts . . . [including] racial, economic, ethnic, political, social, chronological, culinary, ideological, luminous, and stylistic [contexts]" and that "their recognition and celebration of what [Ortega and Sternbach] call 'a matriarchal heritage'" is evidenced in a discourse that pays "tribute to a 'long line' of female ancestors" (11–12).

Mango Street focuses on Esperanza as a daughter in a father-dominated and essentially nuclear family within a neighborhood context that emphasizes male power and the danger that can pose for women; *Menu Girls* presents Rocío as part of a household that is female centered, but in which the father ("your Daddy, que Dios lo cuide" Nieves says each time she mentions him) is conspicuously—and therefore only partially—absent, and Regino is present in each story. Set beside these two texts, the female focus of *Intaglio* seems absolute. Ortega and Sternbach argue that Latina writing often presents an "extended family of women," a configuration that "impl[ies] a restructuring of the traditional patriarchal family . . . the writers often displaced a central patriarchal figure, replacing it with a woman-headed and woman-populated household" (12).

This female focus not only situates *Intaglio* within a recognizably female tradition, it also further redefines the parameters of a *Bildungsroman*. This text is quite clearly about the coming of age of Nenita ("the girl"), yet it spans three generations and has a different title character—never Nenita—for each of the stories. Interestingly, of the six title characters, one is Nenita's maternal aunt, one is her "nanny," and the other four are women from her father's extended family. While this proportion could have enabled Fernández to focus on Miguel Cárdenas (Nenita's father) and the patriarchal line, she does not. Instead, she explores the lessons Nenita learns from each woman and the sorts of creativity that they manifest. In doing so, she—like the other Chicano/a writers described above—creates a sense of collective identity and of the individual as part of a far-reaching community.

In explaining how she arrived at the composite novel as an appropriate genre for this book, Fernández noted that in addition to exploring women's creativity in preliterate societies, she wanted to consider how the women shared that creativity with members of the next generation—for she saw both the artistry and an awareness of the importance of passing on the creative impulse as crucial elements that a foremother shares with a girl as she is coming of age. Therefore, she sought a form that would allow her to deal with a "long time process," while also allowing her to focus closely on one woman and one art form in each story. In that way, she could present each as "an independent story" but also as "part of a whole." She sought to create stories that would independently present "a complete world," while being connected to the others through symbolism and themes so that the text as a whole could be considered "a novel in a new form." She recalled that "about that time . . . Gloria Naylor's book came out, *The Women of Brewster Place*. So then I thought 'aha!' Someone else is doing this, and so it gave me validity. I felt, 'okay, I *can* do this' and treat it like a novel" (Interview).

In addition to the sense of validation that Fernández ascribes to Naylor's work, she says that she valued the examples of Toni Morrison, Leslie Silko, and Maxine Hong Kingston, for the women of color whose writing became well known in the 1980s offered her a community of sorts. Feeling not only that the Chicano movement "had left the women out" but also that in the women's movement of the same time "little was understood about women of color," Fernández resolved to "create a new narrative for women, for Chicanas . . . who are different from men's culture, and also different from white women's culture . . . and different from black culture and Asian culture and so on . . . I wanted to open this space and create a narrative, give voice to a feminist voice, you know, but a third world, a Chicana feminist, voice" (Interview). And while she has done so, and in a way that she feels "doesn't fit with the Chicano movement" (Interview), I would argue that her narrative revisions both continue the tendencies of and critique the assumptions in the most well-known texts of that movement.

In addition to reforming the short story and novel, an endeavor which the other Chicano/a writers included here also undertake, she is also like her Chicano predecessors in writing from a deterritorialized position, the borderland of Texas and Mexico, where Spanish, English, and a hybrid language are the local options. In "Filomena," the children who are visiting tell Nenita that they speak English and Spanish. She suggests that they should all "speak in both . . . We can also use

Tex-Mex" (72). And like the characters, Fernández speaks in both, employing English predominantly but adding so much Spanish that she also includes a glossary to ensure that monolingual English speakers will be able to enjoy her text. This linguistic decision "to use the two languages [was intended] to convey the sense of biculturality" (Interview).

Moreover, her depiction of the extended family as a social unit— one including both blood relatives and *compadres*—prompts the reader to see Nenita's development in relation to a collective identity. Nenita herself emphasizes the aptness of that orientation when she says, in "Filomena," that

> for the moment, I decided to put a halt to the years of abstract thinking and to involve myself more with tangible and communal action. For me these new interests became personified in community activities. I found a real sense of authenticity through new contacts in many different projects but it was in the community arts that I found my most meaningful outlet. (84)

Similarly, at the close of the book, Nenita fills her blue leather book with the stories of the family, commingling details about Mariana and Zulema, constructing a narrative that is "a collection of images of our family's past as it was as we all would have like that past to have been" (154), one in which the truest detail is that the family's stories have been preserved and transformed—the artistry passed to a new generation.

Moving from her grandmother's generation to the girl's, the characters in the composite novel have passed through a "cultural transformation"; whereas the medium for Nenita's mother was the visual image, dance for her aunt, sewing for Amanda, and so on, the medium for Nenita is "the written word." That she can write, that she can "participat[e] in a public discourse" is both her role beyond the end of the text, and Fernández's role, "but it's not the role of the women in the book" (Interview). Because the characters affirm themselves, act as creative beings, without the possibility of participating in a public discourse, Fernández sees them as prefeminist—but pre- also in the sense of engendering Nenita, who can be a feminist, for whom "we suppose there are going to be some changes" (Interview). In the feminist focus of *Intaglio*, Fernández's text may be the most explicit in conjoining political, collective, and aesthetic concerns of the works discussed here.

Not only Fernández's, but all of the Chicano and Chicana composite novels discussed here can be seen as revolutionary and "minor," consistent in both aims and specific narrative techniques with the characteristics that Deleuze and Guattari attribute to such works. When we see these commonalities, we are better able to recognize the internal tradition as well as the challenge to the American canon more generally that these composite novels offer—particularly in terms of narrative structures and deterritorialized language practices. Yet, as Ramon Saldívar implied when he said that contemporary critics seek to understand these texts in order to "highlight the ideological background of the traditional canon, to bring to the surface the repressed formation that Jameson has called the 'political unconscious'"(17), the effort to define a "minor" literature carries with it the risk of reifying the hierarchy that marginalized these texts initially, of valuing the minor literature only for what it can reveal about the major literature. While this risk is real, I would suggest, following Satya Mohanty, that "the present intellectual moment" has, as an "implicit goal, . . . to define a discursive and epistemic relationship that will be 'noncolonizing,' that will make possible a 'mutual exploration of difference'" (109), and that the focus on positionality that is a necessary condition for attaining this goal may enable us to examine the relationships among major and minor traditions and texts without insisting that "minor" equal secondary. Deleuze and Guattari offer a preliminary antidote to the secondary status simply by paying serious attention to the minor, and a second remedy when they assert that "there is nothing that is major or revolutionary except the minor" (26, 27). Of course, inverting the hierarchy in this manner is just an initial step in generating a thoughtful dialogue between so-called major and minor texts. Phillip Brian Harper suggests the next sort of step in *Framing the Margins*, where he considers the notion of decenteredness in texts by writers who are "socially marginalized" in the context of postmodernism. I suggest that we can inch further forward still by analyzing the specific example of the Chicana fiction writers of the 1980s: they extended the serious consideration of the limits of language and narrativity put forward by Chicano writers in the 1960s and '70s and they developed methods for revising narrative without either adopting a major strategy or giving in to the "impossibility of writing." Their composite novels illustrate one means for revising—without reversing—the relations between major/center/novel and minor/margin/short story. And through these works, the Chicana authors discussed here manage to interrogate the relation between these mutually informing terms without denying the cultural power the terms still hold.

REFERENCES

Anaya, Rudolfo. *Bless Me, Ultima.* New York: Warner Books, 1972.

Bakhtin, M.M. "The *Bildungsroman* and Its Significance in the History of Realism (Toward a Historical Typology of the Novel)," in *Speech Genres and Other Essays.* [trans. by Vern W. McGee] Austin: University of Texas Press, 1986. 10–59.

Castillo, Debra. *Talking Back: Toward a Latin American Feminist Literary Criticism.* Ithaca: Cornell University Press, 1992.

Chavez, Denise. *The Last of the Menu Girls.* Houston: Arte Publico Press, 1987.

___. "Heat and Rain: Testamonio." Eds. Asunción Horno-Delgado, Eliana Ortega, Nina M. Scott and Nancy Saporta Sternbach. *Breaking Boundaries: Latina Writing and Critical Readings.* Amherst: University of Massachusetts Press, 1989. 27–32.

___. Personal Interview. July 14, 1992.

Cisneros, Sandra. *The House on Mango Street.* New York: Vintage Books, 1989.

Deleuze, Gilles and Felix Guattari. *Kafka: Toward a Theory of Minor Literature.* [trans. by Dana Polan] Minneapolis: University of Minnesota Press, 1986.

Fernández, Roberta. *Intaglio: A Novel in Six Stories.* Houston: Arte Publico Press, 1990.

___ Personal Interview. August 1, 1992.

Gómez-Peña, Guillermo. "Documented/Undocumented." *The Graywolf Annual Five: Multicultural Literacy.* St. Paul: Graywolf Press, 1988.

Harper, Phillip Brian. *Framing the Margins: The Social Logic of Postmodern Culture.* New York: Oxford University Press, 1994.

Hinojosa, Rolando. *Estampas del valle.* Tempe: Bilingual Press, 1994. [First published Berkeley: Quinto Sol Publ., 1973].

___. "The Sense of Place." in José David Saldívar. *The Rolando Hinojosa Reader: Essays Historical and Critical.* Houston: Arte Publico, 1985.

JanMohamed, Abdul, and David Lloyd. "Toward a Theory of Minority Discourse: What Is To Be Done?" *The Nature and Context of Minority Discourse.* Oxford: Oxford University Press, 1990. 1–16.

Jussawalla, Feroza, and Reed Way Dassenbrock. *Interviews with Writers of the Post-Colonial World.* Jackson: University Press of Mississippi, 1992.

Kelley, Margot Anne. "Gender and Genre: The Case of the Novel in Stories." Ed. Julie Brown. *American Women Short Story Writers.* New York: Garland Publishing, 1994. 295–310.

McCracken, Ellen. "Sandra Cisneros' *The House on Mango Street*: Community-Oriented Introspection and the Demystification of Patriarchal Violence." in Asunción Horno-Delgado, Eliana Ortega, Nina M. Scott and Nancy Saporta Sternbach, eds. *Breaking Boundaries: Latina*

Writing and Critical Readings. Amherst: University of Massachusetts Press, 1989. 62–71.

Mohanty, Satya P. "Epilogue: Colonial Legacies, Multicultural Futures: Relativism, Objectivity, and the Challenges of Otherness." *PMLA*, 110(1), Jan. 1995: 108–118.

Morris, Ann, and Maggie Dunn. *The Composite Novel: The Short Story Cycle in Transition.* New York: Twayne Publishers, 1995.

Olivares, Julian. "Sandra Cisneros' *The House on Mango Street* and the Poetics of Space." Eds. Maria Herrera-Sobek and Helena Maria Viramontes. *Chicana Creativity and Criticism: Charting New Frontiers in American Literature.* Houston: Arte Publico Press, 1988. 160–169.

Ortega, Eliana, and Nancy Saporta Sternbach. "At the Threshold of the Unnamed: Latina Literary Discourse in the Eighties." Eds. Asunción Horno-Delgado, Eliana Ortega, Nina M. Scott, and Nancy Saporta Sternbach. *Breaking Boundaries: Latina Writing and Critical Readings.* Amherst: University of Massachusetts Press, 1989. 2–23.

Paredes, Raymund A. "Mexican American Literature." Eds. Emory Elliott et al. *Columbia Literary History of the United States.* New York: Columbia University Press, 1988. 800–810.

Pratt, Mary Louise. "The Short Story: The Long and the Short of It." *Poetics* 10 [1981]: 175–194.

Quintana, Alvina E. "Women: Prisoners of the Word." Eds. Teresa Córdova et al. *Chicana Voices: Intersections of Class, Race, and Gender.* Albuquerque: University of New Mexico Press, 1990. 208–219.

Rebolledo, Tey Diana, and Eliana S. Rivero. *Infinite Divisions: An Anthology of Chicana Literature.* Tucson: University of Arizona Press, 1993.

Renza, Louis. *"A White Heron" and the Question of Minor Literature.* Madison: University of Wisconsin Press, 1984.

Rivera, Tomás. *. . . y no se lo tragó la tierra (And the Earth Did not Devour Him).* [translated by Evangelina Vigil-Pinon] Houston: Arte Publico, 1971.

Saldívar, José David. *The Dialectics of Our America: Genealogy, Cultural Critique, and Literary History.* Durham, NC: Duke University Press, 1991.

___. "Our Southwest: An Interview with Rolando Hinojosa." Ed. José David Saldívar. *The Rolando Hinojosa Reader: Essays Historical and Critical.* Houston: Arte Publico, 1985. 180–190.

Saldívar, Ramón. "Narrative, Ideology, and the Reconstruction of American Literary History." Eds. Hector Calderon and José David Saldívar. *Criticism in the Borderlands: Studies in Chicano Literature, Culture, and Ideology.* Durham: Duke University Press, 1991. 11–20.

Sikes, Shannon. "Narratorial Slippage and Authorial Self-construction in Sandra Cisneros' *The House on Mango Street*." Print version of talk delivered at Women of Color Conference, Ocean City, MD. June 1992.

Todorov, Tzvetan. *Genres in Discourse.* [trans. by Catherine Porter] Cambridge: Cambridge University Press, 1990.

5. Resistance and Reinvention in Sandra Cisneros' *Woman Hollering Creek*

Susan E. Griffin

In her prefatory poem to *My Wicked, Wicked Ways*, Sandra Cisneros asks, "What does a woman [like me] inherit that tells her how to go?" (x). This question about the cultural inheritance of Mexican American women and how it shapes their perceptions of the choices available to them is central to Cisneros' work. Throughout her poetry and fiction, she has depicted the material and ideological forces that circumscribe Mexican American women's lives.[1] In her novel *The House on Mango Street*, and in several of the poems in *My Wicked, Wicked Ways*, Cisneros portrays women who are trapped by poverty and controlling, often violent, relationships with men. In her second book of fiction, *Woman Hollering Creek and Other Stories*, she explores the cultural as well as the material limitations of the lives of Mexican American women. Like Cisneros herself, her female characters often must come to terms with a cultural tradition that they love but also view as oppressive because of the limited conception of appropriate behavior for women available within Mexican narratives and culture (Rodríguez Aranda 66). In *Woman Hollering Creek*, the role that Mexican popular culture and traditional Mexican narratives play in limiting women's sense of identity becomes one of Cisneros' central concerns.

The limitations of traditional Mexican representations of women are embodied in the dichotomy between two of the most influential women in Mexican myth and culture—the Virgin of Guadalupe and Malintzin Temepal, often referred to as Malinche, the translator for and lover of Hernan Cortes, the Spanish conqueror of Mexico. Cisneros describes growing up with these two female figures—the Virgin of Guadalupe and Malinche—as the two primary role models for women in her culture as "a hard route to go"—a position in which she felt she must choose "one or the other, there's no in-between" (Rodríguez

Aranda 65). Traditionally, Mary is defined primarily in terms of her role as a mother and is associated with family life and the beliefs of the Catholic Church; because of the story of her appearance to Juan Diego in Teyapec, she is also seen by many Mexicans as the protector of their people, their patron saint. Malinche, in contrast, is associated with lust, selfishness, and the betrayal of her race. In "From a Long Line of Vendidas: Chicanas and Feminism," Cherríe Moraga describes how Malinizin's actions are perceived: "To put it in its most base terms: Malinizin, also called Malinche, fucked the white man who conquered the Indian people of Mexico and destroyed their culture. Ever since, brown men have been accusing her of betraying her race" (175).

In Cisneros' depiction of the cultural influences upon Mexican American women in *Woman Hollering Creek*, it is not only the literal figures of the Virgin and Malinche that influence women's views of identity, however. The women in her stories are also influenced by all the contemporary forms of popular culture, like movies, television, and songs—particularly genres within these media that emphasize romance—which utilize the Virgin/Malinche, good/evil, pure/fallen paradigm and define women primarily in terms of their relationships with men. In stories like "Woman Hollering Creek," television is the primary medium that embodies beliefs about appropriate behavior for women. In this story, Cisneros depicts a world in which television, along with movies and songs, is becoming our common mythology (77).[2] But she portrays these forms of popular culture as reinforcing the same limited roles for women as narratives about Malinche and the Virgin. These limitations are illustrated by the two types of women depicted in the *telenovelas*[3] of "Woman Hollering Creek" and "*Bien Pretty*," the evil scheming woman and the pure, passive, long-suffering woman who must endure great hardships for love.

Cisneros and other Mexican American women authors and feminist critics have noted that Mexican women who reject traditional familial roles are often perceived by those within their culture as Malinche has been, as traitors to their race. The question that Sandra Cisneros attempts to work out in *Woman Hollering Creek* is how Mexican American women can create new roles for themselves—ones that reject the Virgin/Malinche dichotomy and the definition of women mainly in terms of their relations with men—without wholly rejecting Mexican culture. For Cisneros, this means not abandoning the narratives of her culture but reinventing and revising both traditional myths and the narratives of current popular culture. Through the short stories in this collection, Cisneros is able to illustrate different ways in which women can reject and even rewrite traditional narratives.

Cisneros' title story, "Woman Hollering Creek," is the story in which she most clearly illustrates the negative effects of popular romance genres' portrayal of women, and it is also the story in which she begins to illustrate how women can resist the romance narrative. Within this work, Cleófilas, the story's central character, interprets the events that happen to her in the literal, chronological narrative of the story within the context of another narrative—one she has absorbed from the *telenovelas* she watches and the romance novels she reads. Cleófilas's actions in "Woman Hollering Creek" are constructed by— and eventually in resistance to—this type of romance narrative.

Cleófilas, like several of the girls in *The House on Mango Street*, believes in a view of romantic love that is perpetuated through the media and the popular culture of both Mexico and the United States. This view is connected to what she reads in romance novels and sees in the *telenovelas*. Like American soap operas, *telenovelas* focus on women characters and romance, but, because they have endings and include a limited number of characters, they have more in common with romance novels—both the Spanish-language Corín Tellado type, which Cleófilas reads, and the similar English-language Harlequins—than with American soap operas.

Cleófilas accepts the idea promoted by the *telenovelas* that love is the ultimate good, "the most important thing" (44). She daydreams about the characters in the *telenovelas*—handsome men who finally confess their love and devotion to the women who adore them—and she imagines this kind of passion in her own life. What Cleófilas has been waiting for all her life is "passion . . . passion in its purest crystalline essence. The kind the books and songs and *telenovelas* describe when one finds finally the great love of one's life" (44).

The love of the *telenovelas* and romance novels, however, is linked with images of wealth and escape and, at the same time, connected with suffering and self-sacrifice. Like the ideas of the women in *The House on Mango Street*, Cleófilas' ideas about romance and her decision to marry are connected to her desire to be materially better off. The girls on Mango Street are aware of the shabbiness of their shoes and clothes and the houses they live in, and, with the exceptions of Esperanza and Alicia, they believe that marriage is their best opportunity to have better things. This wish for more material wealth is intertwined with romantic visions of being rescued by a man who will carry them away from their present lives. What they desire most is a means of escape, so love, distant places, beautiful clothes, jewelry, and houses all become part of the same fantasy. Marín, a friend of Esperanza, the narrator of *The House on Mango Street*, tells Esperanza that the best jobs for girls are downtown because there you "get to wear nice clothes and can meet someone in the subway who might marry you and take you to live in a big house far away" (26). This is the kind of fantasy—a man rescuing a woman from a dreary life and taking her away to a life of love and luxury—toward which romance novels' plots build. As Ann Barr Snitow explains in "Mass Market Romance: Pornography for Women Is Different," romances like Harlequins are based on "a sustaining fantasy of rescue, glamour, and change" that includes descriptions of exotic places and detailed descriptions of consumer items, like furniture, clothes, and gourmet food (248, 250).[4] It is this fantasy of glamour and change that Cleófilas believes in when she marries. After hearing the name of the town where Juan Pedro, the man who has proposed to her, lives, she thinks it has "[a] nice sterling ring to it. The tinkle of money. She would get to wear outfits like the women on the *tele*, like Lucía Mendez. And have a lovely house . . . " (45).

Cleófilas daydreams about the passionate professions of love on the *telenovelas*, but there is a sharp contrast between this romantic passion and her thoughts about her husband with acne scars and a pot-belly "whose whiskers she finds each morning in the sink, whose shoes she must air every evening on the porch, this husband . . . who doesn't care at all for music or *telenovelas* or romance or roses or the moon floating over the *arroyo*" (49). In even greater contrast to the perfect passion of the *telenovelas* is the violence that Cleófilas is a victim of in her own life and is aware of in the world around her. The first time her husband hits her—an incident in which he slaps her "again and again" until her lip splits and bleeds "an orchid of blood" (47)—is only the first of many beatings that begin soon after he and Cleófilas are married and sometimes leave her with black and blue marks all over her body. Cleófilas also notices that the newspapers seem filled with tales of women being beaten and killed:

> This woman found on the side of the interstate. This one's cadaver, this one unconscious, this one beaten blue. Her ex-husband, her lover, her father, her brother, her uncle, her friend, her co-worker. Always. The same grisly news in the pages of the dailies. (52)

Although the combination of the myths of romantic love and the reality of men's control over and violence against women initially may appear to be antithetical, the romantic myths play a role in perpetuating the cycle of violence in "Woman Hollering Creek" because both are dependent upon male action and female passivity. At one point in "Woman Hollering Creek," Juan Pedro throws one of Cleófilas's

Spanish romance novels across the room, hitting her and leaving a raised welt on her cheek. In this scene, the language of romance embodied by the book and the reality of violence literally intersect, and the romance novel becomes something that Juan Pedro uses as a weapon against his wife, but *telenovelas* and romance novels also function as destructive forces in more subtle, less literal ways in "Woman Hollering Creek." They bring love and sacrifice or love and suffering together. After the *telenovela* episode when Lucía Mendez from *Tú o Nadie* confesses her love, Cleófilas thinks that the sacrifices this character has made and the hardships she has endured are worth the price "because to suffer for love is good, The pain all sweet somehow. In the end" (45). Although Cisneros does not indicate whether this woman from the *telenovela* is suffering physical abuse, one of the ideas that Cleófilas absorbs from the *telenovelas* is that suffering for love is a good thing—immediate sacrifice and suffering lead the women on television to a final happy ending.

This idea that love is the ultimate good and therefore worth suffering for is embedded in the plots of romance novels and *telenovelas*. The romance blends love and suffering because, as Ann Barr Snitow argues, romance novels—and I would extend this to *telenovelas* as well—"Make bridges between contradiction; they soothe ambivalence" (253). In them, love magically converts "a brutal male sexuality" to romance (253); through his relationship with the heroine, the hero softens. Snitow argues that, in romances, cruelty, callousness, and coldness are equated with maleness, and the novels' happy endings offer the "possibility that male coldness, absence, and boredom are not what they seem" (250). In the end, a rational explanation for the male hero's behavior appears, and it becomes apparent that "in spite of his coldness or preoccupation, the hero really loves the heroine and wants to marry her" (250). Before the happy resolution, the heroine may suffer as a result of the hero's indifference or his anger and abuse, but the emphasis is on the happy ending, and the heroine's suffering becomes just part of the plot that leads to this ending. In *Reading the Romance: Women, Patriarchy, and Popular Literature*, Janice Radway describes the message inherent in this process:

> When a romance presents the story of a woman who is misunderstood by the hero, mistreated and manhandled, and then suddenly loved, protected, and cared for by him because he recognizes that he mistook the meaning of her behavior, the novel is informing its readers that minor acts of violence can

be similarly reinterpreted as the result of misunderstandings or
jealousy born of "true love" (75).

This view of love allows Cleófilas to see the suffering of the character
in the *telenovela* as " . . . all sweet somehow. In the end"; she
believes that for "the great love of one's life," a woman does "whatever
one can, must do, whatever the cost" (44). For most of "Woman
Hollering Creek," her belief in romance allows Cleófilas to retain the
hope that, beyond her own suffering, there may be a happy ending.

Because of this belief in happy endings, Cleófilas does not reject
the romance plot when her husband begins to beat her as Esperanza does
when she is raped in *The House on Mango Street*. After Esperanza's
rape, the gap between the romance plot and her own life becomes too
great to reconcile, and she feels betrayed by the images of love and sex
she has seen in the media. "They all lied," she thinks, "All the books
and magazines everything that told it wrong" (100). Even after her
husband has begun to beat her regularly, however, Cleófilas clings to
the romance plot and tries to reconcile it with her own life. She begins
thinking of her life as a *telenovela* in which "the episodes got sadder and
sadder. And there were no commercials in between for comic relief. And
no happy ending in sight" (52–53). She imagines romance and happy
endings as things that happened to someone with a romantic name and
thinks that if she were to change her name to something "more poetic
than Cleófilas," her life might be more like the lives of the women in
the *telenovelas* (53).

Radway argues that romantic violence arises from an inability to
imagine "a situation in which a woman might acquire and use resources
that would allow her to withstand male opposition and coercion" (72),
and, for most of "Woman Hollering Creek," Cleófilas is in this very
position. She is simply unable to imagine rejecting the romance plot
and resisting her husband. Along with the violence of Cleófilas's life
and the images and language of the *telenovelas*, however, there is a third
narrative that emerges in "Woman Hollering Creek." The creek itself
comes to represent the voices of real women who are silenced by
violence and by the myths the *telenovelas* and romance novels
perpetuate. After moving to Texas, Cleófilas is always aware of the
creek's presence and is fascinated by its name, but it is only when she
meets Felice at the end of the story that the creek becomes linked with
resistance to the romance plot. When Cleófilas moves to Seguín, she is
puzzled by the name of the creek—*La Gritona*, Woman Hollering.
"Such a lovely name for a creek," she thinks, "Though no one could
say whether the woman hollered from anger or from pain" (46). For

most of the story, these are the only two emotions that Cleófilas can imagine as this woman's motivation—anger or pain, rage or suffering—because these are the only explanations her life or the *telenovelas* offer her for a woman's shout. She speculates about whom the creek is named for, imagining it might be *La Llorona*, the weeping woman of Mexican folklore (51).[5] Yet she is unable to come up with an explanation that satisfies her, and the only women she knows in Seguín are unable to or uninterested in helping her. Cleófilas observes that no one in the town "questioned, little less understood" the name Woman Hollering.

Even when she is puzzled by the river, Cleófilas experiences it as "an alive thing, a thing with a voice all its own" (51), and, when she finally seizes an opportunity to leave her husband and return to Mexico, she realizes that the voice of the woman hollering may be a voice of celebration. In the scene in which Cleófilas is leaving Seguín, Cisneros uses a woman's shout, a holler, to represent a voice that resists both male violence and the romance narrative. When Felice, who has promised to give Cleófilas a ride to the Greyhound station, yells as they cross the river, Cleófilas is shocked. Felice yells not out of anger or pain, but because she wants to shout—as a kind of tribute to the woman for whom the river was named and the other women she represents. "Every time I cross the bridge I do that," Felice tells her, "Because of the name, you know. Woman Hollering. *Pues*, I holler" (55). "Did you ever notice," Felice continues, "how nothing around here is named after a woman?" (55). The shout Felice gives is filled with strength, fearlessness, celebration rather than with pain, fear, or pleading—a shout that both Felice and Cleófilas describe as a "a holler like Tarzan" (55–56).

It is appropriate that Felice is the vehicle of such celebration because her emotional and economic self-sufficiency make her unlike any woman Cleófilas has ever met before. When Cleófilas asks if the pickup Felice is driving is her husband's, Felice tells her she does not have a husband; "the pickup was hers. She herself had chosen it. She herself was paying for it" (55). Everything about Felice amazes Cleófilas and helps her begin to imagine alternatives for women beyond either her own life or the lives of love and suffering in the *telenovelas* and Corín Tellado romance novels. By witnessing the power of Felice's shout—a shout that defies the idea of women as silent victims or sufferers—Cleófilas becomes aware of her own voice. After Felice shouts, Cleófilas hears laughter, and her first response to this is to think that Felice must be laughing, but she soon realizes it is not Felice. The sound is "gurgling out of her own throat, a long ribbon of laughter like water" (56). This laughter is a form of expression that cannot be contained or understood within the romance plot that Cleófilas has accepted for most of "Woman Hollering Creek." Like Felice's shout and the creek itself, it represents a voice in opposition to the romance script and implies Cleófilas's potential to reclaim her own life, as well as her voice, by resisting the popular romance narrative. The ending of "Woman Hollering Creek," however, marks only the first step Cisneros depicts in the rejection of equating women with passivity and suffering. While the final scene of this story demonstrates that Cleófilas is beginning to realize that there are other possibilities for women's lives than the ones she has previously imagined, the story does not reveal how she will use this realization, how it will affect her own self-image and her view of the *telenovelas*. In "Little Miracles, Kept Promises," Cisneros portrays a young woman who is not only able to resist a traditional narrative but is also capable of appropriating and rewriting it. In this story composed of different characters' petitions to various saints, including the Virgin Mary, Chayo, the character whom Cisneros describes at the greatest length, feels alienated from the other women of her culture—both the Virgin and the women of the *telenovelas*. Chayo, who wants to devote herself to painting rather than motherhood, tells the Virgin in her letter, "Though no one else in my family, no other woman, neither friend nor relative, no one I know, not even the heroine in the *telenovelas*, no women, wants to live alone. I do" (127). Chayo even confesses to Mary that she has been unable to accept her, to "let you in my house," because she has associated Mary with her mother and grandmother's silent acceptance of suffering (127). Chayo desires an image not of a woman suffering but of a woman who is strong and powerful. She writes to Mary, "I wanted you bare-breasted, snakes in your hands. I wanted you leaping and somersaulting the backs of bulls. I wanted you swallowing raw hearts and rattling volcanic ash. I wasn't going to be my mother or my grandma. All that self-sacrifice, all that silent suffering" (127).

Chayo is able to accept Mary only by revising or reinventing her image of her. She begins to see her as the spiritual force that is incarnated in images of Aztec deities as well as in portraits of the Virgin. She views her as *Nuestra Senora de Soledad*, Our Lady of the Rosary, Our Lady of Perpetual Sorrow and also as Tonantzín, Coatlaxopeuh, Teteoinnan, Toci, Xochiquetzal, and she addresses her as Mighty Guadalupana Coatlaxopeuh Tonantizín. To Chayo, Mary becomes a figure who embodies both the suffering and endurance of women and their strength and power, and this frees her not only to love

Mary but to love herself—to choose not to repeat the lives of her mother and grandmother without feeling like a traitor to her race.

The central character in Cisneros's *"Bien* Pretty" also engages in this process of rewriting or reinventing, both in relation to a traditional Mexican myth and in relation to contemporary romances. Like Chayo, Lupe is an artist. She is a painter who is using her lover, Flavio, as a model for Prince Popocatépetl in her "updated version of the Prince Popocatépetl/Princess Ixtaccíhuatl volcano myth"[6] until her lover leaves her and returns to his wife and children in Mexico (144). After Flavio leaves, Lupe continues her job as an art director for a community cultural center but is unable to paint and begins watching television when she comes home from work—first old Mexican movies and then *telenovelas*—and begins buying Corín Tellado romance novels and magazines with stories about *telenovela* stars.

Her response to the *telenovelas* is different than Cleófilas's, however. Lupe realizes what the attraction of *telenovelas* is, but she also realizes that the images of women in the *telenovelas* reinforce traditional stereotypes of women. After a conversation with a cashier at Centano's Drugstore about one of the latest *telenovelas,* "Si Dios quiere," Lupe thinks:

> *Amar as vivir.* What it comes down to for that woman at Centano's and for me. It was enough to keep us tuning in every day at six-thirty, another episode, another thrill. To relive that living when the universe ran through the blood like river water. Alive. Not the weeks spent writing grant proposals, not the forty hours standing behind a cash register shoving cans of refried beans into plastic sacks. (163)

But what the *telenovelas* can provide is only a severely limited version of what it means to be alive—living as devising ways to attain the attention and favor of men and, as in "Woman Hollering Creek," romance linked with suffering. Lupe's frustration with these limitations is illustrated in the dreams she begins having about the *telenovelas* she is watching—dreams that express her desire to revise the actions of the *telenovela* characters:

> I started dreaming of these Rosas and Briandas and Luceros. And in my dreams I'm slapping the heroine to her senses, because I want them to be women who make things happen, not women who things happen to. Not loves that are *tormentosos.* Not men powerful and passionate versus women

either volatile and evil or sweet and resigned. But women. Real
women. The ones I've loved all my life. (160)

In "*Bien* Pretty," Cisneros implies both that women can find a
different kind of female figure in some popular culture narratives and
that where these models are unavailable they can choose to create their
own. Lupe can listen, not to "Lola Beltran sobbing '*Soy infeliz*' into
her four *cervezas*. But Daniela Romo singing '*Ya no. Es verdad que te
adoro, pero mas me adoro yo.*' I love you, honey, but I love me more"
(163). By the end of this short story, Lupe realizes that she must make
an effort to "right the world and live . . . the way lives were meant to
be lived" (163)—not the way lives are portrayed in the *telenovelas*. This
means living with self-respect, independence, and strength as well as
with passion, desire, and pain.

When Lupe returns to her volcano painting to finish it, this need to
rewrite the kinds of stories told about women affects her work, and she
decides to switch the positions of Prince Popocatépetl and Princess
Ixtaccíhuatl because "after all who's to say the sleeping mountain isn't
the prince, and the voyeur the princess, right?" (163). What Lupe, like
Cleófilas, and Chayo has discovered is a different way of viewing an old
story, a process that can be applied both to traditional Mexican and
Aztec stories and to popular romance genres in order to yield new
narratives.

NOTES

1. Cisneros has published three collections of poetry, *Bad Boys* (1980),
    My Wicked, Wicked Ways (1987), and *Loose Woman* (1994); one
    novel, *The House on Mango Street* (1983), composed of forty-four brief
    narratives of vignettes; and one collection of short stories, *Woman
    Hollering Creek and Other Stories* (1991). She was born in 1954 in
    Chicago and, like Esperanza Cordero, her narrator from *The House on
    Mango Street,* grew up there. Cisneros is a 1978 graduate of the
    University of Iowa Writer's Workshop, which she attended after
    graduating with a BA in English from Loyola University. From 1978 to
    1980 she taught creative writing at an alternative high school in
    Chicago. Since the early 1980s she has received several grants and
    fellowships, including two from the National Endowment for the Arts.
2. In her interview with Pilar E. Rodríguez Aranda, Cisneros discusses the
    possibility that "the visual is taking the place of oral myth" and
    explains that, while she was teaching, she realized she must resort to
    references to television characters in order to make her points because

"that was our common mythology, that's what we had in common, television" (77).

3. Literally translated *telenova* means "a novel transmitted by television" (Rector and Trinta 194). Although in the United States they are often referred to as Spanish-language soap operas, *Telenovelas* differ from American soap operas because they have endings—usually happy ones. A *telenovela* usually runs for several months, and then a new one begins in the same time slot.

4. In her article "The Incorporation of Women: A Comparison of North American and Mexican American Popular Culture," Jean Franco asserts—using the work of Carola Garcia Calderon's *Revistas Femininas, La mujer como objeto de consumo*—that Harlequins and Corín Tellado romance novels are similar but notes that in the Corín Tellado romance novels, the kind of Spanish romance novels Cleófilas reads in "Woman Hollering Creek" and Lupe reads in "*Bien* Pretty," luxury items, expensive clothes, and jewelry are emphasized even more than in Harlequins (Franco 124).

5. Llorona is a mythical apparition of a weeping woman. Many versions of the Llorona legend exist throughout Mexico and the Pacific and Southwestern portions of the United States. Explanations of the reason for Llorona's sorrow vary greatly among the different versions of the story. In several of these variants, she mourns drowned children and is sighted near a river, creek, or other body of water.

6. Popocatépetl and Ixtaccíhuatl are dormant volcanoes in central Mexico named after legendary Aztec lovers, Ixtaccíhuatl, an Aztec emperor's daughter, and Popocatépetl, an Aztec warrior. For a description of the myth, see Frances Toor's *A Treasury of Mexican Folkways*. Mexico, D. F.: Mexico Press, 1947.

REFERENCES

Cisneros, Sandra. *The House on Mango Street*. New York: Random House, 1989.

___. *My Wicked, Wicked Ways*. New York: Random House, 1992.

___. *Woman Hollering Creek and Other Stories*. New York: Random House, 1991.

Franco, Jean. "The Incorporation of Women: A Comparison of North American and Mexican American Popular Culture." *Studies in Entertainment: Critical Approaches to Mass Culture*. Ed. Tania Modleski. Bloomington: Indiana University Press, 1986. 119–138.

Moraga, Cherríe. "From a Long Line of Vendidias: Chicanas and Feminism." *Feminist Studies/Critical Studies*. Ed. Teresa de Lauretis. Bloomington: Indiana University Press, 1986. 173–190.

Radway, Janice. *Reading the Romance: Women, Patriarchy, and Popular Literature*. Chapel Hill: University of North Carolina Press, 1984.

Rector, Monica, and Aluizio Ramos Trinta. "The Telenovela." *Diogenes* 113–114 (1981): 194–204.

Rodríguez Aranda, Pilar E. "On the Solitary Fate of Being Mexican, Female, Wicked and Thirty-Three: An Interview with Writer Sandra Cisneros." *The Americas Review: A Review of Hispanic Literature and Art of the USA*. 18 (1990): 64–80.

Snitow, Ann Barr. "Mass Market Romance: Pornography for Women Is Different." *Powers of Desire: The Politics of Sexuality*. Eds. Ann Barr Snitow, Christine Stansell, and Sharon Thompson. New York: Monthly Review Press, 1983. 245–263.

6. Healing Ceremonies: Native American Stories of Cultural Survival

Linda Palmer

Survival, I know how this way.
This way, I know.
It rains.
Mountains and canyons and plants
grow.
We traveled this way,
gauged our distance by stories
and loved our children.
We taught them
To love their birth.
We told ourselves over and over
again, "We shall survive
this way."

(Ortiz, "Survival This Way," *Woven Stone* 167)

Acoma Pueblo poet Simon Ortiz's "Survival This Way" reveals much about the Native American response to the continuation of their cultures. Survival, not surprisingly, has been a central concern at least since encounters with Europeans first threatened the continuation of their cultural traditions. But Ortiz's first lines exude a confidence in Native Americans' ability to survive, and subsequent lines tell us how it is done: through love of place, the natural world, and "our children" and, perhaps especially, through the stories that tell the people who they are, where they are, and why they are here—the stories that sustain the culture through generations. As Ortiz says, the stories must be told "over and over." Speaking of his own life, Ortiz has noted that "it was the stories and songs which provided the knowledge that I was woven into the intricate web that was my Acoma life" (Swann and Krupat

189). Indeed, telling and hearing the stories are acts of survival, ceremonial acts of remembering, regenerating, and reassuring.

Native American literature from creation myths to contemporary fiction sings with the urgency of ceremony, song, and memory as means of survival. In the Hopi creation story, Spider Grandmother warns the emerging people before she leaves them, "Compose songs to sing in your ceremonies that will remind you how the sun and moon were made. . . . Only those who forget why they came to this world will lose their way. They will disappear in the wilderness and be forgotten" (Courlander 32). Song, ceremony, and memory blend for cultural survival, and forgetting results in destruction of the fragile web of existence.

Grandmother's advice is as urgent for contemporary Native American writers as it was for the newly-emerged Hopi. Writer and critic Paula Gunn Allen points out in *The Sacred Hoop* that "the purpose of traditional American Indian literature is never simply pure self expression" but rather a fulfillment of communal responsibility, an offering of a survival ceremony in an environment inherently destructive to the people (55). In the prologue of her novel *Ceremony*, Laguna Pueblo writer Leslie Marmon Silko reveals that her story is itself a ceremony, a healing gift assuring the people that they "shall survive," that rain will come, plants will grow, and the people will know who they are. In the prologue, Silko suggests that she is a vessel for the ancient stories, accepting the responsibility of storytelling and passing on the stories that Thought Woman, Spider Grandmother, has conceived: "She is sitting in her room thinking of a story now[.] I'm telling you the story she is thinking," says the storytelling voice (1). Stories, the voice goes on to tell us, "aren't just entertainment. Don't be fooled. They are all we have, you see. . . . You don't have anything if you don't have the stories" (2).

Survival in the face of encounters with the dominant society is naturally a recurring theme in Native American fiction. "We persist in living, believing, hoping, loving, speaking, and writing as Indians," says Ortiz (Swann and Krupat 194). We see the persistence in stories by Louise Erdrich ("American Horse"), Leslie Silko ("Lullaby" and "Storyteller"), Gerald Vizenor ("Almost Browne" and "Feral Lasers"), and Thomas King ("A Seat in the Garden"), among others. In contemporary trickster tales, the cultural encounter plays itself out comically, as when Vizenor's trickster, Almost Browne, uses technology to reverse history, both creating and deconstructing Columbus with laser holograms. Says a disconcerted viewer of

Browne's deconstructive laser show in the sky, "Wild men, wild neighborhoods in the sky, me on my back, the tribes above, the whole thing is turned around somehow" (Vizenor 18). In "POWWOW," Cherokee poet Carroll Arnett/Gogisi similarly uses a trickster narrator to neatly play the white world for the fool:

> Hair the color of
> tobacco ash, the fair lady
> anthro asked, Excuse
> me please, . . . sir
> (guess it beats Chief),
>
> Does that red patch
> On your blanket symbolize
> something?
>
>   Yes mam,
> it surely does, it
> symbolizes that once
> upon a time there
> was a hole
> in the blanket.

(Hobson 127)

As often, however, the encounter plays out tragically, as in Silko's "Storyteller" and Lullaby" or Erdrich's "American Horse." These stories are typically marked by traumatic cultural encounters between the dominant Anglo and traditional native cultures and, often, by the apparent victory of the privileged society and discourse. In *Other Destinies*, critic Louis Owens points out that "again and again in this fiction, this conflict [in world views] is epitomized through conflicting discourses, through breakdowns in communication and understanding, failures in articulation" (8). It is this apparently tragic view of cultural encounter that I wish to consider here, examining how conflicting discourses and cultural survival through memory, story, and ceremony shape both the theme and the structure of Native American short story and fiction. Understanding the story as *itself* a ceremony for cultural survival, we see that even when the encounter ends in what might commonly be considered "tragedy" or "defeat," the spirit triumphs, transcending the particular moment, integrating it into a healing vision of wholeness. The story itself repairs the torn web and thus continues the creation. Chickasaw writer Linda Hogan explains both the importance of story to the healing process and the contemporary writer's place in it: "I know this telling is the first part of the ceremony, my part in it. It is story, really, that finds its way into language, and story is at the very crux of healing, at the heart of every ceremony and ritual in the older America" (*Hogan* 37). The ceremony/story thus re-members the community (in Paula Gunn Allen's words), reaffirming the belief that (despite Yeats' suggestion to the contrary), the center does indeed hold.

Leslie Marmon Silko's deeply moving short story "Lullaby" illustrates in structure, image, and theme the intricate play of struggle for survival and transcendence, of everyday affronts and ancient patterns of survival. This article focuses primarily on "Lullaby," yet necessarily moves out from that story to other stories, stories upon stories. To discuss the way in which story heals is necessarily to move not only through the intricate web of a single story but also through the web of many stories, for as Ortiz says, the story must be (and is) told "over and over." At the end of *Ceremony*, grandma says of the story just completed, It seems like I already heard these stories before . . . only thing is, the names sound different" (260). The point is, of course, that the story is in fact never *completed*, it continues, repeating itself in different manifestations again and again, the ceremony never ending. In his poetry collection *Woven Stone*, Simon Ortiz tells us that "there is always one more story" (177):

It Doesn't End, of Course

It doesn't end.

In all growing
From all earths
To all skies,

in all touching
all things,

in all soothing
the aches of all years,

it doesn't end.

(*Ortiz* 147)

For the Native American writer, the story is "all growing . . . all soothing the aches of all years," and stories are richly interconnected to one another, like strands of a beautiful and perfectly balanced (grandmother) spider web, each strand dependent on the other for existence. To listen to Silko's "Lullaby" is to listen to her *Ceremony* is to listen to Momaday's *House Made of Dawn* is to listen to Erdrich's *"American Horse"* is to listen to Ortiz's "Survival This Way" is to listen . . . It never ends, of course. That is precisely the point.

"Lullaby" tells the story of Ayah, an elderly Navajo woman whose children are long gone from her—one killed in war, two dead in infancy, and, most tragically and urgent, two taken from her by white doctors and police whose language, purpose, and explanations she has been unable to understand. Now years later, she is left only with poverty and her husband Chato. Chato, alcoholic and broken after being discarded like broken machinery from the white-owned ranch where he has worked a lifetime, is little comfort; and Ayah can never forget that it was he who taught her to sign her name in English, the act that allowed the white world to take her children from her.

The tragic sense of loss and decline indicated in this brief sketch of the story hardly "fits" the gentle title. But that ironic distance between the mere outline of the story and the title is precisely the distance "gauged by stories" in Ortiz's "Survival This Way": for the love suggested in the word "lullaby"—here love of place, children, and traditional ways of seeing—sustains Ayah in her grief and sweeps the story to a conclusion of transcendent beauty that suggests Ayah's spiritual survival and the survival of the ancient strengths of the people.

"Lullaby" fittingly enough appears in Silko's *Storyteller*, the title of the book implying its regenerative powers. Ayah—all the people—needs Silko's healing story, her lullaby, in order to mend through appropriate ceremony their broken lives. Ayah's world is crushed by poverty, loss, illness, and confusion. In "Lullaby" the web is torn, nearly shattered. According to Navajo and other southwestern creation myths, Grandmother Spider teaches the people to weave, a life-sustaining act of creation, and in doing so spins the web of existence. Imagining Grandmother Spider's beautifully balanced web helps us see the perfect harmony that exists naturally in the world.

"Out of her own body she pushed/ silver thread, light, air/ and carried it carefully on the dark, flying/ where nothing moved./ Out of her body she extruded/ shining wire, life, and wove the light/ on the void . . . (Allen, "Grandmother," Bruchac, *Songs from This Earth on Turtle's Back* 3). All threads are interconnected, each supporting the other, each radiating out and back into the center. The old medicine man Ku'oosh in Silko's *Ceremony* explains the intricacy and the fragility of the web to Tayo, whose responsibility it is to restore its balance,

telling him, "But you know, grandson, this world is fragile." The
narrator continues,

> The word [Ku'oosh] chose to express "fragile" was filled with
> the intricacies of a continuing process, and with a strength
> inherent in spider webs woven across paths through sand hills
> where early in the morning the sun becomes entangled in each
> filament of web. It took a long time to explain the fragility
> and intricacy because no word exists alone, and the reason for
> choosing each word had to be explained with a story about
> why it must be this certain way. That was the responsibility
> that went with being human. . . . (35)

The web, the world, is fragile, easily rent, for when one strand is torn,
the web is weakened, can be shattered, and it is the responsibility of the
individual to sustain the community by maintaining the perfect balance
of the universe. This is accomplished in part by remembering the
stories, the songs, the mythic traditions and using them in healing
ceremonies that are life-giving, regenerative. The people are sustained
by remembering and passing on what is deep in the memory, there to
draw strength from.

Though a simple plot summary of "Lullaby" reveals the shattered
web, the certain knowledge that it can be mended is evident from the
story's opening lines, which subtly offer Ayah and all of us the
appropriate healing ceremony:

> The sun had gone down but the snow in the wind gave off its
> own light. It came in thick tufts like new wool—washed
> before the weaver spins it. Ayah reached out for it like her own
> babies had, and she smiled when she remembered how she had
> laughed at them. She was an old woman now, and her life had
> become memories. She sat down with her back against the
> wide cottonwood tree, feeling the rough bark on her back
> bones; she faced east and listened to the wind and snow sing a
> high-pitched Yeibechei song. (*Storyteller* 43)

With this opening passage, storyteller Silko offers to Ayah and the
people the healing ceremony to regenerate the web. Survival is the
recognition of nature's perfect balance, with the snow offering "its own
light" when the life-giving sun has gone down. The snow is like the
wool the weaver (Grandmother Spider) will spin, giving warmth and
life to the people. The weaver's presence in the opening line assures
Ayah and the reader that the spirit world is present, even here in Ayah's

old age and sorrow. Zuni and other creation myths emphasize the ever-presence and accessibility of the spirit world: "Do not worry," the gods tell the people. "We have not perished. . . . We stay near by. . . . Do not worry" ("Talk Concerning the First Beginning," Lauter, et al. 36). Strengthened by her memory of her people's stories, Ayah must recognize the work of Grandmother Spider in the weaving of day and night, warmth and cold, youth and age.

She instinctively reaches out for the snow, grandmother spider's wool, and as she does so, she remembers—circling back, moving along the web's strand to the memories of her children. In her poem "Remember," Creek poet Joy Harjo conveys the importance of remembering, speaking, becoming the contemporary voice for Grandmother Spider's long-ago advice to the newly-emerged Hopi: "Remember that you are this universe and that this/ universe is you./ Remember that all is motion, is growing, is you" (*She Had Some Horses* 40). In remembering, Ayah feels her own connection to the land, feels "the rough bark [of the cottonwood] on her back bones" (*Storyteller* 43). Her close relationship to mother earth is part of the healing, nurturing ceremony that will, the reader knows, restore her. The ceremony that foreshadows the story's transcendence concludes, for now, as Ayah faces east where morning begins and hears the song of her people.

In structure, then, the story has begun with its necessary ending, and the story (as we know it must) ends with a healing song and spiritual transcendence. This circular structure appears frequently in Native American literature: N. Scott Momaday's Pulitzer Prize winning *House Made of Dawn*, for instance, opens with its conclusion. Silko's *Ceremony* opens with affirmation that the contemporary story told here is a retelling of the old stories, not *merely* a retelling (as in rehashing) but *profoundly* a retelling (as in necessary). The prologue ends with the word "Sunrise," positioned alone on the page connecting the ancient world of the prologue and its evocation of Thought Woman to the contemporary story and its crisis of cultural conflict and shattered lives. "Sunrise," like the opening paragraph of "Lullaby," assures both the listener and the people enmeshed in the contemporary conflict that there *is* sunrise, that the world will be born anew in the telling of the story. As *House Made of Dawn* ends with the necessary ritual run that is predicted in the prologue, so *Ceremony* ends at full circle, with the words "Sunrise, accept this offering, Sunrise." Because the story has been offered, sunrise comes once again, and the ongoing creation continues. This circular structure, with the "solution" appearing before the "problem" unfolds, reflects not only the traditional belief in circularity but also the certainty that "appropriate" behavior, as Momaday calls it, or ceremony, can mend the fragmented web: "I know how this way. This way, I know" (Ortiz 167).

But the implicit struggle for survival in Ortiz's poem correctly suggests that survival, cultural and spiritual, isn't easy. In Silko's *Ceremony*, as Tayo struggles to recover and in doing so to heal the drought-scarred land of his people, he is reminded repeatedly that "it won't be easy." Though the perfectly balanced web is the natural order of the universe, we humans always manage to pull it askew, often threatening the stability of its very center: "It took only one person to tear away the delicate strands of the web, spilling the rays of sun into the sand, and the fragile world would be injured" (*Ceremony* 38). In "Lullaby," the delicate web of existence is torn away and the fragile world shattered for Ayah, and by extension for her people, by the encounter with white culture.

Many of Silko's stories focus thematically on this encounter ("Storyteller," "Geronimo's Story," *Ceremony,* and *Almanac of the Dead*, for instance). In some of these, trickster Indians get the best of whites trying to get the best of them, as in this brief vignette from *Storyteller:*

> The Trans-Western pipeline vice president came
> to discuss right-of-way.
> The Lagunas let him wait all day long
> because he is a busy and important man.
> And late in the afternoon they told him
> to come back again tomorrow. (238)

More frequently, as in "Lullaby," the encounters result in material, spiritual, and cultural loss. When Ayah touches the bark of the cottonwood in the opening scene of the story, she finds strength and turns to the place of new beginnings, but every touch of white society bruises the spirit and brings great loss. Ayah knows that contact with the whites brings only grief, "because it was like the old ones always told her about learning their language or any of their ways: it endangered you" (47). Her oldest son, Jimmie ("they named him for the summer morning and in English they called him Jimmie") died in the white man's war, leaving her only a regulation army blanket and a message she can't understand from "a man in a khaki uniform trimmed in gold" (44). She has lived her married life in a "box-car shack where the [boss] rancher let the [worker] Indians live," a "gray boxcar shack with the paint all peeled from the wood," and "the stove pipe on the roof . . . rusted and cracked" (46). Chato has lost that meager work with the white rancher telling him "he was too old to work for him anymore, and Chato and his old woman should be out of the shack by the next afternoon" (47).

The story begins with the promise of spiritual renewal and concludes with its fulfillment (with the certain coming of sunrise), but cultural chaos fills much of the story, just as it fills much of Ayah's life. Achieving that sunrise ending, the story's theme and structure remind us, "won't be easy." Within its essential circularity, "Lullaby" moves structurally between the "conflicting discourses" of Ayah's encounter with white society and the "process of reconstruction, of self-discovery, and cultural recovery" that is at the heart of most contemporary Native American fiction (Owens 5). The greatest tearing of the web results when Ayah loses her children, Ella and Danny, to the white doctors, who take them for reasons that Ayah (and the reader) cannot fully understand. The personal loss is painful enough; but the reader aware of Native American reliance on storytelling realizes that the loss is even greater than Ayah's personal loss: for without children there is no one to inherit the story. As Ortiz's survival poem suggests, survival requires teaching the children to love their birth, but without children to become listeners to the story of their birth and their people's birth, the story, and thus the culture, dies. Like the army men who had come years earlier to tell her in an incomprehensible language that Jimmie was dead, the doctors who came to take Ella and Danny "were wearing khaki uniforms and they waved papers at her and a black ball-point pen, trying to make her understand their English words" (45). Language is sacred to the people; it creates the world. As Spider Grandmother, or Thought Woman, names things in *Ceremony*, they become; when in the Wintu creation myth Peheipe and Turtle help the World Maker create the world, they do so by "singing their power song"; when the sisters Uchtsiti and Iatiku in the Acoma Creation myth name all the seeds and plants of the earth, they (the seeds, the plants— and the sisters) *become* (Stirling, *Origin Myth*). In Momaday's *House Made of Dawn,* the priest of the sun understands the power of words, reminding Abel that "words were medicine; they were magic and invisible. They came from nothing into sound and meaning" (96). But as Tosamah also warns, white man words can destroy the people, too, as they destroy Abel: "Word by word by word these [white] men were disposing of him in language, their language" (102).

In "Lullaby," the doctors destroy Ayah with words: they have mastery of the privileged discourse; she is forced to use their discourse but cannot fully understand it. Thinking that if she puts her name on their paper, they will stop looking at her children "like the lizard watches the fly," Ayah signs her name, a skill Chato has taught her and which represents her only knowledge of the incomprehensible language which now controls her destiny. She has, of course, been tricked by words.

Once again, story sustains Ayah, circling her back to that which regenerates. "Mountains and canyons and plants grow," Ortiz's survival poem assures us, and for the moment Ayah is able to escape the doctors and move in her struggle for personal and cultural survival to the mountains and plants that grow and heal, where

> sitting on a black lava boulder in the sunshine . . . she could
>   see
> for miles all around her. The sky was light blue and cloudless,
> and it was warm for late April. The sun warmth relaxed her
> and took the fear and anger away. She lay back on the rock
> and watched the sky. It seemed to her that she could walk into
> the sky, stepping through clouds endlessly. (46)

Ayah's long relationship to the land sustains her in this moment of crisis and terror: she watches the hawk "soar high above them, dark wings gliding," watches the children "play with pebbles and stones, pretending they were birds' eggs and then little rabbits" (46). The story circles in this moment of crisis back to beginnings, to the people's emergence from and intimacy with the land and, in the structure of the story, to the opening passage which suggests the healing conclusion. Time is again erased by the story's movement. It opens with Ayah and an old woman sitting in the mountains "feeling the rough bark on her back bones" (43), facing east toward the sunrise, and circles within the story backward to an almost identical healing moment years earlier, as she sits "on a black lava boulder in the sunshine" (46). As the two moments of contact with the earth blur and are lifted by non-chronology out of time, the reader and Ayah are both reminded of continual healings on the land.

But the web tears again, this time seemingly irreparably, when the children are finally, inevitably taken by the white doctors and social workers who apparently suspect their exposure to tuberculosis:

> It was worse than if they had died: to lose the children and to
> know that somewhere, in a place called Colorado, in a place
> full of sick and dying strangers, her children were without her.
> (47)

The children are gone, not only from her but from their place, their land, and "somewhere" away from the center they are alone, with strangers, removed from their culture, their mother, and Grandmother Spider's creation. Ortiz says that "the language [he] spoke was that of a struggling people who held ferociously to a heritage, culture, language, and land despite the odds posed them by the forces surrounding them. . . . " (Swann and Krupat 187). But Ayah cannot hold on to her children, who are taken "somewhere," to be cured not only of their suspected disease but of their "heritage, culture, language, and land" (Swann and Krupat 187).

Later, in a brief, doomed visit home, Danny tries to answer her questions in Navajo, but "he could not seem to remember and he spoke English words with the Navajo" (*Storyteller* 49). As the children leave with "the blonde woman" who wears "a dainty gold watch," Ayah knows that "they [are] already being weaned from these lava hills and from this sky" (49). Ayah's anguish is intense: she does not sleep, and she hates Chato, "not because he let the policeman and doctors put the screaming children in the government car, but because he had taught her to sign her name" (47), to unwittingly use the white man's language against herself and to see her children (the culture's children) lost to their sustaining land and language.

In the midst of chaos and despair, the story moves again into a subtly healing act: in her grief, Ayah moves up "on the hill where they had fled the first time, and she sle[eps] rolled up in the blanket Jimmie had sent her" (47). Instinctively, (Momaday would call it an act of "blood memory") she returns to the natural world in her grief, away from the "fine-sounding English talk" that has destroyed her and into the land that sustains her. If we circle forward in chronological time (but backward in the circular structure of the story), we see Ayah at the beginning of the story and later in her life again on the hill with the "old Army blanket over her head like a shawl" (43). Circles upon circles bring Ayah to the land of her people's creation in three movements that in their repeated images blend into one.

In a healing ritual on the mountain, Ayah thinks then not of Jimmie's blanket but about "weaving and the way her mother had done it" (43). Silko describes in detail the act of memory and the "way her mother" had woven,

> on the tall wooden loom set into the sand under a tamarack tree
> for shade. She could see it clearly. She had been only a little
> girl when her grandma gave her the wooden combs to pull the
> twigs and burrs from the raw, freshly washed wool. And while

she combed the wool, her grandma sat beside her, spinning a
silvery strand of yarn around the smooth cedar spindle. (43)

Ceremonial in importance and mythic in scope, Ayah's memory heals
her. She remembers her mother, as her own children might remember
her, weaving blankets for survival in the traditional way, close to the
same sacred earth she sits on now, the loom seemingly growing out of
the sand alongside its sister, the tamarack tree. Ceremonially, her
grandmother teaches her, giving her wooden combs to pull the twigs
from the wool, and in following her grandmother's teaching, she
participates in the creation.

As time blurs in the story, so do the material and spiritual
grandmother of her memory, for this grandma is "spinning a silvery
strand of yarn," reminding us that she is Grandmother Spiderwoman,
the creator, the teacher; between the grandmothers, there is no
distinction. In Allen's poem "Grandmother," after Grandmother Spider
has done her work of "weaving the strands/of her body," the people
become her, take on her role: "After her,/ the women and the men
weave blankets into tales of life,/ memories of light and ladders,/
infinity-eyes and rain." In this blurring, all of creation becomes one and
the web is healed, as is suggested by the last lines of Allen's poem:
"After her I sit on my laddered rain-bearing rug/ and mend the tear with
string" ("Grandmother," Bruchac, *Songs from This Earth* 3). It is
precisely this tear that has fragmented Ayah's world, and it is
specifically Ayah who must, through ceremony, memory, and song,
"mend the tear," become the Grandmother, continue the fragile web of
existence.

Pulling Jimmie's blanket around her, "the green wool . . . faded"
the blanket "unraveling on the edges" (*Storyteller* 43), Ayah remembers
that the "blankets her mother made were soft and woven so tight than
rain rolled off them like birds' feathers"; she remembers "sleeping warm
on cold windy nights, wrapped in her mother's blankets on the hogan's
sandy floor" (44). The blankets, one wholly inadequate, the other
mythic in its creation—world-awakening in its sunrise colors of
yellow, red, and gold, and protecting in its perfection—become one, and
the blurring of worlds, time and space, heal, as Ayah "fe[els] peaceful
remembering [and] d[oes]n't feel cold any more" (44).

Silko's story has re-membered for Ayah and the reader the creation
story of blankets created so fine that "rain rolled off them like birds'
feathers" (44). Thinking of creation and of women passing on stories
and acts of creation to their children, Ayah's memory turns naturally to
birth, for as the creation of the perfect blankets gives birth to the world,

so too had she given birth to children. Memory, telling the creation-birth story to herself, brings her back to a sense of the healed web: "She felt peaceful remembering. . . . She could remember the morning [Jimmie] was born. She could remember whispering to her mother. . . . she could remember [the smell of] the bee flowers blooming and the young willow growing at the springs" (44). The repetition of the word "remember" reminds us in its rhythm that remembering is a ceremonial act, as it is in Harjo's "Remember" and suggests that in remembering Ayah is re-membering her shattered life. The memory of Jimmie's birth appropriately "merge[s] into the births of the other children and to her [becomes] all the same birth" (44). In remembering the early morning birth(s), Ayah becomes herself Grandmother Spider, the creator, or the woman Joy Harjo calls in "Early Morning Woman":

> early morning woman
> rising the sun
> the woman
> bending and stretching
> with the strength of the child
> that moves
> in her belly . . .
>
> early morning woman
> she begins that way
> the sun
> the child
> are the moving circle
> beginning with the woman
> in the early morning.

(What Moon Drove Me to This? 3)

The woman in Harjo's poem is mythic in her life-giving gifts, associated with morning, sun, birthing, and the ongoing circle of existence which begins with the creating woman. Ayah similarly takes on the responsibility of mending the web with her string through her nurturing protection of first the children and then Chato. In *Spider Woman's Granddaughters*, Paula Gunn Allen notes a history of Native American "women's tales," tales of women who enter battle, suffer defeat and/or captivity, but who resist in the face of despair in order to save the children, save the community. In "Lullaby," then, the story's movement from despair to continual healing is made possible in part by Ayah's warrior woman determination and strength. She is, in Joy

Harjo's words, "taking on this journey" of life (Harjo, "Rainy Dawn," *In Mad Love and War* 32).

Chippewa writer Louise Erdrich writes into the same tradition with her short story "American Horse" (Allen, *Spider Woman's Granddaughters*). In the story, Albertine, like Ayah, is about to lose her child, her "best thing," to police and social workers who do not understand and make no attempt to understand the world into which they have stepped: "They are after us," Buddy tells his mother, and Albertine responds, "Lay low. They're outside and they're gonna hunt" (51). Like Ayah, Albertine is doomed to lose this battle to save Buddy from a world that wants to "salvage him" and will take him from her with "some type of form" containing incomprehensible words in a "perfect-bound notebook" (55). Still, warrior woman Albertine acts to preserve family, and as in "Lullaby," memory of ceremony gives her strength. Long ago, her father had given her the gift of "grace" by ceremoniously rubbing a "butterfly, a black and yellow one, . . . on Albertine's collarbone and chest and arms until the color and the powder of it were blended into her skin" (58). Remembering that ceremony and the story of the butterfly's grace in the moment she is about to lose Buddy, "she felt so light and powerful" that "on the wings of her father's hands, on dead butterfly wings, Albertine lifted into the air and flew toward the others" (60). It is a doomed effort to save Buddy, who emits a "great rattling scream" as he is taken from his mother, but it is an effort that gives the reader hope for the survival of warrior women like Albertine and Ayah, hope for the survival of a culture with women like them. In *American Indian Women,* Gretchen Bataille and Kathleen Sands quote a traditional Cheyenne saying that suggests the strength of women in preserving culture:

> A Nation is not conquered
> Until the hearts of its women
> Are on the ground.
>
> Then it is done, no matter
> How brave its warriors
> Nor how strong its weapons. (n.p.)

Both Albertine and Ayah watch their children taken from their center in cars they finally can't pursue into the white world. But in the warrior woman tradition, Ayah will survive, through her bravery and through her memory of her place in the web, in the land, in the stories of her people.

Years after losing her children, Ayah is faced with another tear in the web, as Chato is lost to the bars of the town. Though "the bar owner didn't like Indians there" (*Storyteller* 48), Ayah enters the alien and hostile space, crossing boundaries from her natural world into the world that continues to destroy her family and culture. Again, in hostile territory, memory of creation and birth sustain her:

> She stood by the stove and shook the snow from her blanket and held it near the stove to dry. The wet wool smell reminded her of new-born goats in early March, brought inside to warm near the fire. She felt calm. In past years they would have told her to get out. But her hair was white now and her face was wrinkled. They looked at her like she was a spider crawling slowly across the room. They were afraid; she could feel the fear. (48)

Once again, the story circles back to the sustaining memory of birth, and Ayah is calmed. In old age, she has *become* Grandmother Spider the creator, white haired, wrinkled, looking like a spider. We know that like the generations of spider women who in Allen's poem "mend the tear," Ayah will push "out of her own body . . . silver thread, light, air, and carr[y] it carefully on the dark . . . on the void" (Allen, "Grandmother," Bruchac, *Songs from This Earth* 3). Ayah's search for Chato takes place on the evening the story opens, as the snow falls around her. After having looped repeatedly forward and backward as memory weaves its intricately connected web, the story returns to its beginning and to a final challenge to Ayah to mend the torn web with her thread.

At the foot of ancient "caves above the canyon with yellow painted buffaloes on their walls" (50), Ayah walks in the old way on the newly paved road. Ayah must find Chato "because she had the blanket, and there would be no place for him except with her and the blanket" (49). There would be no place for him except in his appropriate place on the web, and without him the web would remain torn. Like a lost sheep, Chato must be brought back to his proper place if the world is to survive. Old as she is, cold as the world has become, warrior woman Ayah finds Chato, and appropriately, leads him away from the white man's road, the road that has taken her children, led Chato to the bars, "away from the road and up the slope to the giant boulders that had tumbled down from the red sandrock mesa throughout the centuries of rainstorms and earth tremors" (50). As Ayah invites Chato to "rest awhile," the story at its conclusion circles back to its beginning, with Chato now joining Ayah amidst the rock and sand of their center, where they sit down "with their backs against the rock" (51) just as, at the story's opening, she had sat on the boulders with "her back against the wide cottonwood tree" (43).

In Momaday's *House Made of Dawn*, Abel must heal his fragmented life by returning, much like Ayah and Chato, to the sacred earth, "right there in the center of everything, the sacred mountains, the snow-covered mountains and the hills, the gullies and the flats, the sundown and the night, everything . . . where you were and had to be" (157). Ayah must be here, on her sacred land, must perform for Chato—for herself, for all of us—a healing ceremony. As the story closes (or is it opening? Or is it going on, over and over?), it moves in a perfect circle toward a vision of the universe and her place in it:

> The sky cleared. Ayah saw that there was nothing between her
> and the stars. The light was crystalline. There was no
> shimmer, no distortion, through earth haze. She breathed the
> clarity of the night sky; she smelled the purity of the half
> moon and the stars. [Chato] was lying on his side with his
> knees pulled up near his belly for warmth. His eyes were
> closed now, and in the light from the stars and the moon, he
> looked young again. (*Storyteller* 51)

Ayah's children had been born in the spring morning, amidst the smell of "the bee flowers blooming" (44), in a promise of birth and beginnings. Death will come for Chato in the winter, in the wake of a winter snowstorm. The winter scene, however, suggests rebirths upon rebirths, with Ayah merging into the crystalline light of the stars, the world's "distortion" of the web erased, with "clarity" and "purity" all around. Resting in the position of a new-born child, Chato is restored to youth, looks "young again" (51). When Death comes, Ayah "recognize[s] the freezing," knows it as a part of life's circle, knows that "its journey was endless" (51). In this epiphany of recognition of love and wholeness, Ayah "remember[s] how it was when Ella had been with her; and she felt the rush so big inside her heart for the babies" that "she sang" a song she knew "her grandmother had sung" and "her mother had sung" (51).

Returns and mergings. Chato has become the child, reborn in a vision of "clarity" and "purity"; Ayah has become Spider Grandmother, spinning her comforting web into the void; her song has become her mother's song, her grandmother's song, Grandmother's song. Ayah and the story Silko has made of her both move in circles, move out across the void, drawing the strands of the web into the perfect harmony of her healing lullaby, the song that is the appropriate and necessary conclusion and continuance of the story:

> The earth is your mother,
>   she holds you.
> The sky is your father,
>   he protects you.
> Sleep,
> sleep.
> Rainbow is your sister,
>   she loves you.
> The winds are your brothers,
>   they sing to you.
> Sleep,
> sleep.
> We are together always
> We are together always
> There never was a time
> when this
> was not so. (47)

As Abenaki poet and storyteller Joseph Bruchac tells us in "The Remedies," "The remedies for all our pains/ Wait for the songs of healing" (*Entering Onandaga* 22). Ayah's lullaby and Silko's "Lullaby" intertwine to become one song, a song of healing, a ceremony for the living and for the dying. Ayah's ceremonial lullaby (her mother's lullaby, her grandmother's, Grandmother's) is a creation song, a song that "re-members" singer (storyteller) and listener, that "re-collects" the web's strands by establishing the oneness of all things. "We are all together," it reminds us, with our mother earth, our father sky, our sister rainbow, our brother wind. They sing to us, and in singing, they once again create the world. Always this unity of all things has existed, always—in all ways. The song transcends time, space, and material existence. The spirts are there, protecting, holding, loving, singing to us.

REFERENCES

Allen, Paula Gunn. *The Sacred Hoop: Recovering the Feminine in American Indian Traditions*. Boston: Beacon Press, 1992.
___. ed. *Spider Woman's Granddaughters: Traditional Tales and Contemporary Writing by Native American Women*. New York: Fawcett Columbine, 1989.

Bataille, Gretchen, and Kathleen Sands. *American Indian Women: Telling Their Lives.* Lincoln: University of Nebraska Press, 1984.

Bruchac, Joseph. *Entering Onandaga.* Austin, TX: Cold Mountain Press, 1977.

___. ed. *Songs from This Earth on Turtle's Back: Contemporary American Indian Poetry.* Greenfield Center: Greenfield Review Press, 1983.

Courlander, Harold. *The Fourth World of the Hopi.* New York: Crown Publishers, Inc., 1971.

Harjo, Joy. *In Mad Love and War.* Middletown: Wesleyan University Press, 1990.

___. *She Had Some Horses.* New York: Thunder's Mouth Press, 1983.

___. *What Moon Drove Me to This?* New York: I. Reed Books, 1979.

Hobson, Geary, ed. *The Remembered Earth: An Anthology of Contemporary Native American Literature.* Albuquerque: University of New Mexico Press, 1979.

Hogan, Linda. *Dwellings.* New York: W.W. Norton & Co., 1995.

Lauter, Paul et al., eds. *The Heath Anthology of American Literature*, Vol 1. Lexington: D.C. Heath and Company, 1990.

Momaday, N. Scott. *House Made of Dawn.* New York: Harper and Row, Publishers, 1968.

Ortiz, Simon. *Woven Stone.* Tucson: The University of Arizona Press, 1992.

Owens, Louis. *Other Destinies: Understanding the American Indian Novel.* Norman: University of Oklahoma Press, 1992.

Silko, Leslie Marmon. *Ceremony.* New York: Viking Penguin Inc., 1977.

___. *Storyteller.* New York: Arcade Publishing, 1981.

Stirling, Matthew W. *The Origin Myth of Acoma and Other Records.* Bureau of American Ethnology Bulletin 135. Washington, D.C.: U.S. Government Printing Office, 1942.

Swann, Brian, and Arnold Krupat. *I Tell You Now: Autobiographical Essays by Native American Writers.* Lincoln: University of Nebraska Press, 1987.

Vizenor, Gerald. *Landfill Meditation: Crossblood Stories.* Middletown: Wesleyan University Press, 1991.

7. Asian American Short Stories: Dialogizing the Asian American Experience

Qun Wang

In a 1983 interview with University of California-Berkeley Professor Paul Rabinow, French scholar Michel Foucault responded to the criticism that his critical study of modern power structures lacked "an overall theory" and, therefore, was anarchistic in nature. Foucault argued that he believed that "the forms of totalization offered by politics are always, in fact, very limited." What he attempted to achieve was "apart from any *totalization*—which would be at once *abstract* and *limiting*—to *open up* problems that are as *concrete* and *general* as possible"; he was interested in studying "problems that approach politics from behind and cut across societies on the diagonal, problems that are at once constituents of our history and constituted by that history . . . " (Foucault 375–76).

It is interesting to notice that in discussing Edward W. Said's *Orientalism*, scholars such as Raman Selden and Peter Widdowson raise questions that resonate with the criticism of Foucault's theoretical approach. In *Contemporary Literary Theory*, Selden and Widdowson observe that, while warning against "the danger that anti-dominant critiques will demarcate separatist areas of resistance and struggle," Said, nevertheless, calls "for a critical 'decentred consciousness' and for interdisciplinary work committed to the collective libertarian aim of dismantling systems of domination." However, since Said's credentials do not "reside in the presumed authenticity of ethnic or sexual identity or experience, or in any purity of method, but elsewhere," where and what this elsewhere is, "is the major problem of postcolonial criticism, and of other differently directed forms of radical 'ideology critique'" (191).

Both Foucault and Said's theoretical approach to the study of the archaeology of knowledge is as dialectical as their belief in the importance of opening up problems that are "as concrete and general as possible" is strong. Since both build their argument on "a decentralizing that leaves no privilege to any center," to suggest that they develop a new theory to replace those which Foucault and Said challenge is to misunderstand the very basic premises of their argument. In "Subject and Power," for instance, Foucault states that the key issue "is not to discover what we are, but to refuse what we are." For "the political, ethical, social, philosophical problem of our days is not to try to liberate the individual from the state, and from the state's institutions, but to liberate us both from the state and from the type of individualization which is linked to the state."[1] In the closing chapter in *Orientalism*, Said also accentuates that his "project has been to describe a particular system of ideas, not by any means to displace the system with a new one"; he has "attempted to raise a whole set of questions that are relevant in discussing the problems of human experience," questions such as these:

> How does one *represent* other cultures? What is another *culture*? Is the notion of a distinct culture (or race, or religion, or civilization) a useful one, or does it always get involved either in self-congratulation (when one discusses the "other")? Do cultural, religious, and racial differences matter more than socio-economic categories, or politicohistorical ones? How do ideas acquire authority, "normality," and even the status of "natural" truth? What is the role of the intellectual? Is he there to validate the culture and state of which he is a part? What importance must he give to an independent critical consciousness, an *oppositional* critical consciousness? (325–26)

Said's questions reveal the basic premises on which postcolonial criticism builds its tenets. The questions are intended not so much to search for what British scholar Raymond Williams in *Marxism and Literature* calls the "recognition of the essential" and "through this recognition" "its desirability and inevitability, according to the basic laws of reality" (102) as to bring our attention to the dynamics of a constitutive and constituting process that challenges the very foundation on which modern power structures are established. In other words, what is so problematic about questions raised in Selden and Widdowson's observations of Said's critical methodology in specific and that of the postcolonial criticism in general is that they follow the approach of what Chinese American writer King-Kok Cheung in *Articulate Silences* calls "either/or binarism" (170). The approach not only fails to recognize the immense plurality of human experience (the word "purity" used in Selden and Widdowson's statement is itself question-begging), it also threatens to remove the dynamics from "the constitutive and constituting" process of literary criticism.

In the essay "Discourse in the Novel," Russian critic Mikhail Mikhailovich Bakhtin explains how "the internalized double-voiced discourse" works in the novel: heteroglossia, as it is incorporated in the novel, "is *another's speech in another's language*, serving to express authorial intentions but in a refracted way." Since such "speech constitutes a special type of *double-voiced discourse*," it "serves two speakers at the same time and expresses simultaneously two different intentions: the direct intention of the character who is speaking, and the refracted intention of the author." In discussing the emergence of conscious thought in the individual mind, Bakhtin again uses the trope of dialogism to signify the dialectical relationship between what the author calls the *I* and the *other*: the supraperson, the *supra-I*, is "the witness and the judge *of the whole* human being, of the whole *I*, and consequently, someone who is no longer the person, no longer the *I*, but the *other*"; in order to reach *I-for-myself*, the development of individual consciousness must "allow the self to know the self, as if it were an observing other" and must pass through the "reflection of the self in the empirical other" (137).[2]

Bakhtin's interest in examining the dialogic relation between characters' voice and the authorial voice and between existence and consciousness is refreshing in the postcolonial study of language and literature. To compare the Bakhtinian theoretical paradigm and the development of Asian American literature in postcolonial America is to discover a dialogic richness. It is generated by Asian American writers' recognition of the dynamics of a process through which meaning is generated, transcribed, transmitted, and (re)created and demonstrated by their attempt to reclaim their sense of history and identity as well as by their willingness to cross borders in search of an approach which can accurately portray the Asian American experience.

Many Asian American short stories describe characters' close connection with their ethnic cultural heritage and the price they have to pay when they lose touch with it. Japanese American writer Hisaye Yamamoto's "Las Vegas Charley" sketches a character whose hope for the future is shattered by the harsh reality of the relocation camp during World War II. Kazuyuki Matsumoto lived a happy life before he lost his wife with the birth of his second son, his first son to World War II, and his second son to his American way of life. Matsumoto had a farm in California before the war. Like 120,000 Japanese Americans, however, he was ordered to sell his farm and move into a relocation camp.

After the war, Matsumoto decided to settle in Las Vegas. He worked as a dish-washer in a restaurant. Matsumoto had disappeared. He was replaced by a new person known to everyone in the city as Charley. Both Charley's American name and his new appearance promised a new beginning and a bright future. His new teeth made him "look ten years younger" (83) and won admiration from the waitresses. But what was missing from Charley's life was his faith in his own cultural heritage, his closeness to his family, and his belief in himself as having control of his own destiny. Now those voids could only be filled by his desire for money and alcohol.

Filipino American writer Bienvenido N. Santos's story "Scent of Apples" portrays another first-generation immigrant's mixed feelings about his home country. The narrator of the story was sponsored by the U.S. government to give talks on Philippine culture during World War II. In Kalamazoo, Michigan, he met Celestino Fabia, a Filipino American farmer who immigrated to the United States twenty years ago. During the lecture, Fabia asked the narrator if the Filipino women were "the same like they were twenty years ago" (163). Later, the narrator learned that Fabia's American wife, Ruth, was Caucasian.

Fabia and Ruth had a very complicated relationship. They sincerely loved each other. Fabia once had an attack of acute appendicitis. Ruth saved his life by carrying him through the snow to the main road and waiting with him for the U.S. mail car in below-zero temperature. But when Fabia told Ruth the narrator "a first-class Filipino" was going to visit them, she snickered: "there's no such thing as first-class Filipino" (165). By asking the narrator the question about Filipino women, Fabia was not only wondering about the road not taken but also trying to preserve a memory as beautiful as the way he remembered his parents' house:

> But sometimes, you know, I miss that house, the roosting chickens on the low-topped walls. I miss my brothers and sisters. Mother sitting in her chair, looking like a pale ghost in a corner of the room. I would remember the great live posts, massive tree trunks from the forests. Leafy plants grow on the sides, buds pointing downwards, wilted and died before they could become flowers. . . . (167)

In the article "Come All Ye Asian American Writers of the Real and the Fake" (*Big AIIIEEEEE!*), Chinese American writer Frank Chin divides Chinese and Japanese American writers into two groups: Asian

American authors and Americanized Asian authors.[3] He posits that only those Asian American writers who are not susceptible to "Christian conversion" (18) and uphold traditional Chinese and Japanese values such as Confucianism, "the Japanese sense of honor," and "the samurai sense of nobility" (69) can be considered as the real voices in Asian American literature. But Asian American writers who use the "exclusively Christian form" of autobiography (11) and revise Asian "history, culture, and childhood literature and myth" (29) are fake. For in their depiction of the "Christian yin/yang of the dual personality/ identity crisis" (26), these writers not only misrepresent their own cultural heritage but also betray the values of that culture.

It is true that Asian Americans can not find their true identity without embracing culturally what they cannot reject ontologically. One advantage of being Asian American is that we are blessed with two cultures and have the freedom and luxury to be selective. Or as Brave Orchid, the dynamic character in *The Woman Warrior*, puts it: "When you come to America, it's a chance to forget some of the bad Chinese habits" (139). Confucianism, for instance, with its emphasis on courtesy, individual responsibility, and familial and social harmony, has played an instrumental role in maintaining stability and peace in China which, for centuries, had been torn by endless wars and meaningless deaths. But the kind of "harmony" Confucius had envisioned was built on the feudal ethical code of the three cardinal guides (ruler guides subject, father guides son, and husband guides wife) and the five constant virtues (benevolence, righteousness, propriety, wisdom, and fidelity) and its infrastructure was supported by patriarchy and primogeniture.

In Asian American literature, many writers have raised questions about ancient Asian traditions and customs, especially those that are moribund. Similar to Chinese American writer Louis Chu's *Eat a Bowl of Tea*, Chinese American writer Monfoon Leong's story "New Year for Fong Wing" describes a first-generation Chinese immigrant's struggle in the United States. The protagonist Fong Wing has been working hard all his life to support his family. But he feels his life is empty. It appears that many of his problems, such as the money problem and his relationship with his wife, are caused by his gambling habit. But as the story develops, the reader learns that Fong Wing has lost three sons to two world wars. After his third son is killed in the Second World War, Fong Wing becomes despondent. Fong Wing's friend Lee Mun reminds him that he still has a daughter and his third son "returned from War on Fourth of July heroes' ship and received hero's burial." Fong Wing laments that there will be no sons, no grandson to "tell of his heroism" and there is no future for an "old man without sons" (120).

In the story "Paths upon Water," Pakistani American writer Tahira Naqvi takes a similar thematic approach. The protagonist Sakina Bano is visiting her son Raza in the United States. She believes that it is not proper for a woman to be "skipping in a public place" and "exposing the outline of her thin calves" (207). She has never seen the sea. The first time she visits the ocean, she is embarrassed by the scantily clad people on the coast. But she finally realizes how ridiculous she looks on the beach fully clothed. She gathers enough courage to pull up her *shalwar* and dip her feet in the water and feels a happiness she has never experienced before. The ocean in the story becomes synonymous with openness, freedom, and natural beauty.

Indeed, to recognize the dialogic richness of Asian American literature is to understand tradition's hegemonic impulse. In *Articulate Silences*, King-Kok Cheung suggests that the "two-toned language" used by many Asian American writers results from the distrust of inherited language and that of traditional myth with patriarchal ethos. This distrust brings many Asian American writers to the conclusion that they must cross cultural borders in search of ways to not only "revise history," but also "transfigure ethnicity," for "the point is never to return to the original but to tell it with a difference" (170). The use of "two-toned language" (16), thus, concretely objectifies Asian American writers' attempt to negotiate a ground on which they can find their own identity.

In appearance, Fukunaga, the protagonist in Japanese American writer Toshio Mori's short story "Japanese Hamlet" is caught in the clash between American culture (boundless optimism and individual freedom of choice) and traditional Japanese culture which places practicality above ideals and dictates that in the collision between individual aspiration for self-fulfillment and a person's social and familial obligation, the person should forfeit his/her claim to individual freedom in exchange for communal harmony. But Fukunaga's ambition of becoming a ranking Shakespearean actor and the identifiability of his experience and that of Hamlet suggest that the story's thematic appeal is as specific as universal. Both Fukunaga and Hamlet are mediocre actors; both are trapped in the world of inaction and procrastination, wasting a lot of time and energy in fantasizing about what might and could happen instead of making things happen; both are "play-acting," but not "acting"—their self-created unreality impugn the ontological significance of their relationship with reality. If, in the article "Hamlet, Prince of Denmark," Frank Kermode is right in positing that it is in the perplexed figure of Hamlet, "just because of our sense that his mind lacks definite boundaries, we find ourselves" (Kermode 1135), Fukunaga's experience is indeed as Japanese as American. For the tragicomic power of the story is generated by conflicts between dream and reality, between commitment and effort, and between individual choice and communal pressure, conflicts which are as indigenous to the Japanese American community as to the United States.

Hisaye Yamamoto's "Seventeen Syllables" again portrays Asian Americans' complicated relationship with their cultural heritage. Rosie's mother is an aspiring *haiku* poet. She believes that it is very important for Rosie to keep in touch with Japanese culture. Rosie goes to a Japanese school to study Japanese twice a week in the summer, although her English, or even her French, is better than her Japanese. As the story develops, Rosie learns that her mother used to have a lover in Japan who was from a well-to-do family. Because her grandfather was poor, the lover's family did not approve of their relationship. They arranged his marriage, and Rosie's mother gave premature birth to a stillborn son who would be seventeen now. Between suicide and America, she chose the latter.

Yamamoto's use of juxtaposition in the story is very effective. Rosie's mother is torn between *haiku* and the tomato fields, between Japanese culture and American culture, and between the past and the present. Her confusion is revealed at the end of the story by her forcing Rosie, who is in love with Jesus Carrasco, to promise that she will never marry. The failure of her love affair in Japan and the promise of Rosie and Jesus's friendship invite readers to draw a comparison, reminding them of the dialectical relationship between physical displacement and cultural disorientation.

As is demonstrated by Asian American short stories, what many Asian American writers are searching for is a ground on which they can find their own identity, whether the identity is Asian or American, or American Chinese or Chinese American. In Amy Ling's article, "Creating One's Self: the Eaton Sisters," the author reiterates "what has by now become almost a truism": "the self is not a fixed entity but a fluid, changing construct or creation determined by context or historical conditions and particularly by power relationships" (306). By using the example of the Eaton Sisters who had adopted identities of their choice in creative writing, Ling convincingly reveals the dialectical relationship between creation and recreation and between the permeability of the boundaries of the self and the influence of historical conditions.[4] To understand Asian American literature in the postcolonial period is, indeed, to resist the temptation of totalization, to accept the plurality of the Asian American experience, and to appreciate Asian American writers' effort to democratize American literary voice by (re)presenting what has been mis(sing)-represented, by celebrating the cultural diversity of American society, and by calling readers' attention to the peculiarity and uniqueness of the Asian American experience.

NOTES

1. Cited by Paul Rabinow in the "Introduction" to *The Foucault Reader*, p. 22.
2. "From Notes Made in 1970–71" is included in Mikhail Mikhailovich Bakhtin's *Speech Genres*. The quotation is used in Amy Mandelker's article, "Semiotizing the Sphere: Organicist Theory in Lotman, Bakhtin, and Vernadsky."
3. Frank Chin's insistence on using the term "Chinaman" represents a tenacious effort on the writer's part to celebrate the Chinese cultural heritage. On August 2, 1970, Chin and Chinese American writer, Virginia Lee, openly discussed the use of the term in a TV interview. Lee argued, as Kai-yu Hsu recalls in *Asian-American Authors*, that she was "not so much concerned about being either Chinese or American or Chinese-American or American-Chinese" as she was "about being human." Chin responded by asking a rhetorical question: "Where's your identity, then?" (1).
4. Both Edith Maud Eaton and Winnifred Eaton were Eurasian. In creative writing, however, Edith wrote under the Chinese pseudonym Sui Sin Far, whereas Winnifred adopted a Japanese identity. For further information, see Amy Ling's *Between Worlds*.

REFERENCES

Bakhtin, Mikhail Mikhailovich. "Discourse in the Novel." *The Dialogic Imagination*. Ed. and trans. Michael Holquist. Austin: University of Texas Press, 1981. 259–422.

Cheung, King-Kok. *Articulate Silences*. Ithaca: Cornell University Press, 1993.

Chin, Frank. "Come All Ye Asian American Writers of the Real and the Fake." *The Big AIIIEEEEE! An Anthology of Chinese American and Japanese American Literature*. Ed. Frank Chin, et al. New York: Meridian, 1991. 1–69.

Foucault, Michel. "Politics and Ethics: An Interview." *The Foucault Reader*. Ed. Paul Rabinow. New York: Pantheon, 1984. 373–80.

Kermode, Frank. "Hamlet, Prince of Denmark." *The Riverside Shakespeare*. Ed. G. Blakemore Evans. Boston: Houghton Mifflin, 1974. 1135–1140.

Kingston, Maxine Hong. *The Woman Warrior.* New York: Vintage, 1975. 139–65.

Leong, Monfoon. "New Year for Fong Wing." *Imagining America.* Eds. Wesley Brown and Amy Ling. NY: Persea Books, 1991. 117–24.

Ling, Amy. *Between Worlds.* New York: Pergamon, 1990.

___. "Creating One's Self: The Eaton Sisters." *Reading the Literatures of Asian America.* Eds. Shirley Geok-lin Lim and Amy Ling. Philadelphia: Temple University Press, 1992. 305–18.

Mandelker, Amy. "Semiotizing the Sphere: Organicist Theory in Lotman, Bakhtin, and Vernadsky." *PMLA* 109.3 (1994): 385–96.

Mori, Toshio. "Japanese Hamlet." *Imagining America.* Eds. Wesley Brown and Amy Ling. New York: Persea Books, 1991. 125–27.

Mudimbe, V. Y. *The Invention of Africa: Gnosis, Philosophy, and the Order of Knowledge.* Bloomington: Indiana University Press, 1988.

Naqvi, Tahira. "Paths upon Water." *Forbidden Stitch.* Eds. Shirley Geok-lin Lim, Mayumi Tsutakawa, and Margarita Donnelly. Corvallis, OR: Calyx Books, 1989. 207–17.

Rabinow, Paul. Introduction. *The Foucault Reader.* By Michel Foucault. New York: Pantheon, 1984. 3–29.

Said, Edward W. *Orientalism.* New York: Vintage, 1979.

Santos, Bienvenido N. "Scent of Apples." *Asian-American Authors.* Eds. Hsu, Kai-yu and Helen Palubinskas. Boston: Houghton Mifflin, 1972. 161–70.

Selden, Raman, and Peter Widdowson. *Contemporary Literary Theory.* 3rd Ed. Lexington: University Press of Kentucky, 1993.

Wallace, Michele. *Invisibility Blues: From Pop to Theory.* London and New York: Verso, 1990.

Williams, Raymond. *Marxism and Literature.* London: Oxford University Press, 1977. 116–17.

Yamamoto, Hisaye. "Seventeen Syllables." *Seventeen Syllables.* Latham: Kitchen Table, 1988. 8–19.

___. "Las Vegas Charley." *Seventeen Syllables.* Latham: Kitchen Table, 1988. 70–85.

8. The Invention of Normality in Japanese American Internment Narratives

John Streamas

Of imprisoned Jews, Bruno Bettelheim writes, "How silent one's voice becomes under totalitarianism is well known by those who were inside concentration camps" ("Eichmann" 263). Of imprisoned Japanese Americans, Ronald Takaki writes, "Memories of the internment nightmare have haunted the older generation like ghosts. But the former prisoners have been unable to exorcise them by speaking out" (484). These two imprisonments are part of the story of the Second World War. Significantly, Franklin Roosevelt, "on at least three separate public occasions," referred to relocation camps for Japanese Americans as "concentration camps," and "informally officials often called them concentration camps" (Daniels, Conference Keynote Address 6; Culley 57). I do not mean to equate the imprisonment of 120,000 Japanese Americans with the imprisonment and massacre of millions of Jews and other oppressed groups in Nazi Europe: Roger Daniels aptly reminds us that internment camps and relocation camps "were not, thank God, death camps or extermination camps" (Conference Keynote Address 6). I mean, rather, to draw from Bruno Bettelheim's moving study of Holocaust survivors a lesson in silence, so that we may more compassionately know the condition of oppressed people as well as the expression—or failures of expression—of this condition. Here I apply the lesson to Japanese American short stories of internment, discovering that, when these stories revolve around children and teenagers, their writers often use an internal narrative perspective to construct a politics of protest.

In the work of sansei, third-generation Japanese Americans, such protest advances the imperative of breaking silence—an imperative announced in titles of poems, anthologies, conferences, and chapters of popular histories. Janice Mirikitani's book *Shedding Silence* contains the poem "Breaking Silence," whose headnote reads, "After forty years of silence about the experience of Japanese Americans in World War II concentration camps, my mother testified before the Commission on Wartime Relocation and Internment of Japanese American Civilians in 1981" (33). Introducing the anthology *Breaking Silence*, Joseph Bruchac celebrates young Asian American poets for "breaking both silence and stereotypes with the affirmation of new songs" (xv). Takaki cites nisei parents and issei grandparents who in recent years have been prodded for their story by sansei and by government commissions. One woman claims that, as a "stereotype [sic] Japanese American," she "kept quiet" for thirty-five years, and now realizes that "it doesn't pay to remain silent" (485).

Of course issei, the immigrant generation, bring a culture whose attitude toward silence differs greatly from mainstream America's. Among writers naming the difference, D. T. Suzuki identifies a Zen silence that is God and wisdom; Michihiro Matsumoto describes a silence that guides and impels Japanese commerce; and Deborah Tannen and Muriel Savile-Troike recognize in Japanese discourse a "wordless communication" in silences that punctuate conversation.[1] But to focus exclusively on this cultural difference, King-Kok Cheung shrewdly reminds us, risks subscribing to stereotypes of "the inscrutable Oriental" and neglecting the *American* part of Japanese Americans (17, 18). Japanese American silence is informed by, but does not duplicate, Japanese silence.

Surely this silence was *transformed* by imprisonment. Among Holocaust survivors, Bettelheim identifies a "concentration camp syndrome" that, in its final stage, leads to managing "the trauma of the concentration camp experience through repression and denial" ("Trauma and Reintegration" 31, 33). Though removed by many lesser degrees of trauma, Japanese American internees must recognize in their silence a version of "camp syndrome."

But even these two factors—cultural legacy and imprisonment— may not account for all Japanese American silence. Constructing a theory of minority discourse, JanMohamed and Lloyd recognize a "nonidentity experienced by minorities as the oppressive effects of Western philosophies of identity" (16). Such "nonidentity" is surely marked by smothering silence.

Yet even as they name and identify "nonidentity," JanMohamed and Lloyd further identify "discourses emerging from that nonidentity" (16). Silence's trajectory, then, begins with powerlessness as a function of class, gender, race, or ethnicity; arcs through functions of survival, then of "repression and denial" and perhaps even of culture; and sweeps back in "emerging" discourse.

Sometimes silence *becomes* the discourse, inverting Bettelheim's depiction of it as a signal of repression and denial.[2] George Steiner advances a sort of confrontational silence as the appropriate response to real genocide and threatened nuclear annihilation.[3] And Leslie Kane observes that, in much modern drama, silence—"indicated by ellipses, pauses, and wordless responses"—systematically stands for the unspeakable (15). What is unspeakable, then, turns against itself. Oppression is not imitated but reproduced. An art that is unable to articulate oppression must reproduce and embody it. But silence as a discourse option exists mostly for alienated but otherwise dominant-culture postmodernists.[4]

Minority literature exists. Women such as Tillie Olsen write about their silence, thus breaking it. There is a literature of Holocaust survival. And there is a literature of Japanese American internment, a significant part of which is the work of nisei internees. I am mindful that the number of Japanese Americans imprisoned is much smaller than the numbers of many other peoples oppressed in our century for their racial, ethnic, religious, or national identities. The number killed in Hiroshima by the atomic bomb is significantly larger; many times greater still is the number of Armenians massacred in the first two decades of this century. Surely, though, we must reexamine Japanese American silence. To the extent that internment imposed silence, it also provoked an emerging discourse.

We detect patterns in the literature of internment. The novels are overtly political. John Okada's *No-No Boy* is loud and angry in its depiction of a young man learning to live with the consequences of his wartime decision to forswear loyalty to the United States.[5] Even Joy Kogawa's quiet and lyrical *Obasan*, a novel of Japanese Canadian internment, has a character whose crusading, though loud and coarse and even ridiculous at times, necessarily confronts us with a government's injustices. Some internment literature for children gently explores racial politics in scenes wrenching Japanese American children away from white friends. In Yoshiko Uchida's *The Bracelet*, for example, interracial friendship triumphs over internment.

Shorter forms—lyric poems and short stories—afforded Japanese American writers their earliest and, perhaps even now, their finest expressions of their internment story. Camp publications existed under the scrutiny of the War Relocation Authority, and so overt protest during the war was impossible. But Susan Schweik, in her study of American women's poetry of the war, locates in Japanese American women's writing a "*civilian* 'war poetry of experience'" (174).

Particularly, she locates in the ardent lyrics of Toyo Suyemoto "a coded narrative of Nikkei [Japanese American] experience on American land" (188).

Short stories, too, have been good vehicles for internment literature. Frank O'Connor argued that the genre is congenial to "submerged population groups," oppressed people, often "outlawed figures wandering about the fringes of society" (xii). Mary Louise Pratt counterargues that marginalized people do not exactly *choose* the short story, that they accept it as the only available vehicle proffered by a niggardly culture: "When it comes time for a dominant class to bring what Frank O'Conner [sic] likes to call 'submerged population groups' to the surface, the short story comes into play" (189)—to which O'Connor might retort that Pratt confuses cause and effect, that submerged people appropriate the form as congenial to their needs and that dominant classes, for whom the form is less congenial, see no harm in the appropriation. Surely internment short stories, like internment poems, embed a politics under a husk whose spare breadth might have seemed quaint and "Japanesey" and probably seemed unthreatening to the War Relocation Authority.

Okada's *No-No Boy*, not only the first Japanese American novel of internment but also generally regarded as the first Japanese American *novel*, was published in 1957. Yet even in the 1920s and 1930s, according to Valerie Matsumoto, a "flood of poetry, fiction, articles, and essays by the Nisei" saturated Japanese American community newspapers and magazines ("Desperately" 20). Tailoring their work to the limited space in such publications and lacking access to the mainstream book publishing industry, these writers, in their fiction, quite naturally produced short stories rather than novels. Economies of expediency and disposition, then, dictated that early nisei fiction take the form of short stories.

Two of the best internment stories, Hisaye Yamamoto's "The Legend of Miss Sasagawara" and Lonny Kaneko's "The Shoyu Kid," bear close examination for their recreation of the perspectives of young internees, thus wedging their politics under a thicker husk of seemingly artless narration. Two other stories, Valerie Matsumoto's "Two Deserts" and Toshio Mori's "The Long Journey and the Short Ride," offer the reflections of adults many years after the war. Politics in Yamamoto and Kaneko, though much more deeply embedded beneath everyday contingencies of camp life, are more persuasively subversive.

"The Legend of Miss Sasagawara" was first published in *The Kenyon Review* in 1950, thus staking an early claim to both Japanese American literary achievement and the literature of internment.[6] It is set in the Poston camp in the Arizona desert, and its first-person narrator Kiku tells her story apparently *after* the war, though in the camp scenes that occupy most of the story she is nineteen years old. Its central character is Mari Sasagawara, a thirty-nine-year-old dancer who is beautiful and brilliant and erratic. Very simply, it tells the story of Mari's life in Poston. Mari instantly becomes a subject of gossip and rumors, for her colorful form-fitting clothes, her tours as a dancer in a ballet company, and her eccentricities. Twice she is sent away, "to a state institution," for madness: her second banishment seems permanent (Yamamoto 30).

But the story is not so simple. Kiku's narration is limited partly by limitations in her experience and sympathetic understanding— though surely she understands more sympathetically than other internees, including Mari's father—and mostly by her unfamiliarity with her subject: much of what she tells us about Mari has been passed on to her by internees whose unreliability she readily acknowledges. The episodes leading to Mari's final banishment are related to Kiku's friend Elsie by "giggling" Mrs. Sasaki and "drawling" Joe Yoshinaga: "Elsie's sources," says Kiku, "were not what I would ordinarily pay much attention to" (32). Elsie herself "knew all about Miss Sasagawara" by learning "a morsel here and a morsel there" (24). She too eagerly joins the chorus of gossips and busybodies who declare Mari mad. Kiku herself has only one extended conversation with Mari, a friendly chat in the community shower in which they laugh about their fumbling on musical instruments. With such limited acquaintance, Kiku's story's reliability depends on her skill in extracting truth from gossip.

To what extent can we trust Kiku? Hearing the second-hand account of Mari's final scandals, she questions Elsie's sources but admits, "I was impressed" (32). By this time Kiku has herself left camp, for a semester in college in Philadelphia and has returned only long enough "to spread the good word about higher education among the young people" (30). Showing off her new learning in psychology, she "sagely explained" the scandals to Elsie: "Miss Sasagawara had no doubt looked upon Joe Yoshinaga as the image of either the lost lover or the lost son" (32). But in the next sentence she confesses that "my words made me uneasy by their glibness" (32). King-Kok Cheung notes that readers are here swayed by Kiku's ambivalence: "Kiku at least allows that she could be mistaken. Yet partly for that reason her explanation remains tantalizing" (61).

But we must be careful not to trust Kiku too much. King-Kok Cheung is right to argue that Mari is "thrice-muted"—"as a daughter by the father, as a single woman by the community, and as a member of a persecuted people by the government" (69)—but we must not forget that Kiku, who herself suffers the muting of internment, is surprisingly uncritical of all three injustices. She is not only an unreliable narrator, as several critics observe; she is also a naive character, at least while in camp. Her very return to camp to promote education is probably sponsored by camp authorities: "it had been decided to close down the camps," she says, "and I *had been asked* to go back and spread the good word about higher education" (30; italics mine). By this time Kiku's language and tone tell us that she is older, more mature. She is *adult*. The assumption of some critics that she is twenty years old means that only a year passes between the Sasagawaras' arrival and Kiku's narration. Chronologically this is remotely possible. But even in the beginning Kiku says she and Elsie were "pushing twenty" and fantasizing their "mission in life . . . to finish college somewhere when and if the war ever ended and we were free again" (21). Also at this time the camp population is "15,000 or so" (22)—close enough to Poston's maximum population of 17,814 to suggest that these scenes take place long before war's end, especially considering that as early as the fall of 1942 "hundreds of students were allowed to leave to attend colleges" and that, "after the beginning of 1943, a process of controlled resettlement in the interior states" was initiated (Daniels, "Chronology" xxi; "Forced Migrations" 73). Also some indefinite but considerable time passes between the Sasagawaras' arrival and Kiku's discovery of Mari's poem "some time after I had gone back to Philadelphia and the family had joined me there" (32). The events cover well over a year; and the narration—in the past tense—happens later still, quite likely after the war.

The significance of this chronology is that it clarifies Kiku's different maturities. Yamamoto here plays with narration in a manner familiar to readers of short stories: an adult first-person narrator, recalling childhood scenes, occasionally lapses into the language and perception of childhood. The difference here is that these recollected scenes are possibly only eighteen months distant—certainly no more than three or four years—and the "children" in these scenes are nineteen years old. Yet critics refer to the Kiku of the opening scene as a "girl"; McDonald and Newman emphasize Kiku's youth:

> The young narrator sits on the front stoop with her best friend, using such phrases as "Oooh" and "Wow!" while watching the other people and slapping mosquitoes. (137)

Charles L. Crow more quaintly distinguishes between Kiku the first-scene character and Kiku the narrator:

> The narrator, as she writes, is no longer the callow bobby-soxer who once fantasized with her friend Elsie about "two nice, clean young men, preferably handsome, preferably rich, who would cherish us forever and a day." (124)

And King-Kok Cheung observes that "Elsie and Kiku have managed to take imprisonment in their stride, as though the detention camp were a summer camp" (63). Such behavior was, she says, among "survival strategies" of internees (63).

Childlike behavior as a survival strategy is not unique to Japanese American internees. Bruno Bettelheim is again instructive, for he connects childlike behavior to denial:

> The small child, confronted with some unpleasant fact, will insist that it is not so. Usually as we get older, we no longer use this primitive defense when confronted with incontrovertible facts. But when anxiety becomes overwhelming, even normal adults tend to regress to using it. ("The Holocaust— One Generation Later" 90)

Stanley Elkins identifies an equally compelling example in African American slavery: he says that absolute power for the slaveholder dictated "absolute dependency for the slave—the dependency not of the developing child but of the perpetual child" (112).

Silence and childlike behavior are thus twin manifestations of a denial that is, for oppressed and submerged people, a survival strategy. Kiku the narrator is not much older than Kiku the dreamer of a nice clean young husband, but she *is* out of camp, free and independent. Maturity has caught up to chronology, so that now she may tell Mari's story, lapsing only occasionally into her recent childlikeness. Her unreliability now is mostly a function of her failures in understanding—her references to "the good old days" of camp are, for example, only vaguely sardonic (30)—but we can rightly applaud when, almost literally released into maturity, she earns enough understanding merely to tell the story. Furthermore, her moral sensibility never allows her to agree with her community and label Mari mad; her literary sophistication prompts her to call Mari's story a "legend" and drives her to read Mari's poem with surprising self-effacement and grace; and her education in and out of camp compels her to become, like Mari, an artist, a storyteller. She may not grasp the significance of her legend-making, but telling Mari's story so soon after the war makes her a pioneer silence-breaker.

It is in the very gaps in Kiku's understanding—the margins of her unreliability as a narrator and her naivete as a character—that Yamamoto embeds the story's political protest. This is truest at the very end, as Kiku the adult, educated narrator offers an apparently faithful paraphrase of Mari's poem that so impresses us with its objectivity and lyrical sophistication that we can easily miss Kiku's refusal to interpret the poem. She describes the work only as "a *tour de force*, erratically brilliant and, through the first readings, tantalizingly obscure" before launching her paraphrase with "It appeared to be about a man whose lifelong aim had been to achieve Nirvana" (32). Her words "appeared to be" may betray uncertainty; more likely, they are Kiku's wink suggesting that, while the poem seems to concern "a man"—a generic indefinite man—we in Kiku's audience know that it *really* concerns the Reverend Sasagawara. From this point on, Kiku vanishes out of her story and the paraphrase of the poem takes over. The man in the poem clearly mirrors Mari's father; but is Kiku aware of the irony in the claim that, during imprisonment, the man "felt free for the first time in his long life" (32)?

The language of the last paragraph is less Kiku's than Mari's, assuming the dancer's flourishes and cadences. The language of girlish nuptial fantasies surrenders to a "saint, blissfully bent on cleansing from his already radiant soul the last imperceptible blemishes" (33). In the poem the noble man's companion feels "passions rising, subsiding, and again rising, perhaps in anguished silence" (33). And the last two sentences convene the story's multiple ironies:

> The poet could not speak for others, of course; she could only speak for herself. But she would describe this man's devotion as a sort of madness, the monstrous sort which, pure of itself, might possibly bring troublous, scented scenes to recur in the other's sleep. (33)

Invoking King-Kok Cheung's analysis of the triple muting of Mari as well as JanMohamed and Lloyd's theory of minority discourse, we note that the poet/speaker's "anguished silence" is transformed into an emerging discourse, even if she speaks only "for herself." But of course Kiku speaks for her too, even if only in paraphrase, and her countercharge of her father's imprisoning madness reminds us that oppression here ripples across concentric circles, the outermost ring being internment itself. Mari does not speak just for herself; Yamamoto here shrewdly lets the poet's voice suffuse Kiku's. For the poet who suffers "anguished silence" contrasts sharply from the narrator who constructs an internment camp as a summer camp.

Lonny Kaneko's story "The Shoyu Kid" was first published in 1976, well into the years of ethnic consciousness-raising and the emergence in universities of ethnic studies programs. In fact the story appeared in *Amerasia*, a pioneer journal of Asian American scholarship and literature. Kaneko is a sansei who spent part of his youth in the Minidoka camp in Idaho. His story concerns three boys—children, not lapsing adolescents—whose apparently normal boyhood play uncovers dirty secrets of racial and sexual oppression that, we come to realize, are a mere variation on the public degradations of internment.

I stress here the apparent *normality* of the play of the three boys Jackson (whose Japanese name is Hiroshi), Itchy (named Ichiro), and the narrator Masao. They are merely playing army, or spies, or cowboys and Indians; and, at least for Jackson, the swaggering John Wayne persona perverts—and mirrors—their first encounter with adult sexuality. We must be careful not to read the story so politically that we ascribe the boys' behavior to an inescapable matrix of sociopolitical injustices. Sau-ling Cynthia Wong acknowledges that Kaneko's point is "that the potential for domination and violence is universal, found within even the weakest and most oppressed," but still she too readily "highlights ethnicity-bound rejection and projection" (101, 102). The problem with such a reading is that it ignores the significance of the boys' attempts to construct a "normal" life. To be sure, much of the story's irony depends on the contrast between this normality and the abnormality of internment. When we consider the boys' behavior apart from its sociopolitical context—playing army, throwing stones at signs they have stolen, leering at the little girl bathing, teasing each other about "queerness," even taunting and "pantsing" the weak Shoyu Kid— we realize that, even at their worst, they are acting like many "normal" mainstream American boys. That is, they are not responding to a hostile environment with hostile, "uncivilized" tumult, as do the British boys in William Golding's *Lord of the Flies*. We can imagine them engaging in such play even if there were no internment precisely because it *is* so "normal." Unlike Kiku and Elsie, who in "The Legend of Miss Sasagawara" survive by reverting to childlike behavior, these boys need only act naturally to survive. This leaves open a possibility that "The Shoyu Kid" aims to expose "normality" as cruel and unaccommodating—but only if Kaneko accepts the universal standard of dominant-culture normality. More likely, Kaneko aims to advance a universe of many, often overlapping normalities, each defined by an originating culture, and to suggest that children must not be condemned for the normalities they adopt.

Thus the boys are largely unconcerned with the difference between their adapted mainstream American normality and their parents' Japanese normality. In fact their most serious cultural friction shows in Jackson's obsequiousness before three old women who praise the "fine lads" and in his nose-thumbing when they call him by his Japanese name (Kaneko 305–06). Otherwise the boys are too absorbed in their play to worry about cultural conflicts or to notice irony. Jackson gives the name "Kraut" to the Kid's dachshund, and neither he nor the narrator Masao notes the irony in appropriating America's bitter epithet for its European enemy (305). Itchy peers "around the corner like an Indian from behind a tree," and again the narrator is oblivious to irony in his racial allusion (306). And when Itchy, knowing the Kid's secret, reveals only that the red-haired soldier has been providing the Kid's chocolate bars, Jackson tries "to sound like his older brother" in complaining that the soldiers "don't patrol here anymore. They're supposed to stay by the gate" but then he drops his older-brother pose to add, "Let's check it out tomorrow. Maybe he'll give us some too" (307).

To be sure, the boys' Japanese American normality bears little resemblance to their parents' Japanese normality. Still, its familiarity to most of Kaneko's readers, Japanese Americans and others, establishes a commonness across many cultures of boys' behavior in play. These boys may be, as Elaine Kim observes, "cruel and ruthless" because of their "wild and decadent life," but surely many sons of the white soldiers confining them are similarly cruel, roughly strutting and taunting (262). Significantly, neither the narrator Masao nor the author Kaneko condemns the boys' general behavior as deviant. Kaneko saves his condemnation for symbols and ironies of internment such as the animal that internees trap and, mob-like, want to kill, or the distant range fire that Japanese American men are "freed" from camp to fight, a fire that seems to Masao like "the sun rising from the wrong direction" and to Itchy like the "end of the world" (304, 312).

Kaneko therefore suggests that the boys' normality, however cruel, benignly mocks adult abnormalities. Jackson at play "flattened himself against the wall and like a soldier in a war movie, peered around the corner," but real "soldiers used to march around the fence" that surrounds "the blocks of barracks" that house internees (305, 306). The boys steal "the hastily painted government signs" that, bearing the words "Off Limits" and "MINIDOKA RELOCATION CENTER," announce their imprisonment (312, 313). Even Jackson's lurid fascination with sex—his ogling of little Joyce Furuta's body, his taunting and stripping of the Kid—mocks the red-haired soldier's trading chocolate bars for the Kid's sexual favors. The abnormality of the soldier—who is significantly red-haired, to underscore his whiteness—is further marked by his breaking a rule "to stay by the gate" in order to meet the Kid behind the garage, and also by his own peculiar army-playing in which, says Itchy, "he used to stand there at the fence and point his gun at me like he was going to shoot" (307, 308). Still, Itchy's confused and bitter lament that "everyone's queer" obviously refers to something more than the soldier's sexual preference: because the story is set in the 1940s—that is, before the word "queer" assumed its nearly exclusive association with homosexuality, but also when homosexuality was generally regarded as no less deviant than the soldier's pedophilia—Itchy may as well be complaining that "everyone" is abnormal. In a world in which boys' cruel play is the most natural and normal behavior, who can blame Jackson for asking, in a voice that is "quiet, almost a curse," "Who cares" (312)? Appropriately, then, in the closing image it is Jackson who, already exposed as a boyish oppressor, is literally in the spotlight as a symbol of adult racist oppression. Unlike the animal trapped by internees beneath a building—an animal identified by the Shoyu Kid himself as "maybe" a jack rabbit, with an escape route of "a burrow under the barrack" (310)—Jackson is trapped by "everyone's" "queerness": "He was sitting very still, and his eyes were soft and wide like a rabbit's" (313).

Like the Reverend Sasagawara in Yamamoto's story, Jackson is both oppressor and oppressed. The boys in "The Shoyu Kid" are victims of several oppressions: particularly of white adults' racial and sexual entrapment, more generally of clashing white and Japanese adult standards of normality. Unlike Yamamoto's Kiku and Elsie who, reverting to childhood, reclaim only innocence and curiosity, these boys ruthlessly project their normality into an adult world whose own ruthlessness has dangerous consequences. For Kaneko's boys no less than for Yamamoto's young women, childlike behavior is a strategy for survival. We may surmise that, after the war, it may metamorphose into the denial that Bettelheim identifies in many Holocaust survivors, into the silence that sansei like Kaneko identified in many nisei, and that much later it may evolve into emergent discourse. But, while we may claim that Kiku's emergence as a storyteller occurs shortly after the war, we cannot know exactly when Masao tells his story: it too may be shortly after the war, but it may also be coterminous with

Kaneko's own 1970s emergence as the author. Like Kiku, however, Masao as an adult narrator revisits a childlike consciousness. His first sentence—"We were ready for him" (304)—alerts us to the language and perspective of this consciousness.

To better recognize the political implications of this narrative reconstruction of childlike consciousness, we may look briefly at two other stories that consider internment. "The Long Journey and the Short Ride," by Toshio Mori, who is hailed by Yamamoto herself as "the pioneer of Japanese American literature," is the first-person story, rendered many years after the war, of both the narrator's wartime ride in a generous white family's car and his brother's postwar adjustment to a paralyzing injury suffered in combat (Yamamoto, Introduction 14). It is a gentle remembrance, whose narrative perspective is defined in the first two sentences: "The other day my brother and I got to talking of the World War II days. It seemed so long ago, we agreed" (Mori 123). This perspective does not change: it remains in the voice of a man in late middle age who, though fully aware of the sorrows of war and the injustices of internment, feels no bitterness and casts no blame. Significantly, the narrator and his brother, though nisei, are young adults during the war. The brother is already a member of the all-nisei 442nd Infantry Regiment, and will be wounded in Italy. The narrator recognizes the irony of his brother's fighting for the country that imprisons his family "in a dump like Topaz War Relocation Center" and realizes that "the vast emptiness of the desert sunset" provides a "fitting description for my 'inside' life" (123, 125). But his question "How will a camp resident be received on the 'outside'?" is answered minutes later by the friendly white family offering him and his mother a "short ride" from the station into town: "It was a short ride, sure enough, but the most memorable, coming at the right moment for us— especially for me" (124, 125). In the end even his paralyzed brother speaks, like him, "[n]ot with bitterness and despair but with calm and contentment" (126). Here is a narrator who will not pair off his present-tense storyteller's consciousness with a reconstructed subjective childlike consciousness. Here is no reversion to Kiku's childlike daydreaming, no reinvention of Masao's "wild and decadent" play. This story directly concerns, then, neither politics nor internment: it concerns Japanese American people, for whom, "within the shelter" of their community, "dignity has been possible" (Yamamoto, Introduction 10). It may thus be, in a modern sense, less *literary*—simple, naive, almost like a folk tale. Such simplicity does permit Mori a politics of omission. Yamamoto says, "In Toshio Mori's stories, it is the white who is marginal" (Introduction 10). Lawson Fusao Inada explains bluntly:

> The point is, this is a Japanese American community—the people do not define themselves as nonwhite, nor do they need to rely on whites. Whites are just there, like street names, like racism—they come with the territory. Japaneseness is also taken for granted. (xvii)

But such a gentle politics of omission resides only in the "calm and contentment" of nostalgic adulthood. It is not ironic or confrontational; it cannot construct characters who, like Jackson and the Reverend Sasagawara, are both oppressors and oppressed.

Valerie Matsumoto's short story "Two Deserts" is *very* confrontational—to the extent that, surprisingly like Mori's story, it abides no implied ironies. Its third-person narration focuses on Emiko, who lives with her husband Kiyo and daughter Jenny in California's Imperial Valley, which is "just like the Topaz Relocation Camp . . . but without the barbed wire fence and crowded barracks" (Matsumoto 45). Neither the narrator nor Emiko notes that the absence of barbed wire and barracks should make a tremendous difference, for we come to understand that Emiko's new imprisonment is the relentless sexual harassment by the retired white neighbor Roy. Unlike the oppressing and oppressed Jackson and the Reverend Sasagawara, Emiko is doubly oppressed. Her adult oppression seems more manageable than her girlhood internment—she feels "caged, pent up, restless," but at least she can often avoid her oppressor—until Roy racializes his harassment, comparing her to "the cutest *geisha* girl" he had met in Tokyo (51, 52). The narrator also racializes gender oppression; in the climactic moment as Emiko expels her anger and frustration in killing a scorpion, she compares Emiko to "a *samurai* in battle . . . battering her enemy to dust" (52). Now both enemies, the scorpion and the white man, are "battered" by the shovel-wielding samurai Emiko. This triumph may be, finally, ambiguous, for though surely "Emiko stood tall" before the desert whose sand is now "glittering like an ocean," still she says only "Maybe" when Jenny asks whether they may find gold, and still she must shade "her eyes from the deceptive shimmer" (53). It is a triumph nevertheless, more than any conceivable to her as an internee. Matsumoto's story, dense with symbols, is more political than Mori's; but, like his, it is a story of Japanese American adulthood long after the war, in which internment is an essential, but not an exclusive, aspect of a protagonist's current life. Normality is thus

defined by Mori as the brothers' postwar "calm and contentment," and
by Matsumoto as the assertive Emiko.

We may regard adult nostalgia as practiced by Mori and Matsumoto
as a Japanese American manifestation of what Bettelheim calls denial,
or as an answer to the sansei call to break silence. Charitably, we read
in Mori's compassion and Matsumoto's urgency an assertion that we
must not define nisei only as victims of internment.

Yamamoto's and Kaneko's stories are more strictly protests against
internment, but here protest is silent, implied in an adult narration that
recreates the perspectives of children. The mere presence of "normal"
children in the camps must seem abhorrent to those white racists who,
even today, justify internment as a brake against espionage. Of course
we must not forget that these children understood the pains of
internment (Kawakami, interview). Masao and Kiku acknowledge the
barracks and fences of camp and the open spaces "outside." But these
children, better than their elders, can adapt and assert their normalities in
their new environment. And Kaneko and Yamamoto, circumscribing
adult narrators around them, can evince an awareness of both normal
play and abnormal pain. These narrators are silent breakers of silence,
practicing what Mori calls in his story "Slant-Eyed Americans" "the
silence which was action" (134). Their authors are heroes of emergent
Japanese American discourse.

NOTES

1. See Suzuki's *An Introduction to Zen Buddhism*; Matsumoto's *The Unspoken Way: Haragei: Silence in Japanese Business and Society*; and *Perspectives on Silence*, eds. Tannen and Savile-Troike.
2. See Susan Sontag's "The Aesthetics of Silence," in *Styles of Radical Will* for insights into silence in postmodernism.
3. See Steiner's *Language and Silence*.
4. An example: mime artist Marcel Marceau once recorded an *audio* album.
5. The War Relocation Authority required all adult internees to indicate both their willingness to serve in the military and their unqualified allegiance to the United States, and to renounce any allegiance to Japan. Okada's protagonist answers "no-no," indicating no loyalty to the nation that has imprisoned him unjustly.
6. Some Asian American critics suggest that its appearance in such an influential journal indicts the presumably white male editors for obliviousness to what Schweik calls a "coded narrative." But this denies the possibility that the story's achievement is so obvious that even *The*

Kenyon Review staff recognized it, and it surely forecloses the possibility that the editors might have appreciated its politics.

REFERENCES

Bettelheim, Bruno. "Eichmann: The System, the Victims." *"Surviving" and Other Essays.* New York: Vintage, 1979. 258–73.
___. "The Holocaust—One Generation Later." *"Surviving" and Other Essays.* New York: Vintage, 1979. 84–104.
___. "Trauma and Reintegration." *"Surviving" and Other Essays.* New York: Vintage, 1979. 19–37.
Bruchac, Joseph. Preface. *Breaking Silence, An Anthology of Contemporary Asian American Poets.* Ed. Joseph Bruchac. xiii–xv.
Cheung, King-Kok. *Articulate Silences: Hisaye Yamamoto, Maxine Hong Kingston, Joy Kogawa.* Ithaca: Cornell University Press, 1993.
Crow, Charles L. "The *Issei* Father in the Fiction of Hisaye Yamamoto." *"Seventeen Syllables."* By Hisaye Yamamoto. Ed. King-Kok Cheung. New Brunswick: Rutgers University Press, 1994. 119–28.
Culley, John J. "The Sante Fe Internment Camp and the Justice Department Program for Enemy Aliens." *Japanese Americans: From Relocation to Redress.* Eds. Roger Daniels, Sandra C. Taylor, and Harry H. L. Kitano. 2nd ed. Seattle: University of Washington Press, 1991. 57–71.
Daniels, Roger. "Chronology of Japanese American History." *Japanese Americans: From Relocation to Redress.* Eds. Roger Daniels, Sandra C. Taylor, and Harry H. L. Kitano. 2nd ed. Seattle: University of Washington Press, 1991. xv–xxi.
___. "The Conference Keynote Address: Relocation, Redress, and the Report—A Historical Approach." *Japanese Americans: From Relocation to Redress.* Eds. Roger Daniels, Sandra C. Taylor, and Harry H. L. Kitano. 2nd ed. Seattle: University of Washington Press, 1991. 3–9.
___. "The Forced Migrations of West Coast Japanese Americans, 1942–1946: A Quantitative Note." *Japanese Americans: From Relocation to Redress.* Eds. Roger Daniels, Sandra C. Taylor, and Harry H. L. Kitano. 2nd ed. Seattle: University of Washington Press, 1991. 72–74.
Elkins, Stanley M. *Slavery: A Problem in American Institutional and Intellectual Life.* 3rd ed. Chicago: University of Chicago Press, 1976.
Inada, Lawson Fusao. "Standing on Seventh Street: An Introduction to the 1985 Edition." *Yokohama, California.* By Toshio Mori. 1949. Seattle: University of Washington Press, 1985. v–xxvii.
JanMohamed, Abdul R., and David Lloyd. "Introduction: Toward a Theory of Minority Discourse: What Is To Be Done?" *The Nature and Context of Minority Discourse.* Eds. Abdul R. JanMohamed and David Lloyd. New York: Oxford University Press, 1990. 1–16.

Kane, Leslie. *The Language of Silence: On the Unspoken and the Unspeakable in Modern Drama*. Madison, NJ: Fairleigh Dickinson University Press, 1984.

Kaneko, Lonny. "The Shoyu Kid." *The Big AIIIEEEEE! An Anthology of Chinese American and Japanese American Literature*. Eds. Jeffery Paul Chan, Frank Chin, Lawson Fusao Inada, and Shawn Wong. New York: Meridian, 1991. 304–313.

Kawakami, Toyo Suyemoto. Personal interview. 30 May 1995.

Kim, Elaine. *Asian American Literature: An Introduction to the Writings and Their Social Context*. Philadelphia: Temple University Press, 1982.

Matsumoto, Valerie. "Desperately Seeking 'Deirdre': Gender Roles, Multicultural Relations, and Nisei Women Writers of the 1930s." *Frontiers* XII (1991): 19–32.

___. "Two Deserts." *The Forbidden Stitch: An Asian American Women's Anthology*. Eds. Shirley Geok-lin Lim, Mayumi Tsutakawa, and Margarita Donnelly. Corvallis, OR: Calyx, 1989. 45–53.

McDonald, Dorothy Ritsuko, and Katharine Newman. "Relocation and Dislocation: The Writings of Hisaye Yamamoto and Wakako Yamauchi." *"Seventeen Syllables."* By Hisaye Yamamoto. Ed. King-Kok Cheung. New Brunswick: Rutgers University Press, 1994. 129–41.

Mirikitani, Janice. *Shedding Silence*. Berkeley: Celestial Arts, 1987.

Mori, Toshio. "The Long Journey and the Short Ride." *"The Chauvinist" and Other Stories*. Los Angeles: Asian American Studies Center, 1979. 123–26.

___. "Slant-Eyed Americans." *Yokohama, California*. 1949. Seattle: University of Washington Press, 1985. 127–35.

O'Connor, Frank. *The Lonely Voice*. 1963. New York: Bantam, 1968.

Pratt, Mary Louise. "The Short Story: The Long and the Short of It." *Poetics* 10 (1981): 175–94.

Schweik, Susan. *A Gulf So Deeply Cut: American Women Poets and the Second World War*. Madison: University of Wisconsin Press, 1991.

Takaki, Ronald. *Strangers from a Different Shore: A History of Asian Americans*. New York: Penguin, 1989.

Wong, Sau-ling Cynthia. *Reading Asian American Literature: From Necessity to Extravagance*. Princeton: Princeton University Press, 1993.

Yamamoto, Hisaye. Introduction. *"The Chauvinist" and Other Stories*. By Toshio Mori. Los Angeles: Asian American Studies Center, 1979. 1–14.

___. "The Legend of Miss Sasagawara." *"Seventeen Syllables" and Other Stories*. Latham, NY: Kitchen Table: Women of Color Press, 1988. 20–33.

9. No Types of Ambiguity: Teaching Chinese American Texts in Hong Kong

Hardy C. Wilcoxon

The responses of Chinese readers in Asia to works of Chinese American literature have more than documentary interest, for they may offer fresh insight into the relations between the ethnicity of the authors and the stories they tell.[1] More specifically, the ways Hong Kong Chinese readers typically analyze and praise Amy Tan's stories in *The Joy Luck Club*, which will be the centerpiece for discussion, and disparage Maxine Hong Kingston's *The Woman Warrior* suggest that as a storyteller, Amy Tan is, from their point of view, more Chinese. The stories in *The Joy Luck Club* conform more readily to the expectations Chinese readers have about what "good stories" are, and above all conform in their values with a Chinese world view. In terms of genre, that is, Amy Tan's stories seem to Chinese readers consonant with the Confucian traditions that even now strongly influence their values and habits of interpretation, inclining them to take a moralistic view of literature, in general, and story-telling, in particular. To them, *The Joy Luck Club* is an unambiguously homiletic book. And in terms of its content, the book pleases Chinese readers by reinforcing the values Chinese people—but by no means only Chinese people—traditionally place on family ties and by apparently aiming to show that one's sufferings, perhaps especially at the hands of one's parents, are ultimately beneficial. *The Woman Warrior* is by comparison a threatening book: it wilfully subverts genre, rebels against parental authority from the opening sentence, questions the value of a Chinese ethnic inheritance, and resolves only ambiguously the issues of Chinese American identity that it takes up.

The readers central to the discussion are a group of seventy English majors at The Chinese University of Hong Kong: fifty fourth-year students—or about two-thirds of the entire fourth-year class—who had elected to take a course in "The Asian American Experience" (the first

of its kind ever to be offered in Hong Kong) and twenty first-year
students in a "Writing About Language and Literature" course in which
I re-read some of the same texts. Like virtually all university students
in Hong Kong, they have come up through the Anglo-Chinese stream
of the school system, in which, after primary school, they study all of
their school subjects (except Chinese) in English. Of the seventy in
question, only a few were born in mainland China; virtually all call
themselves "British" on the dotted lines of official forms; and about one
in ten have, in fact, acquired foreign passports that will enable them to
settle overseas, at least before the British flag comes down at
Government House in the summer of 1997, and Hong Kong is handed
over to what most local people perceive to be a very uncertain future
under the control of The People's Republic. All of these students,
however, are native speakers of Cantonese who are proud of their
language, their city, which is 98 percent Chinese, and, for the most
part, their culture. Although many of the patterns of response revealed
by the current analysis might very well represent attitudes of Chinese
on the mainland as well, no Asian cultural monolith or hegemony is
here supposed. On the contrary, the particularly fascinating twist in the
analysis, suggestive of much genuine individual pathos, is that
especially in Hong Kong, the colonial, soon to be postcolonial, nature
of the territory forces a great many people into an ambivalent, at times
uncertain, relation to their "Chineseness," which strongly influences
their reading.

 That all of the readers but one are women certainly needs to be
mentioned also, not because the fact is in itself surprising—almost all
English majors at the three tertiary institutions that offer literary studies
in Hong Kong are women—but because Amy Tan's stories and other
works of Chinese American literature engage their deepest and most
ambivalent feelings when traditional views about the status of women
in Chinese culture are at issue. A parable, for example, in *The Joy
Luck Club* about a frog swallowing the tears shed by women provoked
a typically intense, ambivalent tendency to feel simultaneously
empowered and threatened by the text: the parable "shows that women
always are victims in male-dominated China," one student wrote. "They
adapt to keep silent and eat their own tears. As a female, I do not like to
see this scene which is so contradictory to my wish. I hate to be this
kind of Chinese woman." Others, in a similar vein, quoted again and
again, both in the "Worksheets" and in essays, the hurtful maxims that
make the speaker of *The Woman Warrior* so justly indignant: "'Girls
are maggots in the rice.' 'It is more profitable to raise geese than
daughters'" (46). Having quoted these maxims and the one about how

"there is an outward tendency in females," one student said "I still
remember how I read these pages with blurred eyes, and how the line
'Did you have a full-month party for me?' struck me, since only my
younger brother but not me had such a party." "The message," one
student said of *The Joy Luck Club,* though it would apply no less to
The Woman Warrior, "is that even though Chinese women must suffer
without power, they can attain power, or at least speak out about their
suffering, which can be a way of attaining power."

The students, in short, felt a strong sense of personal connection
with feminist issues embodied in Amy Tan's text and in *The Woman
Warrior,* and these define the one region of cultural values where the
forces of tradition are felt to be a terrible constraint. "Misogyny does
not only confine itself to the old and the less educated," as one student
noted in an essay. "Even though most women in Hong Kong receive
western education, deep inside their hearts they feel they are inferior to
men. . . . We are terribly afraid of the routine life of a housewife
because it is a sign of failure. We refuse the traditional role of
submissive women not because our parents call us maggots but because
of a drive which urges us to prove ourselves better than the boys. I
think we have this drive not because we have experienced suppression,
but because we are unconsciously influenced by the sexual inequality
which is an accustomed belief in our environment." From this
perspective, both *The Joy Luck Club* and *The Woman Warrior* seemed
to the students empowering, clarion calls for change. Maxine Hong
Kingston, as one student wrote, "is speaking on behalf of many
Chinese women, who are showing that they have the ability to be
woman warriors and are crying for equality." Another hoped that *The
Joy Luck Club* could be translated into Chinese so that Chinese on the
mainland, both male and female, could be prompted "to overthrow this
custom of suppressing women, and liberate themselves." "Voices for
human rights are getting louder and louder," still another wrote. "It is
really the right moment for us to speak for women, especially in China
where they have been suppressed for thousands of years. We should face
this problem instead of hiding from it."

Perhaps especially in the context of such a favorable disposition
towards feminist concerns, the challenge is to understand as fully as we
can the students' uneasy response to the stories in *The Joy Luck Club*
and their intense dislike of Kingston's text. At least the starting point
for the discussion is that from the students' point of view, even the
relatively more reassuring stories by Amy Tan sometimes misrepresent
and defame Chinese culture and Chinese people. The students frequently
alleged, for example, that in creating the narratives by the mothers,

Amy Tan exaggerates the superstitiousness and primitivism of traditional Chinese life. Singled out for the most intense criticism was one of An-Mei Hsu's narratives, "Scar," at the end of which she recalls seeing her outcast mother return to visit her own mother's deathbed and, in a gesture of filial piety, perform "magic in the ancient tradition" by cutting "a piece of meat from her arm" and stirring it into the dying woman's soup (40–41). Some students resisted what seemed to them an implicit demand in the text: "This scene makes me scared. . . . I don't know why Chinese think that . . . you should cut your flesh to feed your parents. . . . We do not choose to be born, so we are not indebted." "Love and affection are already enough to show our '*hsiao [xiao]*,'" another said, and the primitive magic is "too bloody and inhuman." Most students, however, expressed their distaste in terms such as these: "The author is using this kind of exaggeration to fascinate the Western reader . . . [which is] quite hateful." Readers, she continued, "will think that Chinese are irrational and barbarian."

Virtually innumerable examples of similarly distasteful "exaggerations," "distortions," "misconceptions," "biases," and the like, can be found in *The Woman Warrior,* according to the students. They were especially aggrieved about the centrality that Maxine Hong Kingston gives to "ghosts," "real" and metaphorical;[2] the portrait that she draws of social tyranny, suicide, and infanticide in "No Name Woman"; the comments that she makes about the frequency of lying in Chinese culture; and the distortions, however intentional and expressive, that she makes of traditional Chinese legends, which led one student to compare her explicitly to Salman Rushdie, and say: "It is as if she has betrayed her Chinese community by violating cultural myths and legends that are considered sacred. . . . " This was a most extreme view.

Two main issues underlie such defensiveness and the students' apparent need to separate what they admire about the feminist criticism of the misogyny in Chinese tradition from other criticisms, real or imagined, that they feel compelled to fend off. The first issue, to be taken up later, involves the students' sense of their own "Chineseness," which, though proud, is vulnerable and open to question, especially in a community like Hong Kong, which is in some ways a community in diaspora. The second, as I have said at the outset, involves the persistence of Confucian traditions, in which moral philosophy is embodied in stories, parables and homilies, and ways of reading are correspondingly allegorical and moralizing in their tendency. The students respond strongly and rather defensively to texts, in other words, because their socio-cultural context defines literature for them as a kind of discourse that by nature has "illocutionary force," as speech-act theorists would call it: ordering, exhorting, or warning. Literature has designs on them.

Given the power and authority of history in Chinese culture, it should not surprise us that the most potentially important, morally influential stories would also be those that are taken to be "true." At first it struck me as a little odd, for example, that one of the most pressing issues for students from the outset, as readers of *The Woman Warrior,* was whether it was fact or fiction. "How much is pure imagination?" they wanted to know; how much is "with her imagination added?" Aesthetically, their expectations seemed to dictate a rigid separation. But the issue turned out to be largely a moral one. Along with the general tendency to dismiss the book as "subjective" and "merely personal" went comments from a few of them about how the book "after all is not a history book." Conversely, more than one student found the "exaggerations" in *The Joy Luck Club* more "hateful" than those in *The Woman Warrior* because in the former, "we see what is supposed to happen in real life." If such remarks give to stories a moral weight or authority that may strike Western readers as unusual, they confirm in a dramatic way how absolutely right Amy Tan, Maxine Hong Kingston, and other Chinese American writers are to dwell upon and thematize the power of storytelling in Chinese culture.

Affectively, my Chinese students respond to these texts with an intensity and immediacy that is enviable, as when one of them remarked that she intensely disliked the scene of Bing's drowning in *The Joy Luck Club* because she wanted "to shout to Bing's parents and sisters that he is drowning." But whereas I would mean to praise a work by calling it "terrible," my students most certainly would not. Often the things that they most intensely disliked were things the texts were not inviting them to "like," exactly, such as incidents or characters in *The Joy Luck Club* that seem intended for disparagement. When a student wrote, for example, that she disliked above all Amy Tan's story about the marriage of Rose and Ted because he is "such a terrible and disgusting husband," a possible response would have been to write in the margin, "Who ever said you should like him?" But the underlying issue, as the students helped me to see, was a difference (once again) in their *moral* responsiveness to the act of storytelling, a responsiveness arising from the supposition that in storytelling, an "ought" lurks behind every "is."

For a few students, these designs that Amy Tan's stories implicitly had on them seemed vividly personal, evoking memories of hearing stories used in their family as "psychological threats," as one expressed it. Here, evoked by one scene from *The Joy Luck Club*, is a fairly extended recollection of this sort:

> I dislike the story "Scar" because it is full of myth, which I hate most. I hate the elders using the story as a means to teach the children to be obedient. They make the stories into something terrible, and make children unable to forget their horrible endings. The stories mark the dark side of one's childhood. When I was young, my grandmother told many stories to me and all the endings were so horrible that I would have nightmares after I heard them. . . . I think that Chinese use this myth of cutting one's flesh to feed one's parents to control us. You have to cut your own flesh . . . so as to leave them and live in your own way.

No less personal, but more general in their criticism, are a couple of other comments suggesting that Amy Tan's stories, however "realistic," may be culpably discouraging. "I don't like the philosophy Amy Tan expresses at the beginning of the section 'Queen Mother of the Western Skies,'" one said. "At the end of this passage, the little Queen teaches the girl 'How to lose your innocence but not your hope.' This is something in Chinese culture which I dislike. Chinese parents force children to learn more about the evils in the world so they will not be hurt by others. I think their method forces you to be unhappy so you will not feel sad if misfortune falls on you. But in this way, you are *doomed* to lose your hope, so I find this teaching a very confusing one." More generally still, another said, "I cannot think of a passage I especially dislike, but it seems to me that life in this book is full of all kinds of problems. There is always great pressure from surroundings and difficulties in getting along with people, even within one's own family. I do really wonder if life is like this. . . . Amy Tan also shows us the hopeful and bright aspect of life, but when compared with the suffering portion, it is quite unbalanced. *Is this the way life should be?*" Every story, it would seem, is at least potentially a fable, an exemplum, or a possibly influential stereotype in the offing.

That Amy Tan herself would largely sympathize with this view of literature may define an important aspect of her ethnicity as a storyteller. Her underlying sympathy with the Chinese mothers in *The Joy Luck Club* and *The Kitchen God's Wife,* who instruct and were instructed in part by stories, is reinforced in her reflections by the Christian homiletic traditions inculcated by her father, who was a preacher and her "very early writing teacher," as she realized when writing *The Joy Luck Club:* "Every week he wrote sermons and he would read them out loud to me and the quality of his sermons was very much like stories. . . . He had an absolute belief in what these stories had to mean" (Davis 98). In "good stories," as she puts it, "there [is] always a reason for telling the story. . . . In fairy tales and fables there is often a moral attached. [In the stories of *The Joy Luck Club*] I didn't want to have something that was exactly the moral, but I wanted to have something that was equivalent. . . . " (Davis 101–02). This she refers to as "a frame," which is "'the reason' for telling the story" (Davis 101) and may take the form of a one-sentence question that the story will address or a one-sentence statement of what the story to be composed will be about (Davis 101–02).

The concentration or "over-determination" of meaning she describes as an aspect of her practice as a writer is certainly compatible with, if not indeed attributable to, habits of mind and feeling that Amy Tan would readily identify as "Chinese." In *The Kitchen God's Wife,* for example, the young narrator of the first section describes her mother as "like a Chinese version of Freud, or worse," in that "*nothing* is an accident," and "everything has a reason" (29). The mother sees the world and her own life as a text that must be read allegorically to grasp "the lessons of my life" and comprehend "the fate that was given me" (62). In her own growing up, and in her effort to make her experience useful to her daughter, the "lessons" of her life take the form of stories, which form the bulk of the novel itself, which is addressed to the daughter. The main difference between the stories that she was told as a girl and the stories she would tell to her daughter, perhaps, is that the stories of her own youth were of the sort that my Chinese students have complained about: stories "giving threats . . . [and] handing out warnings about another kind of life, too terrible to imagine. . . . This is how you made children behave" (133). The mother, and implicitly Amy Tan herself, wants to hold tenaciously to the possibility that these largely grim stories "with scary morals given at the end" may be false, and that happy endings are possible (340).

Such a possibility animates the desires of the mothers in *The Joy Luck Club* as well, and takes the form of their hoping, in their different ways, that their American-born daughters will find happiness through acknowledging and embracing their "Chineseness": their root or *"gen,"* which is inextricable from family ties and ultimately from one's ancestral home. On the largest scale, this is enacted by the progress of Jing-Mei Woo, whose narratives frame the whole collection. She begins estranged from her roots by the death of her mother and by denial ("What can I tell . . . about my mother? I don't know anything" [31]). She goes on, of course, to visit her long-lost sisters in China and

to discover "what part of me is Chinese. It is so obvious. It is my
family. It is in our blood" (331). And in the closing sentences of the
collection, as the narrator watches the Polaroid snapshot develop, "our
three images sharpening and deepening all at once," she and her sisters
all see that "together we look like our mother. Her same eyes, her same
mouth, open in surprise to see, at last, her long-cherished wish" (332).
Simple identity or fusion, in other words, becomes the triumphant way
of answering how past and present, East and West, are to be related.
Although this may be, as it seems to me, a rather simplistic answer,
explicitly full of wishful thinking, the nature of its appeal to Chinese
students is powerful and complex.

First of all, the students are readily inclined to think in racial terms
about their identity and that of ethnic Chinese in diaspora, regardless of
their place of birth and upbringing. For Chinese in Asia, in other
words, a Chinese American is an American Chinese: an "ABC"—
"American Born Chinese," of course—or to invoke a Mandarin term,
"Meiji hua ren," which with stiff literalness can be translated as
"American citizen Chinese person." Here is one analysis of *The Joy
Luck Club* that is heavily freighted with assumptions of this sort:
"When the ABC's refuse to accept their native culture, they have
nothing to depend on except the American one. They do not understand
why they have to obey their culture without questioning. Since they do
not understand the way Chinese people insist on loyalty, they cannot
conform themselves to their native culture. It is not until they discover
the strength of their mothers and the values already inscribed in them by
the stories told by their mothers that they begin to change." This
entirely typical use of "ABC" and above all of the phrases "native
culture" and "their culture" is an index of my failure as a teacher to
vivify the issues central to many Asian American texts.

And yet it is important to note that Amy Tan herself would seem
inclined to a similarly racial or essentialist view of her own ethnic
identity, having said proudly that "as soon as my feet touched China, I
became Chinese."[3] In this she is just like her creation Jing-Mei, or
"June" in *The Joy Luck Club,* who, crossing the border into China
feels instantly different: "I can feel the skin on my forehead tingling,
my blood rushing through a new course, my bones aching with a
familiar old pain. And I think, My mother was right. I am becoming
Chinese" (306). Maxine Hong Kingston, by contrast, does not feel this
way, as I know from conversations with her in Hong Kong in 1995, and
finds it very odd indeed to be referred to as an "ABC": her "essence"
is not Chinese, nor is her American-ness adjectival, a matter of accident
rather than substance. In thinking and writing she rather subverts the

essentialism on which this kind of discourse rests. That her texts display this by their polyglossia, insisting on the diversity of voices that make up one's identity, "questioning the values of the autonomous self and definitions of racial and sexual identity" (Schueller 424) is in fact one of the things Chinese readers find so disquieting about her writings and forms the basis of one of the firmest distinctions one could draw between Maxine Hong Kingston and Amy Tan as storytellers. The tendency of Amy Tan's stories is towards an ever firmer, ever more affectionate embrace of her ethnicity.

The appeal this makes to Hong Kong students derives not just from cultural habits of thinking about identity in racial terms but from the insecurity that Hong Kong people in general suffer in relation to the "hand-over" or perhaps "take-over" of Hong Kong in 1997, which will free them of their colonial bonds and return them to the motherland but also will decidedly subject them and sacrifice their freedoms to an extent that cannot yet be determined. Underlying the defensiveness of the students in response to Chinese American texts that are sometimes critical of Chinese culture and informing their fondness for the stories of *The Joy Luck Club* is the affinity the students feel with the "between worlds" condition—to borrow the title of Amy Ling's book—of the Chinese in diaspora. In contemplating the change of sovereignty in the near future, the Hong Kong people to some extent fear the loss of their origins.

Most commonly, these feelings were expressed indirectly by the students, as in the ways they articulated their great fondness for the morally reassuring strategy of *The Joy Luck Club,* which I have already described: a strategy in which Amy Tan repeatedly shows the women of the younger generation learning that their sufferings at the hands of their elders were for the best and that a stable, redeemed sense of self can be achieved only by acknowledging one's Chinese root. Students frequently expressed their positive responses with constructions in the pattern, "I used to think . . . but now I see," where what they see, as if seen afresh, reinforces tradition and conservatism. One young woman, for example, expressed her fondness for a fortune-telling story in *The Joy Luck Club* by recalling her own experience with fortune-tellers and underscoring the filial lesson of the novel: "Every time they told me that I would have a harsh life because my nose is a bit flat, like that of my mother. My mother would then blame herself. . . . When I was young, I could never understand why my mother pushed me so hard in my studies, but now I realize that she wants me to be better, despite my destined harsh life."

In a similar vein, students said repeatedly, as if in danger of
forgetting something, that the book is "a reminder." It "is a reminder
that we need to try and see things from our parents' point of view," one
said; it "reminds us," said another, "of how important it is . . . to
realize ourselves by connecting ourselves with our root." "*The Joy
Luck Club* reminds us that we must stay integrated with our families.
This is the way Chinese people identify 'self.'" Amy Tan inspired the
students, in sum, with various images of triumphs over divided selves,
triumphs which have involved parents successfully "trying to make
children retain their culture in the face of outside influences," as one
expressed it.

Many of the students' comments on the subject of their identity as
Hong Kong Chinese and on the relation of this subject to their feelings
about Amy Tan and other Chinese American writers are much more
direct and reflective than these just quoted. As they themselves at times
explained, their defensiveness in response to these texts arises in part
from their own ignorance of things Chinese. "To be honest," one said,
"I myself cannot say for sure whether the writer is exaggerating or not.
I'll say that even we Chinese ourselves are not wholly familiar with our
own culture." "Hong Kong people's understanding of China and its
culture," another averred, "is pretty shallow and superficial." "Usually,
the one who criticizes others about being disloyal," a student reflected,
"makes use of this to conceal his own ignorance and pretend to be the
one who tries very hard to save the traditional culture." She dubbed such
a one (in Chinese) "The Great Pretender."

Underneath these responses, as I suggest, runs an anxiety about
being very much betwixt and between. "In Hong Kong," as one of them
put it, "we are living within the tensions and contradiction of
cultures. . . . We reject and even hate the government of our Mainland
China. We are also caught in the dilemma of Eastern and Western
education which teach us different cultural and moral values. Which
value or perspective should we adopt in making a decision?" "Our
parents always condemn us," another said, "for being 'half human, half
foreign ghost.'"

Particularly for Hong Kong students, to be anxious about being
betwixt and between is to be anxious about being left nowhere at all, in
the end. "Hong Kong is, at least in spirit, part of the Chinese diaspora,"
Professor Tu Wei-ming has written. "Despite Hong Kong's impending
return to its homeland in 1997," he observes, "an overwhelming
majority of the working class as well as the intellectuals, if offered the
opportunity, would not choose to identify themselves as citizens of the
People's Republic of China" (13–14). The Hong Kong Chinese,

however, cannot identify themselves as British in the ways—however complex—that Amy Tan, Maxine Hong Kingston, and other Asian American writers identify themselves as Americans. Further, perhaps more acutely for the people of Hong Kong than for Chinese elsewhere, the meaning of being Chinese in the aftermath of the Tiananmen "incident" has become a pressing question.

For many years, of course, in Hong Kong as in the Taiwanese Republic of China, "lurking behind the scenes . . . [has been] the overwhelming presence of mainland refugees and their experiences of persecution, loss, escape, renewal, and uncertainty" (Tu 10). "Hong Kong people are proud of their great tradition," one student wrote, "but when they talk about life in Communist China, they tell a lot of suffering stories. This may be why they flee from 1997." Responses by the Hong Kong students to Asian American texts often brought some of these "experiences of persecution" and "suffering stories" into the foreground, as when one student felt constantly reminded by stories in *The Joy Luck Club* of "my grandmother and mother who sailed into Hong Kong from China in a small boat during the Japanese invasion of the late 1930s. My mother always tells me vividly that when she and my grandmother arrived in Hong Kong, they had no proper clothes to wear and were bare-footed." Another remarked that she found the character of Brave Orchid in *The Woman Warrior* "entirely believable" because her own mother's experiences were so similar: "Like Brave Orchid, my mother came from a well-off family in Shanghai. The Cultural Revolution forced my mother to Hong Kong where her life was marked with hardship. She always felt discontented but helpless in being made to internalise Cantonese language and customs at the expense of Shanghaiese." Still fresher memories of the brutal suppression of the pro-democracy movement mingle with reflections on the pains of family life in response to Amy Tan's stories: the love of the mothers and daughters "contains pain that cannot be removed; and it is because of the pain that their love is so deep and so moving, just like my love for my native country. I love China and have painful feelings because of the fate of the June 4th movement. I can only hope that some ultimate reconciliations will be possible."

In some respects, my students are like "reformers in the tradition of Hu Shi," who are "critical-minded intellectuals who try to pick and choose what to keep and what to discard from the Chinese cultural inheritance" (Schwarcz 94). Most emphatically, it seems, they have felt empowered by their encounters even with texts they do not like, such as *The Woman Warrior*, to speak out against the misogyny that is a part of their inheritance and to speak in favor of ideals of equality that they suppose to be realized in the West. But anxiety about the prospect of having no culture to inherit or of having their inheritance confiscated by the takeover in 1997 has made them deeply conservative in other ways. The moral imperatives of their reading incline them to eschew works like Kingston's that to some extent celebrate ambiguity and interrogate values and to embrace warmly only works consonant with the values of *The Joy Luck Club*, in which "parents try to make children keep their cultural heritage in the face of outside influence," as I have already quoted one student as saying in praise of the novel. These moral imperatives arise in part from traditional Chinese ways of construing the function of literature, with which Amy Tan's own writings are compatible. But they also arise from or are reinforced by the exigencies of politics and history, which make the uncertainties and criticisms of Kingston's text perhaps more than usually unsettling and make the clarities and affirmations of Tan's text a reassuring confirmation of their hopes for a stable future.

"It is a natural psychological tendency and especially important in times of difficulties," one student wrote in an essay, to have "a sense of *embodying* one's own culture." This "internalization," as she put it, "gives a sense of security and stability that is of supreme value and can compensate for all of its defects." Amy Tan's responsiveness to just such a theme, which runs through the stories of *The Joy Luck Club* and structures the novel as a whole, and her willingness to celebrate with unambiguous moral force the Chineseness that is "in the bones" (31) helps define the ethnicity of her writings and makes many Chinese readers proud to claim her as one of their own.

NOTES

1. Very little has been done to assay the responses of Asians to works of Asian American literature. *Asian American Literature: an Annotated Bibliography* (New York: Modern Language Association of America, 1988), by King-Kok Cheung and Stan Yogi, contains no entries of such studies; and an issue of *Melus* (18.4 [1994]) has only recently been devoted to "Asian Perspectives." This issue contains one essay relevant to the present undertaking, John J. Deeney's "Of Monkeys and Butterflies: Transformation in M.H. Kingston's *Tripmaster Monkey* and D.H. Hwang's *M. Butterfly*" (21–39). Deeney has discussed Chinese American literature with Chinese students in Asia and notes "that many of them react to these writers with indignation and even hostility" (34). Analyzing these responses is not central to his larger enterprise, however, and his main argument about them, different from my own, comes down to this: "These native Chinese are more bound by time

(they tend to look to the past and to be more traditional in their thinking) and by space (they usually have not travelled very far beyond their cultural borders). Consequently . . . they are detached from the Chinese American experience and dismayed by something about which they have limited understanding" (34).

To explain my own procedures, it is worth stressing at the outset that for the most part the students chose for themselves the scenes or moments to discuss from the texts central to the analysis here and decided for themselves what criteria to apply in interpreting and judging them. What has been lost thereby in methodological rigor has been made up for, as I hope to show, in the expressiveness and diversity of many students' responses. Their responses were registered on "Worksheets" of questions which were always completed before launching discussions about the texts, and were originally conceived only to help in the preparation of lectures and tutorials. My "Worksheets" were analogous to those used by David Bleich to solicit "response statements" for his study *Readings and Feelings: An Introduction to Subjective Criticism* (Urbana, Illinois: National Council of Teachers of English, 1975), in which he developed the reader-response theory elaborated more fully in his later book, *Subjective Criticism* (Baltimore: Johns Hopkins U.P., 1978). My questions, however, tended to give students more latitude for negative responses and to focus at times on some feature or issue relating exclusively to the text in hand. More specifically, the "Worksheets" for each text were purposefully open ended in asking students to locate and discuss: (1) the most confusing thing to them about the work; (2) a scene or moment that they particularly liked, and why; and (3) a scene or moment that they particularly disliked, and why. And in a move analogous to Bleich's questions about feelings of "identification" with protagonists, students were also asked (4) to describe their responses to central characters who, in the works we are presently concerned with, were Brave Orchid in *The Woman Warrior* and their favorite narrator in *The Joy Luck Club*. Originally with the aim of providing a focus for later discussion, one other text-specific question was posed about each text. For *The Woman Warrior*, the question was how to explain Maxine Hong Kingston's motives in writing the book to a "traditionally-minded" Chinese person who has read it and is dismayed by the way it portrays Chinese culture. For *The Joy Luck Club*, the students were asked how to describe the "ideal audience" for the book and to say whether they considered themselves the sort of persons Amy Tan had in mind as an audience. These last, text-specific questions had the diverse but simple aims of anticipating and exploring rumored hostility to Maxine Hong Kingston's work, and satisfying curiosity about how directly Chinese students felt addressed by Amy Tan's work. Although not posed systematically, these questions sometimes occasioned brilliant analyses and responses imbricating the pattern of their responses to other questions. Over three hundred handwritten pages were generated in response to the "Worksheets." The present essay also draws upon some remarks in a set of fifty essays by students in the "Asian American Experience" course. Because these essays were important to their grades, however, and because they were written after we had finished discussing the text, I have not considered the remarks in them equal to the "Worksheets" in reliability as an index of the students' true feelings and more or less spontaneous opinions and have quoted from them only sparingly and with specific reference to the nature of the source.

2. To understand the centrality of "ghosts" in *The Woman Warrior*, see Gayle K. Fujita Sato, "Ghosts as Chinese-American Constructs in Maxine Hong Kingston's *The Woman Warrior*," in *Haunting the House of Fiction: Feminist Perspectives on Ghost Stories by American Women*, eds. Lynette Carpenter and Wendy K. Kolmar (Knoxville, Tennessee: University of Tennessee Press, 1991), 193–214.

3. This comes from a "Note About the Author" printed on page 333 of the edition of *The Joy Luck Club* cited above.

REFERENCES

Bleich, David. *Readings and Feelings: An Introduction to Subjective Criticism*. Urbana, IL: National Council of Teachers of English, 1975.

___. *Subjective Criticism*. Baltimore: Johns Hopkins University Press, 1978.

Cheung, King-Kok, and Stan Yogi. *Asian American Literature: An Annotated Bibliography*. New York: Modern Language Association of American, 1988.

Davis, Emory. "An Interview with Amy Tan: Fiction—'The Beast that Roams,'" *Writing on the Edge* 2.2 (Spring 1991): 96–111.

Deeney, John J. "Of Monkeys and Butterflies." *Melus* 18.4 (1994): 21–39.

Kingston, Maxine Hong. *The Woman Warrior*. New York: Alfred Knopf, 1975; London: Pan Books, 1981.

Ling, Amy. *Between Worlds: Women Writers of Chinese Ancestry*. The Athene Series. New York: Pergamon Press, 1990.

Schueller, Malini. "Questioning Race and Gender Definitions: Dialogic Subversions in *The Woman Warrior*," *Criticism* XXXI, no. 4 (Fall 1989): 421–437.

Schwarcz, Vera. "No Solace from Lethe: History, Memory and Cultural Identity in Twentieth-Century China." *Daedalus* 120.2 (Spring 1991): 85–112.

Tan, Amy. *The Joy Luck Club*. New York: Ballantine Books, 1989.

___. *The Kitchen God's Wife*. New York: Putnam's, 1991.

Tu, Wei-ming. "Cultural China: the Periphery as the Center." *Daedalus* 120.2 (Spring 1991): 1–32.

10. "Wavering" Images: Mixed-Race Identity in the Stories of Edith Eaton/Sui Sin Far

Carol Roh-Spaulding

The hybrid flower is the saddest flower of all.

—"Leaves from the Mental Portfolio of an Eurasian," 1909

From tales of the tragic mulatto (or quadroon or octoroon) to Harlem Renaissance novels of passing, from Injun Joe to Joe Christmas, and from Leslie Silko to Louise Erdrich, race mixture has long been a subject in American fiction. Most literary depictions and critical discussions of race mixture, however, have focused on the African American mulatto and the "half-blood" Indian—on characters best known as cultural symbols of American historical and racial conflict. Comparatively few discussions of mixed race focus on individuals of Caucasian and Asian parentage, even though Eurasians have been a presence in American literature and film since the beginning of the century.

The half-Chinese, half-English, Canadian-born writer Edith Maude Eaton, or Sui Sin Far (1865–1914) was the first Eurasian in North America to address the subject of mixed race.[1] Between 1987 and 1913, Eaton published dozens of short stories in magazines such as the *Independent, Good Housekeeping, Century,* the *Westerner,* and *Land of Sunshine* (later, *Out West)* and, near the end of her career, collected these in a volume titled *Mrs. Spring Fragrance,* which appeared in 1912. In her own day, Eaton was read primarily by a white middle-class audience inspired by an Orientalist taste for the exotic (White-Parks, *Sui Sin Far* 7). As the first American of Chinese ancestry to write in defense of the Chinese, Eaton has recently been the focus of several literary recovery projects in Asian American literature, most notably by Elizabeth Ammons (*Conflicting Stories*, 1992), Amy Ling *(Between*

Worlds, 1990), and Annette White-Parks (*Sui Sin Far*, 1991).[2]
Contemporary readings of Edith Eaton are driven not by Orientalism,
however, but by the multiculturalist approach of ethnic literary studies,
an approach that fails to account for Sui Sin Far's evasiveness regarding
Chinese-American identity and for the complexities of her own racial
self-definition.

In North America, where race is scripted in absolute terms, racial
designations cannot accommodate race mixture. Homi Bhabha explains
that the in-between—which lacks designation—is difficult to identify,
and its potential is not yet fully understood. Edith Eaton was a writer
who attempted to explore that potential. The manifest purpose of most
of her work is to champion the cause of her mother's people; at the
same time, she continually undermines the permanence and singularity
of the notion of ethnic identity. Far from regarding herself as a Chinese
American writer, Sui Sin Far resists this designation by continually
shifting her authorial stance in relation to a Chinese American ethnic
locale, by creating hybrid motifs and characters, and by depicting
Eurasian consciousness as one that wavers between but remains
permanently resistant to either culturally-imposed notion of categorical
purity, Anglo or Chinese. In her short fiction, the particular focus here,
Eaton maintains a sense of ethnic disequilibrium in two ways. First,
her stories represent a variety of ethnic stances in relation to Chinese
American identity, such that no single implied ethnic version of the
author predominates. Second, Eaton creates several "wavering" heroines
who struggle between two sides of a conflicted or liminal identity,
thereby literalizing the inevitable tensions arising from the historical
encounter between Chinese emigrants and white Americans on the
Western coast in the early part of the century. Because she was sickly
all of her life and because she nearly always had to support herself
through means other than her writing, Sui Sin Far was unable to devote
the time and energy necessary to fulfill her dream of completing the
novel she left unfinished at her death in April 1914 at the age of 49.
"Appetite must be gratified before ambition," she wrote in a letter to
her editor, Charles F. Lummis, in 1897. But her jobs as stenographer
and typist barely paid the bills. As late as 1911, she wrote Lummis that
she was still "trying to write a novel." Therefore, one explanation for
Sui Sin Far's concentration in the genre of short fiction was sheer
physical exhaustion and economic necessity. But an equally compelling
explanation lies in the author's formal as well as thematic expression of
a mixed-race sensibility.

Eaton's stories appeared far more frequently in magazines and
newspapers than they would have as novels, enabling her to create

various depictions of Chinese Americans, some of which were complicitous with and some of which were resistant to the stereotypes current in her day. It is difficult to pin down exactly what version of Chinese American identity Sui Sin Far means to affirm or whether she means to affirm one at all, but this difficulty is precisely the point. Taken as a whole, as in the collection *Mrs. Spring Fragrance,* the stories negotiate the tensions between competing and contradictory versions of an ethnic category that was characterized primarily by stereotype in the minds of many white Americans of Eaton's day. This disjuncture between fictional depiction and social ascription, between documentation and stereotype, evokes the same sense of ethnic disequilibrium that lies at the heart of mixed-race experience. Eaton's project is neither to ennoble her ethnic roots nor to deepen her identification with the Chinese but to reveal the suffering caused by notions of categorical purity for those who find themselves racially, ethnically, or culturally in between.

The author's acute sense of racial displacement has not been appreciated by her critics, primarily because her definition of "Eurasian" is not recognized as distinct from "Asian." For example, Eaton's biographer, Annette White-Parks, notes that Eaton was "ingenious at trickster stylistics, often masking her personal identity under various guises" (Ling and White-Parks, *Mrs. Spring Fragrance* 170); yet White-Parks does not recognize Eaton's "trickster" strategies as central to the question of Eurasian difference. In fact, she dismisses the term *Eurasian* as a "racialized" pejorative (White-Parks, *Sui Sin Far* 9), preferring the term *Chinese American.* Sui Sin Far did become more widely known as a champion of the Chinese in America, but she never identified herself as a Chinese American.[3] "I have no nationality and am not anxious to claim any," she declared in her autobiographical essay "Leaves from the Mental Portfolio of an Eurasian" (Ling and White-Parks, *Mrs. Spring Fragrance* 230). Rather, she positioned herself between identities: "I give my right hand to the Occidentals and my left to the Orientals, hoping that between them they will not utterly destroy the insignificant 'connecting link'" (Ling and White-Parks, *Mrs. Spring Fragrance* 230).

Amy Ling, as well, stops short of the fullest implications provided by Sui Sin Far's treatment of mixed race. Ling does recognize the conflict inherent in being Eurasian:

> Coexisting and unresolvable opposites are daily experiences for bicultural people and particularly for Eurasians. Which language, which nationality, which culture will dominate? By which race shall one be known? (*Between* 112)

Yet it is precisely Ling's preoccupation with the idea that one must choose that obscures Eaton's attempts to define Eurasian as neither white nor Asian. According to Ling, Sui Sin Far chose to assert her Chinese side over her white side, to champion their cause. What "Leaves" and her other work illustrate, however, is that Eaton was a champion of the displaced, from the Chinese Americans torn by the contending forces of Chinese and American culture to the young Eurasian heroines of her fiction, products of Chinese and American unions.

"Illuminating and Obscuring"

The Chinese were a little-admired ethnic minority in the early part of the century, a time when public awareness about things Oriental ran toward the exotic and the stereotypical, at best. The first immigrants, their numbers overwhelming male, were forced into Chinatowns by exclusionary employment practices and by the need to create solidarity against racist sentiment (Takaki 13–14). Having suffered pogroms throughout the Western states and vicious anti-Chinese legislation in the years since their arrival, the Chinese were finally banned from entering the United States altogether, with only a few exceptions, by the Chinese Exclusion Act of 1882. Even more educated and progressive Americans proved they were no sinophiles. In the three volumes of the *Independent* in 1909, for example, Eaton's essay, "Leaves," is the sole article to address the subject of Chinese Americans, while several articles on Japan and other international interests appear. And where this journal is merely dismissive, William F. Wu's thorough study of the literary representation of Chinese Americans, *The Yellow Peril* (1982), demonstrates the recurring anti-Chinese sentiment in the novels of Jack London, Frank Norris, Gertrude Atherton, and Ambrose Bierce as well as a host of lesser-known authors.

Read in light of dominant turn-of-the-century images of the Chinese as "heathen, unassimilable, hatchet-waving rat-eaters and pipe-smoking opium addicts who had no right to live in the United States or Canada" (Ling and White-Parks, *Mrs. Spring Fragrance* 13), Sui Sin Far's stories are a unified front that works to dispel such negative images and to show the Chinese as fully human. Read against Rohmer Sax's famous series, which began with *The Insidious Dr. Fu Manchu* in 1913, the same year that *Mrs. Spring Fragrance* was published, these stories take on the serious task of countering a proliferation of Chinese stereotyping. When examined more closely, however, it is clear that the author provides no single dominant image of the Chinese with which to counter negative stereotypes. To offer such an opposing image would position her within a binary structure which allows for the flip side of the negative portrayals—exoticism—and leaves the Chinese seeming just as alien and remote. It would also indicate that, indeed, the Chinese can be packaged for readerly consumption—fixed into a "pure and unadulterated" version of Chinese-ness, as the author calls it in her article "Half-Chinese Children" (Ling and White-Parks, *Mrs. Spring Fragrance* 188). Most of the time she positions herself as what James Clifford calls a "traveller" between or "interpreter" of cultures, in this case between white Americans and the American Chinese. However, the author continually shifts that interpretive stance.

Eaton's first published story, "The Gamblers" (1896), feeds directly into Chinatown stereotypes with its descriptions of the opium-addicted "murderous Chinese." Clearly, Eaton's early ambition to write about the Chinese was not yet differentiated from popular portrayals of her day, such as Bret Harte's rendition of the "heathen Chinee" in his poem "Plain Language from Truthful James" (1870), or in Chester B. Fernald's story—also about unscrupulous Chinese gamblers—in "The Pot of Frightful Doom," also published in 1896, and in *The Century*, where many of Eaton's later stories appear. Yet even though she never again created such a purely stereotypical portrayal, Eaton's depictions are not without stereotypical elements. Amy Ling notes, for example, that Sui Sin Far is "occasionally guilty of exoticizing and orientalizing," noting her "frequent use of the adjective *quaint*" and the "flowery, honorific language of the stories that attempt to render for an English reader the flavor of translated Chinese" (Ling and White-Parks, *Mrs. Spring Fragrance* 12–13). In addition, certain details are almost comically rendered in an attempt to add the flavor of authenticity. In "Mrs. Spring Fragrance," for example, the early death of the main character's two babies is described as "transplanted into the spirit land before the completion of even one moon" (20). Ling attributes such portrayals to the fact that Eaton was essentially an outsider to Chinatown and the Chinese community and to her unfamiliarity with the Chinese language, written or spoken. She may also have been attempting to fit within the marketable but limiting genre of "Chinatown tales" of which Helen Clark, author of *The Lady of the Lily Feet and Other Tales of Chinatown*, was a once-famous practitioner. Eaton's slips and blind spots, however, can also be read with more intention: given the "rock" that, as defender of the Chinese in America, Eaton could not rely on dehumanizing or one-dimensionalizing portraits, and the "hard place" that she had to sell her stories in order to be heard, Eaton's solution was to create images which would complicate the extant stereotypes and "Chinatown tales" of her day. As long as she took care to distinguish her public identity from the negative images of the Chinese, she could appeal to what Howard Mumford Jones has called the "cosmopolitan spirit" of the age. At the same time, by alternating and amalgamating competing popular images of the Chinese along with full and sympathetic portrayals, Eaton's stories act to unsettle and resist any totalized version of the American Chinese.

Before 1900, Eaton signed her work "Sui Seen Far," an early spelling of her pseudonym, Sui Sin Far. According to White-Parks, the author's pen name, which means "fragrant water lily," was her mother's name for her as a little girl. But built into her very name are some of the blendings found in her work. In either spelling of the pseudonym, two out of the three words that make up her name are also used in English, *seen*, *sin*, and *far*. The first word, *sui*, is pronounced like the first-person singular form of "to be" (*je suis*) in French, the language Eaton heard as a child during her family's visits in Quebec. The earlier spelling, Sui Seen Far, suggests penetrating insight: "I am," she may be declaring, one who has "seen far" into Chinese culture, into the situation of the Eurasian. The latter spelling, Sui Sin Far, contains the English word "sin," which could suggest the author's "transgression" of the boundaries of ethnic identity. Aside from her own pen-name, Sui Sin Far sometimes invents Chinese-sounding names—"Tie Co," "Oh Yam," "Mag-gee"—yet equally as often employs actual Chinese names. This blending of American and Chinese elements foils identification of the "authentically" Chinese and creates a subtle disjuncture between the exotic and the familiar.

No Chinese customs or traditions predominate in these stories; in fact, they appear contradictory. In "Children of Peace," for example, a couple who want to marry for love dishonor their parents' wishes that they take the mates chosen for them. After a few years, however, the couple long for their families in China and send their twin sons as a peace offering to both sets of grandparents. Family bonds and cultural tradition, it would seem, are not so easily broken. On the other hand, the girl, Fin-Fan, in "Tian Shan's Kindred Spirit" behaves very much like a rebellious American daughter. She refuses to marry the man her father has chosen for her because "the law in this country is so that you cannot compel me to wed against my will." Her father merely acquiesces, explaining to the disappointed would-be bridegroom that, "We are in a country where the sacred laws and customs of China are as naught" (122). Fin-Fan wins the man she chooses, indicating—in opposition to the values promoted in "Children of Peace"—that the laws of the new world and the individual will take precedence over those of family and tradition.

Some of Eaton's stories offer a comforting picture of assimilation, reassuring a white readership that the Chinese are no different than Americans. The cheerful and charming meddler, Mrs. Spring Fragrance, who appears in the title story as well as in "The Inferior Woman," affirms a white middle-class way of life. She and her husband, Mr. Spring Fragrance, live in a well-off suburban neighborhood with gardens and walkways, in a house with a veranda. The couple have both Chinese and white friends, and while Mr. Spring Fragrance attends to his business or reads the paper, Mrs. Spring Fragrance reads poetry and plays matchmaker for young lovers of her acquaintance. "She is just like an American woman," remarks one of Mr. Spring Fragrance's business associates (24). Blended within such domestic bliss, however, are details that remind readers that assimilation is not quite so easy or complete. Although Mr. Spring Fragrance is flattered that his wife is considered so clever, he isn't sure he likes the idea of her becoming Americanized, because it might mean that she will "love as an American woman"—that is, find a mate whom she chooses rather than remain in her arranged marriage. While this fear turns out to be completely unfounded and based on a misunderstanding, the clash between American and Chinese ways of understanding casts its shadow. A longer shadow is cast when the Spring Fragrances' young American friend from next door declares to Mr. Spring Fragrance, "haven't you ever heard that all Americans are princes and princesses, and just as soon as a foreigner puts his foot upon our shores, he also becomes of the nobility—I mean the royal family." Mr. Spring Fragrance dryly replies, "What about my brother in the Detention Pen?" (23).

Eaton doesn't let us forget that even for those Chinese who have made it well beyond immigration detention centers and become established citizens, discrimination is a still a daily fact of life. For example, Mrs. Spring Fragrance shares with her husband the irony that America would be declared in the news as "The Protector of China" while "the barber charges you one dollar for a shave while he humbly submits to the American man a bill of fifteen cents." This is a private ironic remark shared in a letter to her husband, but as readers "eavesdrop" and learn from this communication, they also experience the role of outsider—a reversal of what the Chinese are made to feel daily. Another subtle, but unmistakable reversal is Mrs. Spring Fragrance's ambition to write a book about Americans for her Chinese women friends, because the Americans are such "mysterious,

inscrutable, incomprehensible" people (33). This objectification turns
orientalism on its ear, but it does so within a pair of stories that
ostensibly offer a positive vision of assimilation.

Class differences among Eaton's various depictions of the
American Chinese also complicate the ethnic picture. Some stories
depict characters who live in extreme poverty—"actresses" (probably
prostitutes), laundrymen, slaves, families struggling to pay huge debts,
and men struggling to purchase the freedom of their lovers. Such
characters and settings contrast markedly with depictions of middle-class
contentment as in "Mrs. Spring Fragrance." The concern in many of the
stories containing working-class characters is for the creation of a safe
space of some sort. In "The Story of One White Woman Who Married a
Chinese," the white narrator escapes her abusive American husband and
marries a kind-hearted Chinese man. In "Lin John," a brother scrimps
and saves to buy his sister's freedom from slavery. In "The Land of the
Free," a couple hope to establish their safe American household, only
to have their baby taken from them by authorities. In Sui Sin Far's
stories, the creation of safe spaces almost always ultimately fails. Even
in "Mrs. Spring Fragrance," the threat of racial prejudice, while slight,
is present. The lack of refuge and the instability at the heart of many of
Sui Sin Far's stories mimic the instability of a single ethnic version of
the Chinese.

The reminders of racial prejudice in the two "Mrs. Spring
Fragrance" stories remain like flies in the assimilationist's ointment:
they are neither eliminated by the narrative action nor resolved. The
same uneasy juxtaposition of conflicting details occurs on a broader
scale in the collection *Mrs. Spring Fragrance*. Amy Ling notes how the
physical volume itself depicts a "tug of war" between the "medium and
the message." She describes the book as one "printed on decorated
paper, each page imprinted in a pastel 'oriental' design: a crested bird on
branches of plum blossoms and bamboo with the Chinese characters for
Happiness, Prosperity, and Longevity vertically descending along the
right margin" (*Between* 41). In addition, her publisher, A. C. McClurg,
marketed the volume in an advertisement appearing in the *Century* as
one that contained "quaint, lovable characters" in "unusual and exquisite
stories of our Western Coast." Some of the stories do, in fact, fulfill
the expectations created by the book's presentation, especially the many
lighthearted, orientalist pieces collected in the back section, called
"Tales for Chinese Children."

Yet several bleak and tragic stories foil McClurg's tidy packaging.
In "The Wisdom of the New," Pau Lin, the wife of Wou Sankwei,
suffocates their boy in his sleep rather than allow him to grow up in a

culture that is frightening and alien to her. In "Her Chinese Husband," a white woman who marries a Chinese man loses her husband to the prejudice against intermarriage when he is shot through the head by his own countrymen. In "The Land of the Free," Lao Choo's Little One is taken from her by immigration officials the day she sets foot in the United States. Bureaucratic stalling foils the family's desperate attempts to have the child returned. After many months and many hundreds of dollars, Lao Choo is allowed to see her boy, who runs from her in fear, having completely forgotten her.

In some stories, of course, the difficulties are resolved. "The Americanizing of Pau Tsu," for example, contains the same conflict as "The Wisdom of the New," in which a newly arrived Chinese wife is jealous of her husband's admiration for a white friend, but here the husband recognizes and corrects the problem before tragedy strikes. The overall effect—of the blending of exotic and familiar images, of details of assimilation and marginalization, and of tragic and lighthearted narratives—is one of disequilibrium. Eaton provides readers with depictions that both rehearse and revise the cultural scripts for Chinese Americans, ultimately denying readers a stable or reliable version of Chinese America.

In one of her closing statements to her autobiographical essay, "Leaves," Edith Eaton/Sui Sin Far makes clear the purposefulness of this ambiguity. To those who suggest she should "trade" on her nationality by looking more the part of a Chinese woman, with fan, slippers, and other accoutrements, Eaton responds by mocking that desire for "authenticity":

> I should discourse on my spirit acquaintance with Chinese ancestors and quote in between the "Good mornings" and "How d'ye dos" of editors: Confusious, Confusicous, how great is Confucious. Before Confucious, there never was Confucious. After Confucious, there never came Confucious, etc. etc. (230)

Such playing into white America's expectations is "both illuminating and obscuring" as Eaton puts it (Ling and White-Parks, *Mrs. Spring Fragrance* 230) for, like the mingling of the exotic and familiar, Eaton's Confucian-Western greetings reveal a dual strategy in which she both affirms on behalf of the Chinese and resists on her own behalf the ethnicity she trades upon. Her ambiguous portrayals create a space in which she may both commit herself to the Chinese American cause and yet undermine the culture's insistence on racial and ethnic purity.

In the "Tales of Chinese Children," Sui Sin Far tells the story of a mischievous princess who inquires of all her servants as to the whereabouts of her cat. All of them give the princess a fanciful answer that delights her, but she then decides to assemble them before her, whereupon she demands, "Which of these stories is true?" The joke is on them, for all the while the princess's cat is hidden in her sleeve. "They are all untrue," the princess declares, echoing Sui Sin Far, who wears her own version of ethnic identity up her sleeve.

"Wavering Women"

Aside from the ways in which Edith Eaton/Sui Sin Far's presentation of Chinese Americans underscores the insufficiency and instability of ethnic categorization, a few stories contain her most compelling expressions of mixed-race identity. In Eaton's "Eurasian" stories, her heroines struggle with their culture's expectations of categorical purity as young women who find themselves racially, ethnically, or culturally in between. The first of her stories to feature a Eurasian character was "The Sing-Song Woman," originally published in *Land of Sunshine* in 1898 and later included in *Mrs. Spring Fragrance.* The central character, Mag-gee, has a name that mimics her in-between status, for it is pronounced like the American name Maggie but with a Chinese spelling. Miserable at the thought of her impending marriage to a "Chinaman," Mag-gee wants, like other American girls, to marry whom she chooses. She insists, in a rather breathless litany of characteristics, that her physical appearance and personality testify to a less racially ambiguous and decidedly white self:

> I was born in America, and I'm not Chinese in looks nor in any other way. See! My eyes are blue, and there is gold in my hair; and I love potatoes and beef; and every time I eat rice it makes me sick, and so does chopped up food. (126)

Mag-gee is not only in love with the idea of white America, she has internalized the race prejudice directed at the Chinese, railing, "To think of having to marry a Chinaman! How I hate the Chinese!" (126).

Her resistance pays off when her Chinese friend, an actress called the Sing-Song Woman, whose name recalls child's play, suggests to Mag-gee that they play a trick on Mag-gee's father, Hwuy Yen. As easily as the word "sing" slips into "song," Mag-gee's friend will slip into the role of the bride during the wedding ceremony, while Mag-gee runs off with her meat-and-potatoes man. The irony of this scheme lies within the roles of bride-imposter and true bride. Hwuy Yen expects to betroth his daughter to a Chinese man, at which point Mag-gee must "go away forever to live in China." Her father has forced her to "put the paint and powder on [her] face, and dress in Chinese clothes." She laments, "I shall be a Chinese woman next year—I commenced to be one today" (126). In other words, now that she is of marrying age, the biracial Mag-gee must assume the ethnic status of her father and her future husband (there is no mention of her mother). But if being a Chinese woman is a role that Mag-gee can don like a wedding gown; and if, like a wedding gown, her ethnicity is nothing but a nuptial detail, then Mag-gee is decidedly not already (that is, biologically) Chinese. Mag-gee is the "real" bride, being the legitimate, presumably virgin daughter of Hwuy Yen. Yet her Chinese-ness is real neither to her father nor to herself. Since her father intends to pass her off as Chinese for the rest of her life, the "real" bride is, ethnically, a fake.

The Sing-Song Woman, on the other hand, being an "actress" by profession—a term which implies pretense and which, according to White-Parks, was a euphemism for prostitute (*Sui Sin Far* 171)—is neither the actual daughter of Hwuy Yen nor a virgin. But because she is authentically Chinese and because she actually desires to marry the bridegroom, Ke Leang, she is "real" in the ways that count. After the bride-imposter has been unveiled, Hwuy Yen demands to know where Mag-gee has gone. The Sing-Song Woman replies with "bright, defiant eyes" that Mag-gee has run off with a white man. In the end, the Sing-Song Woman wins Ke Leang as a real husband by being authentic in the two respects in which Mag-gee would have had to fake it—in her desire for and her ethnic suitability for a Chinese husband. Meanwhile, Mag-gee's father seems more concerned about the Sing-Song woman's trickery than his daughter's whereabouts. "See how worthless a thing she is," are his last words, spoken to his would-be son-in-law; they refer not to Mag-gee but to the woman who has beaten him at his own game (127).

Presumably, both women have achieved their heart's desire, but only the Sing-Song Woman's future happiness seems secured. Of Mag-gee's fate, none are the wiser. Her refusal to live out the ethnic future her father intends for her results in Mag-gee's disappearance from the narrative. We see not that choosing whiteness is the solution to Mag-gee's identity crisis, but that Hwuy Yen's insistence on ethnic purity has led to the loss of his only daughter and the destruction of his hopes. Despite her ambiguous sexual purity, the ethnically correct (and unconflicted) Sing-Song Woman wins out in Hwuy Yen's racial economy. White-Parks wisely asks of the story's conclusion, "Who is fooling whom when the trick used to overcome society's demands succeeds only in confirming them?" (*Sui Sin Far* 160). The answer is that within a larger scheme, evasion and disguise—even when they fail—are the trademark of Eaton's strategically conceived self-positioning.

William F. Wu has stated that Sui Sin Far's fictional portrayals are "clearly that of an insider" into Chinese American culture (54), but she was just as familiar with the border between identities. Like "The Sing-Song Woman," Eaton's story, "The Smuggling of Tie Co," employs the elements of disguise in order to call into question the notion of "authentic" identity. Jack Fabian, a contrabander known as the "boldest in deed, the cleverest in scheming, and the most successful in outwitting Government officers," is the amalgamation of Jack London's rough, dashing spirit and Fabian Socialism. In helping Chinese men to enter the United States illegally from Canada, he believes he is taking "a little out of these millionaire concerns" of the government (105). A little down on his luck when the story opens, Fabian meets Tie Co, a frail lad of quick intelligence and an "uncustomed Chinaman" who becomes strongly attached to the burly character and requests to be smuggled to New York city for fifty dollars—no small sum for a turn-of-the-century Chinese laundryman. According to Xiao-Huang Yin, "tie co," translated literally, may mean "pitiful" (69). Furthermore, since Eaton uses names that bring association on many levels, both "tie" and "co" as words of interconnection suggest the desire the boy feels to "bond" meaningfully with Fabian.

On their journey, Fabian asks the "nice-looking Chinaman" why he does not marry, to which Tie Co replies, "I not like woman, I like man." Evidently unaware of the seemingly homosexual overtones of this comment, Fabian retorts simply, "You confirmed old Bachelor!" So Tie Co becomes more explicit. "I like you," the boy reveals, his voice sounding "clear and sweet in the wet woods." He admits that he has no friends in New York and adds, "I like you so much that I want go to New York, so you make fifty dollars" (107). Horrified by this unwonted selflessness, Fabian insists that Tie Co buy a ticket back to Toronto instead of continuing their nighttime trip through the woods at the Canadian border. The sexual anxiety Tie Co causes Fabian to feel intensifies the anxiety of their secret passage across the border. Within minutes, they are stalked by the border patrol. In a flash, Tie Co sacrifices his life for Fabian, leaping from a bridge to distract the officers. Fabian jumps after him, but the boy is lost. The next day's search for the body produces "Tie Co's body, and yet not Tie Co," the essence of this cross-dressing, cross-nationalizing, cross-racializing individual. For dressed in Tie Co's clothes, Fabian and the reader learn simultaneously, was "the body of a girl—a woman" (108).

As in "The Sing-Song Woman," Eaton creates a disjuncture between appearance and "authentic" identity, where the "authentic" is maintained only at the cost of individual human suffering and, in this case, death. Posing as a boy, Tie Co enjoys a certain degree of mobility as the companion of Jack Fabian, but ultimately her crossing of national, gender, and racial boundaries in her love for a white man reveals that the border is a dangerous, if compelling, place to be. Eaton seems fascinated with the subject of identity deception concerning both gender and race in these stories and others, including "Tian Shan's Kindred Spirit," "A Chinese Tom-Boy," and "A Chinese Boy-Girl." While "mistaken identity" is a stock narrative convention, Sui Sin Far heightens its effect. It is the attraction of the border, where identity cannot be fixed, that helps to explain Tie Co's attraction to a man like Jack Fabian. Himself unambiguously white and emphatically male, this trafficker of people moving between nations seems, ironically, to understand the condition of in-betweenness better than anyone. At the same time, the very ease with which he traverses borders makes him unable to sympathize with those for whom the border is a difficult and dangerous space.

Masquerade and deception in "The Sing-Song Woman" and "The Smuggling of Tie Co" are inadequate solutions for survival on the border between identities, yet Sui Sin Far offers little hope that more forthright or honest attempts will fare better, so long as the notion of racial purity endures. An intimate, confessional tone haunts "The Story of One White Woman Who Married a Chinese" and its companion piece, "Her Chinese Husband"—Eaton's only stories narrated in the first person, and the only ones in which the author posits "mixed blood" as the wave of the future. The unique use of first-person narration indicates that Eaton means to be heard differently here; however the stories, unlike her autobiographical writing, undercut her predictions of a mixed-racial future with a conclusion that indicates the world is not ready for such change.

Minnie, the "white woman," begins by stating the question assumed to be foremost in reader's minds: "Why did I marry Lui Kanghi, a Chinese?" Fully half the story explains her motivation for accepting "the lot of the American wife of an humble Chinaman in America" (67). Although she loves her Chinese husband, she takes care to explain that she chose Lui Kanghi only after being driven from her abusive husband, James Carson. This insistence suggests that the act of miscegenation is highly unusual and difficult to justify except as an acceptance of defeat (66–67). Inter-racial marriage was, indeed, highly unusual. In 1903, for example, the *San Francisco Chronicle* reported that only twenty white women were married to "Mongolians" in Chinatown. Edith Eaton, who lived for some years in San Franciso, was a product of the kind of marriage such laws were designed to prevent and, had she herself chosen to marry, her union with a white man would have been, technically, illegal, according to anti-miscegenation laws passed in various states in 1880 and lasting until 1948 (Osumi).

Minnie's working-class, self-educated socialist husband has little but contempt for his "narrow-minded" wife.[4] While Minnie wants nothing more than to cook and keep house, Carson becomes, meanwhile, infatuated with a "Miss Moran," a modern woman and social reformer with "ambition of the right sort" in Carson's opinion (70). After Minnie catches him making a pass at Miss Moran, who rejects him anyway, Carson files for divorce. On the point of drowning herself and her infant child, Minnie is saved at the last moment by Lui Kanghi.

Ostensibly, the old-fashioned Minnie can't compete with the socially progressive "New Woman" her husband admires, so she takes refuge within the Chinese community and Lui Kanghi's household. However, the real progressivism lies with her Chinese husband. At the waterfront where she plans to attempt suicide, Minnie catches sight of her future husband's face by the "flash" of an "electric light," indicating that Lui Kanghi is illuminated not by a dim, ancient culture or by a seedy Chinatown but by a modern light (72). His first words to Minnie express tenderness for her and her child in a voice "unusually soft for a man's" but not weak, for at the same time he lays a "strong hand" upon her arm and firmly swings Minnie around to him (71–72). After they fall in love, Lui Kanghi allays Minnie's fears of his taking a second wife, because his life with her is already a "filled-up cup" (82). At the same time, he has made her and her daughter by James Carson "more independent, not only of others but of himself" by nursing her back to health, giving her child a home, and enabling her to support herself by employing her as a seamstress (77). While Lui Kanghi does not identify himself as a woman's suffragist, he always treats Minnie with "reverence and respect," never pressing her for information about her past nor causing her to feel indebted to him for his kindness. And when he finally asks Minnie if she has "the love feeling" for him, he accepts her answer that she does not yet know. In all of these ways, Lui Kanghi proves that "the virtues do not all belong to whites" (74) and embodies the belief that women should become "comrades to men and walk shoulder to shoulder with their brothers" (67), a belief Carson espoused but completely failed to live by.

In his vision of a mixed-race future, Lui Kanghi again demonstrates his progressivism. Once a son is born to the couple, Minnie feels less able to justify her marriage to a "Chinaman," because she fears that her racially mixed child will only suffer from his parents' union.

> As he stands between his father and myself, like yet unlike us both, so will he stand in after years between his father's and his mother's people. And if there is no kindliness nor understanding between them, what will my boy's fate be? (82)

Lui Kanghi feels more hopeful. An old Jewish mulatto midwife—an interesting choice, given her striking racial and cultural mix—declares, "A prophet has come into the world!" Lui Kanghi adds to the messianic overtones:

> What is there to weep about? The child is beautiful! The feeling heart, the understanding mind is his. And we will bring him up to be proud that he is of Chinese blood: he will fear none and, after him the name of the half-breed will no longer be one of contempt. (82)

This hopeful prediction echoes that in "Leaves," published a year earlier in 1909, in which Edith Eaton/Sui Sin Far declares, "My experiences as an Eurasian never cease; but people are not now as prejudiced as they have been" (Ling and White-Parks, *Mrs. Spring Fragrance* 230); and she adds, "I believe that some day a great part of the world will be Eurasian" (Ling and White-Parks, *Mrs. Spring Fragrance* 224). In "Her Chinese Husband," however, such hope is short lived. If Lui Kanghi is a progressive Chinese man, he is not representative of all Chinese, for the triumphant resolution suggested by the birth of the Eurasian son is destroyed when Lui Kanghi is shot through the head by one of his own countrymen. "There are some Chinese," Minnie explains, "just as there are some Americans, who are opposed to all progress, and who hate with a bitter hatred all who would enlighten or be enlightened" (83). Thus, the story's conclusion indicates that neither whites—as represented by Minnie's former husband, who sneers, "The oily little Chink has won you!" (76)—nor the Chinese, are ready for a racially mixed America.

What Hortense Spillers says of the term *mulatto/a,* applies equally to *Eurasian* or other mixed-race terms: they "tell us little or nothing about the subject buried beneath them but quite a great deal more concerning the psychic and cultural reflexes that invent and invoke them" (166). Eaton's last story of conflicted racial identity, "Its

Wavering Image," tells most compellingly about "the subject buried beneath" and serves as a motif for her view of mixed race. Pan, the central character, "wavers" between a white and a Chinese sense of self and between the things these sides symbolize—romantic and sexual fulfillment on one hand, family and community on the other. Like her namesake, the hybrid man-beast of the forest, Pan is caught between the conflicting forces of nature and culture.[5] Her "wavering" seems so irresolvable and causes her so much anguish that the most meaningful aspect of her racial identity becomes not her choice of either side but the permanent disequilibrium between them.

On the brink of womanhood, Pan, who has always regarded herself as Chinese, lives with her father in Chinatown, her white mother having passed away long ago.[6] Pan's Chinese identity is founded in a dread of the unknown rather than in a conscious decision to identify with her Chinese side. She "always turned from whites," and shrank from the "curious scrutiny as she would from the sharp edge of a sword" (61). But with the arrival of the opportunistic young journalist, Mark Carson (James's hardly less admirable literary "brother"), Pan is forced to deal with the conflict inherent in her racial sense of self. Known as the man who would "sell his soul for a story," Carson has been trying to get an insider's scoop on Chinatown since it became part of his beat.

Pan feels free to associate with her first white friend, Mark Carson, because she was "born a Bohemian, exempt from the conventional restrictions imposed upon either the white or Chinese woman" (62). Her racial ambiguity and her lack of maternal upbringing have allowed her a certain freedom in girlhood. But just as sexual maturity means assuming a Chinese ethnicity for Mag-gee in "The Sing-Song Woman," so must Pan mature by casting off her own racial innocence. She is too young to comprehend Mark's attraction to her, which is centered in Pan's racial ambiguity. As Judith Butler explains, a mixed-race woman's "vacillation" between racial identities serves as an "erotic lure," because she represents "the specter of a racial ambiguity that must be conquered" (172).

Pan begins to trust Mark fully, luxuriating in a newly found intimacy coupled with her native appreciation of the sensual. She "led him about Chinatown, initiating him into the simple mystery and history of many things." And after their walks, "when the afternoon was spent," they retreat to "that high room open to the stars, with its China bowls full of flowers and its big colored lanterns, shedding a mellow light" (62). So well does Mark win over Pan that this once-Chinese girl begins to regard herself as white, precipitating an internal struggle. She feels "at times as if her white self must entirely dominate and trample under foot her Chinese" (62). In a sentimental romance, Pan would eventually marry Mark, choosing the race allied with her sexual maturity and leaving Chinatown and her father behind. But as we have already seen with Mag-gee, such a choice leads to no guarantees of happiness. Maturity is not truly achieved in the choosing of a mate, and racial indeterminacy is not so easily resolved.

Mark soon pushes Pan too hard. He urges her to leave Chinatown with him, insisting, "You do not belong here . . . you are white— white." Not only does he name his lover as racially displaced— repeating the word "white" so that it sounds more like an order than a description—but he suggests that her refusal to leave with him is practically immoral: "You have no right to be here," he pleads. "Your real life is alien to them" (63). In Butler's terms, the white racial purity evidently so important to Mark is constituted only in opposition to Pan's racial ambiguity, which he wants to deny but which he cannot deny and remain white (173). Because Pan demurs, Mark finally gives her an ultimatum; she must decide between living in Chinatown or white society, and he frames this decision as the choice to be with him or without him. "Pan," Mark urges, "don't you see that you have got to decide what you will be—Chinese or white? You cannot be both!" (63). His insistence that Pan leave behind her racial murkiness and "choose" to be white is similar to the expectations of Mag-gee's father, who wants her to "choose" Chinese-ness. Gina Marchetti explains men's need to force a choice and their conflating of women's racial, sexual, and moral identity in *Romance and the Yellow Peril*. As representatives of "taboo sexuality," Marchetti states, Eurasian women pose an implicit threat to "racial boundaries and traditional morality" (71) at the same time that they fascinate white men. Control often involves naming and classifying.

Nearly broken by Mark's coercion, Pan is later calmed when he sings her a love song about the "wavering image" of the moon casting its broken reflection upon the water—a symbol of heaven's perfect love cast imperfectly upon the earth. He wins back Pan's trust and then declares to her, "Those tears prove that you are white" (64). However, his vehement insistence that his beloved completely separate her thoughts and actions from all things Chinese serves only to strengthen Pan's devotion to the people whom whites—like her lover—so easily disregard. Her split loyalties bring her no closer to the decision that both she and her lover believe she must make.

In the end, however, Mark must destroy his connection with Pan. Enticing as she is to him, her racial ambiguity is a taint or taboo that threatens his own whiteness. He reveals his lack of trustworthiness when he publishes Pan's confidences to him about Chinatown's secrets in the newspaper. Betrayed, she sits once more under the "wavering image" of the moon, this time alone. "A white woman!" she whispers. "I would not be a white woman for all the world. *You* are a white man. And *what* is a promise to a white man!" (66). The true "wavering image" is Pan's own unstable image of herself. She fails to recognize that her split racial identity cannot be resolved through Mark, and for that mistake she becomes his victim. And yet Mark is not entirely to blame; he is simply the story's catalyst for the real maturing Pan must do, for the recognition that she is the agent of her own change. Pan feels a rage so fierce it "almost shriveled up the childish frame." But in the end she decides that both the idea of a resolute whiteness and the "wavering" she endured while in love with Mark are too much for her. She retreats, instead, to the "race that remembers" (66).

In the last image of the story, the young Chinese daughter of a friend comforts Pan, climbing into her lap and pressing her head against Pan's "sick bosom." The image calls forth Pan's former uncomplicated Chinese self and a glimpse into her future as a Chinese mother, but it offers no real comfort or solution. If Pan's solution is to salvage her broken identity, she does so by regressing to a "pre-wavering" self, an innocence to which she can never fully return. She has too much knowledge of adult love and loss to be content with the traditional picture of maternal fulfillment. For contemporary readers accustomed to stories that celebrate the return to ethnic origins, this ending may seem quizzical. Sui Sin Far's Eurasians find a wavering identity is too painful to sustain, yet intensifying either side of their ethnic identity is not a satisfactory answer. What "Its Wavering Image" suggests most strongly is that Pan's sense of herself will never be perfect, perhaps never even completely safe. White-Parks notes that Mag-gee and Pan are fixed within roles that offer little chance for growth (*Sui Sin Far* 350). The stories indict the culture, however, and not the character, for in both cases constricting racial categories work to prevent that growth.

For Pan, Mag-gee, and Tie Co, life's experiences are keenest at this border, where there is the chance for love and great risk. These young women seem to live with the same urgent questions at heart that Edith Eaton asked as a child. "Why are we what we are? I and my brothers and sisters," she laments in "Leaves." "Why couldn't we have been one thing or the other?" (Ling and White-Parks, Mrs. *Spring Fragrance* 222). The strong presence of the wavering image throughout Eaton's stories of conflicted identity represents the possibility of a strategically conceived positioning: "My experiences as an Eurasian never cease," she relates, "so I roam backward and forward across the continent. When

I am East, my heart is West. When I am West, my heart is East" (Ling and White-Parks, *Mrs. Spring Fragrance* 230). For Edith Eaton/Sui Sin Far, there is no happy amalgamation of races and cultures; only the continually shifting, wavering frontier between white and Asian, Asian and white, where she positions herself as "but a pioneer" (Ling and White-Parks, *Mrs. Spring Fragrance* 224).

Contrary to a multiculturalist perspective that regards Sui Sin Far as a turn-of-the-century hero for the Chinese, her stories complicate traditional narratives of assimilation and amalgamation with tales of failed cultural mixing and conflicted identity. The short story was the perfect genre in which to illustrate a "wavering" identity, because Eaton could shift her authorial stance quite often, both from story to story and within stories. Her mixed-race and liminal characters embody the cultural tensions Eaton elsewhere expressed through fictional form. While recognizing Edith Eaton/Sui Sin Far's contributions to Chinese American literature is important work, the current regime of multiculturalism tends to concretize writers into categories that efface other ways of understanding their work. In a promotional autobiographical piece published in the *Boston Globe* in 1913, presumably to help sell *Mrs. Spring Fragrance,* Eaton declared that she came to the United States from her home town of Montreal (at the age of 33 in 1898) "with the intention of publishing a book and planting a few Eurasian thoughts in Western literature" (Ling and White-Parks, *Mrs. Spring Fragrance* 288). That book was not *Mrs. Spring Fragrance* but another book that remained unfinished at her death, which Eaton did not describe beyond her declaration that it would "appear next year" (1913) "if Providence [was] kind." Later in the *Globe* essay, she related that at eight years old she "conceived the ambition to write a book about the half Chinese" because she wished to describe to others "that I felt all that I saw, all that I was . . . I was not sensitive without reason" (Ling and White-Parks, *Mrs. Spring Fragrance* 289). Most likely, these were the "Eurasian thoughts" she meant to leave for Western literature, and had they been recovered they might have illuminated the uniqueness of Edith Eaton-Sui Sin Far's self-conception as Eurasian. Without that distinction, a traditionally multicultural order—with its accompanying expectations and assumptions—predominates. The secrets of the Eurasian, the half-blood, the mestizo/a and mulatto/a remain half-told.

NOTES

Many thanks to Tom Lutz, Ned Stuckey-French, and especially Martha Patterson of the University of Iowa, who helped me to articulate my arguments over the course of many drafts and many months.

1. Throughout this article, I will use the names Sui Sin Far, Edith Eaton, and Edith Eaton/Sui Sin Far interchangeably, as does Amy Ling in her chapter on the Eaton sisters in *Between Worlds.* My doing so will underscore my argument that Eaton assumed a variety of authorial positions in her work in order to avoid being centered within a single ethnicity.

2. For a listing of critical discussions of Sui Sin Far's work, see Annette White-Parks "Introduction to Part II" in the edited edition titled, *Mrs. Spring Fragrance and Other Writings,* edited by Amy Ling and Annette White-Parks (University of Illinois Press, 1995). Annette White-Parks's doctoral dissertation, *Sui Sin Far: Writer on the Chinese-Anglo Borders of North America* has recently appeared in book form, published by the University of Illinois Press as *Sui Sin Far/Edith Maude Eaton: A Literary Biography* (1995). In addition, further discussion of White-Parks's "trickster" argument can be found in *Tricksterism in Turn-of-the-Century American Literature : A Multicultural Perspective,* which she co-edits with Amy Ling.

3. The narrator in "Leaves from the Mental Portfolio of an Eurasian" does haltingly declare, "I-I am Chinese!" but it is in response to a scene in which the narrator's speaking out in defense of her mother's people would not be understood unless she declared herself as a member of that same group. See page 225 in *Mrs. Spring Fragrance and Other Writings.*

4. Despite her sympathy with working-class people, demonstrated in her articles and in some of the stories in *Mrs. Spring Fragrance,* Edith Eaton/Sui Sin Far probably had little patience for Carson's brand of working-class man. Labor parties in the Western United States often agitated against Chinese immigration and supported legislation that not only restricted entry into the United States but discriminated against the Chinese already in the States. See Ronald Takaki, pp. 79–132 on the Chinese in nineteenth-century America in *Strangers from a Different Shore* (New York: Penguin, 1989).

5. I am indebted to Ned Stuckey-French for his insight into Pan's connection to the mythological figure of Pan. It is typical of Sui Sin Far to choose for her character a name that is as Eastern as it is Western.

6. Mothers are curiously absent from every story that involves biracial or otherwise liminal characters. While the absence of the mother is part of the sentimental tradition in late nineteenth-century fiction, it is still worth remarking that this absence comes only in the "Eurasian" stories. Sui Sin Far's younger sister, the novelist Winnifred Eaton, also wrote tales of Eurasian women, and in these tales the mother is, again, absent. The Eatons' own Chinese mother, Grace Trepesis, or Trefusis, (1847–

1922) was an unusual woman. While but a toddler, she was kidnapped by circus performers and later adopted by an English missionary couple, who provided her with an English education (*Between* 26). She met the sisters' father, Englishman Edward Eaton (1838–1915) during one of his frequent business trips to China. Settling in first in England and then in Canada, Grace bore Edward a total of sixteen children, all but two of whom survived into adulthood. She seems to have been so beleaguered by child-rearing, according to Winnifred, who describes home as "a place full of howling, roaring, fighting, shouting children and babies" (Eaton, *Me* 113–14), that the girls may have had very little opportunity to relate to the mother or learn of her Chinese background. It is also possible that Edith Eaton felt extremely ambivalent about a woman who offered her little help in understanding her mixed-race identity in childhood. As a girl, when she heard herself called "Chinese" in a derogatory manner, young Sui Sin Far was hurt and confused. "I am a young child. I fail to make myself intelligible. My mother does not understand, when the nurse declares to her, 'Little Miss Sui is a story-teller,' my mother slaps me." In addition, as the eldest of her mother's brood, Eaton was obliged to help her parents and keep house throughout her developing years—a significant burden for a girl who was already in poor health.

REFERENCES

A. C. McClurg and Co. Publishers. Advertisement for *Mrs. Spring Fragrance. New York Times,* 7 July 1912: 405.

Ammons, Elizabeth. *Conflicting Stories: American Women Writers at the Turn into the Twentieth Century.* New York and Oxford: Oxford University Press, 1992.

Bhabha, Homi K. *The Location of Culture.* London and New York: Routledge, 1994.

Butler, Judith. "Passing, Queering: Nella Larsen's Psychoanalytic Challenge." *Bodies That Matter.* New York: Routledge,1993.

Clark, Helen. *The Lady of the Lily Feet and Other Tales of Chinatown.* Philadelphia: Griffith and Rowland Press, under the imprint of the American Baptist Publication Society, 1900.

Clifford, James. "Traveling Cultures." *Cultural Studies.* Eds. Lawrence Grossberg, Cary Nelson, and Paula Treichler. New York and London: Routledge, 1992.

Eaton, Edith/Sui Sin Far. Letter to Charles F. Lummis. 30 January 1897. Southwest Museum Library, Los Angeles.

___. *Me: A Book of Remembrance.* New York: Century, 1915.

___. Letter to Charles F. Lummis. 13 July 1911. Southwest Museum Library, Los Angeles.

___. "The Gamblers." *Fly Leaf.* February 1896: 14–18.

Fernald, Chester B. "The Pot of Frightful Doom." *Century* 52: 3 July 1896: 369–374.

Harte, Bret. "'The Heathen Chinee' or 'Plain Language from Truthful James.'" *Overland Monthly* 5 September 1870: 287–288.

Jones, Howard Mumford. *The Age of Energy: Varieties of American Experience 1865–1915.* New York: Viking, 1971.

Ling, Amy. *Between Worlds: Women Writers of Chinese Ancestry.* New York: Pergamon Press, 1990.

___ and Annette White-Parks, eds. *Mrs. Spring Fragrance and Other Writings.* Urbana and Chicago: University of Illinois Press, 1995.

Marchetti, Gina. *Romance and the Yellow Peril: Race, Sex, and Discursive Strategies in Hollywood Fiction.* Berkeley, Los Angeles, and London: University of California Press, 1993.

Osumi, Megumi Dick. "Asians and California's Anti-Miscegenation Laws." *Asian and Pacific American Experiences.* Asian/Pacific Learning Resources Center and General College. Minneapolis: University of Minnesota Press, 1982: 16–31.

Patterson, Martha. "The Wisdom of the New." Doctoral dissertation, University of Iowa. Program in English.

Spillers, Hortense J. "Notes on an Alternative Model—Neither/Nor." *The Difference Within: Feminism and Critical Theory.* Eds. Elizabeth Meese and Alice Parker. Amsterdam and Philadelphia: John Benjamins Publishing Company, 1989.

Takaki, Ronald. *Strangers from a Different Shore.* New York: Penguin, 1989.

White-Parks, Annette. "The Wisdom of the New by Sui Sin Far." *Legacy: A Journal of Nineteenth-Century Women's Literature* 6. Spring 1989: 34–39.

___. *Sui Sin Far: Writer on the Chinese-Anglo Borders of North America, 1865–1914.* Doctoral dissertation, Washington State University. Program in American Studies. May 1991.

Wu, William F. *The Yellow Peril: Chinese Americans in Fiction 1880–1940.* Hamden, CT: Archon Books, 1982.

Yin, Xiao-Huang. "Between the East and West: Sui Sin Far—the First Chinese-American Woman Writer." *Arizona Quarterly* 47:4. Winter 1991: 49–84.

11. Resistance and Reclamation: Hawaii "Pidgin English" and Autoethnography in the Short Stories of Darrell H. Y. Lum

Gail Y. Okawa

[Rosa] was the bully of the school and ruler of the second floor lavatory. Some haole [Caucasian] kid had told his father and the judge had sent him away to the Boys' Home for three months. When he got out he joined the union and was a laborer. He almost became a carpenter's apprentice when he and half the crew got laid off. That was when he started collecting bottles. For awhile the money from empties was all he had to live on until the welfare came.

After I come out of the Home, the judge tell me I join the Army or go work, 'cause I too old for go back ninth grade. The judge he say I can go night school with older people so I no beat up people no more and then he assign me one social worker, one haole lady, Miss Prussy, for check up on me. I tell Miss Prussy that I like live with Willy, that I gotta take care Willy. She say I no can, that mahus, that home-saxtuals like live with their own kind. I tell her, " . . . but that my bruddah." She tell I gotta get one healthy family relationship and atta-tude.

From "Primo Doesn't Take Back Bottles Anymore"

Goosebumps. Whether I read Rosa Kamahele's words silently or aloud to my students, I found that I reacted physically to the language in Darrell H. Y. Lum's short story "Primo Doesn't Take Back Bottles Anymore." In telling the story of this school bully, who was kicked out of ninth grade and who finally ended up as an unemployed laborer, Lum alternates sections of the narrator's edited American English with

Rosa's narrative cast in "pidgin English," the Island vernacular of
Hawaii.[1] For me, Rosa's language was emotionally charged, powerfully
evocative, hauntingly moving.

Like Lum, a third-generation Chinese American, I, a third-
generation Japanese American, had grown up in Honolulu, a mixed
ethnic community where many acknowledged their own ethnic roots
while crossing readily into the cultural territories of others.

*Every year on New Year's Eve, exactly at midnight, our
Chinese neighbors would chase away the evil spirits by
burning ten thousand firecrackers all at once. They hung them
from a ladder in long, flat strings and lit them together so that
they made a deafening sound going off—a veritable
bombardment of explosions —always jolting to me, no matter
how much I was expecting it. We pressed our hands over our
ears until the din subsided. After the noise would come the
smoke, billowing over into our yard and nostrils, taking over
the neighborhood. One year there was no breeze and it was so
thick that it hung over us all like an impenetrable fog. This
happened like clock-work every year until the City and County
of Honolulu passed an ordinance against burning firecrackers
like that.*

Though there were some discernably ethnic neighborhoods in Honolulu,
different cultures permeated one another like the smoke, weaving an
interdependency and reciprocity among us.

*For a while on our side of the block the Chinese and Japanese
American families lived alternately like the black and red
squares on a Chinese checkerboard: the Changs, then the
Sakamotos, then the Wongs, then the Okawas, then the
Chongs, then the Murakamis. During Chinese New Year or
the Moon Festival, a Chinese neighbor might share festive
food with us and we would reciprocate in the Japanese way
with avocados or mangoes or lychee that my father grew and
harvested from our backyard. In school we learned to sing
songs in Hawaiian from Mrs. Kahananui, a stately Hawaiian
woman who accompanied us on her ukulele. I grew up hearing
dialects of Japanese, Chinese, and Hawaiian, Hawaii Pidgin,
Hawaii Creole, and other varieties of English.*

The goosebumps came from seeing "pidgin English"—something familiar, intimate, yet an oppressed, almost taboo language at one time in Island culture and politics—in print. In the context of Hawaii's social, linguistic, and literary history, Lum's short stories—particularly those written partially or wholly in pidgin English—reflect in the author's choices of subject, language, and form a growing resistance to the dominant society's stereotypes of and colonial attitudes towards Hawaii's multiethnic people, culture, and language. Moreover, I believe these stories represent an autoethnographic reclamation of that culture and language by those who "own" it.

Hawaiian "Pidgin English" and U.S. Colonialism

We can more easily understand and appreciate the extent of that resistance and reclamation, knowing that Hawaii Pidgin English originally emerged as a *lingua franca* out of the need among non-English-speaking sugar and pineapple plantation workers—principally speakers of Chinese, Japanese, Korean, Filipino, Portuguese, and Spanish dialects—to communicate among themselves and with the English-speaking planter oligarchy. In this respect, Hawaii Pidgin English is like many pidgin languages that become creoles in the second generation of speakers, including plantation pidgin and creole forms in the American south that served as the foundation of Black English (see Smitherman, Dillard). The association of immigrant plantation labor with different forms of Hawaii Pidgin English led to the stigmatizing of both the speakers and their language varieties by those in positions of power. As Lawrence Fuchs points out in *Hawaii Pono*, his seminal social history of Hawaii,

> nowhere was the haole sense of privilege and power clearer to the others [non-haoles] than on the plantations. Every living and working arrangement on the sugar and, later, the pineapple plantations was calculated to make haoles as a class feel superior. In almost every instance, plantation officials encouraged segregation of haoles from nonhaoles. (61)

Given this practice and the added factor that this environment was generally the only one known to plantation workers, the English language of the haole became the language of the elite, of power, of oppression. And denigrated languages became equated with denigrated people.

In fact, Fuchs maintains that such racial and linguistic elitism among the white (*haole*) oligarchy became the basis for Hawaii's English Standard School system where linguistic segregation served as but a thin veneer for a racist school segregation for almost a quarter of a century. Linguist Charlene Sato asserts that "the major effect of this system was the further stratification of Hawaiian society along ethnic lines by means of discrimination along linguistic ones. By institutionalizing linguistic inequality in this way, the ES [English Standard] schools legitimized the negative stereotyping of HCE [Hawaii Creole English] speakers" (264).

The damage to generations of Island children and their self-esteem has been portrayed poignantly by contemporary writers like Lois-Ann Yamanaka, in *Wild Meat and the Bully Burgers*. Through Lovey, the narrator, Yamanaka writes:

> I don't tell anyone . . . how ashamed I am of pidgin English. Ashamed of my mother and father, the food we eat, chicken luau with can spinach and tripe stew . . .
>
> And nobody looks or talks like a *haole*. Or eats like a *haole*. Nobody says nothing the way Mr. Harvey tells us to practice talking in class.
>
> Sometimes I secretly wish to be *haole*. That my name could be Betty Smith or Annie Anderson or Debbie Cole, wife of Dennis Cole who lives at 2222 Maple Street with a white station wagon with wood panel on the side, a dog named Spot, a cat named Kitty, and I wear white gloves. . . .
>
> *Now let's all practice our standard English, Mr. Harvey says. You will all stand up and tell me your name, your grade, and what you would like to be when you grow up. Please use complete sentences. . . . All of you were terrible, and we will have to practice and practice our standard English until we are perfect little Americans.* (9–11, 12)

Such colonialist attitues toward nonstandard language varieties and their predominantly non-white speakers led to the subordination and disparagement of generations of Island people and cultures, immigrant and Native Hawaiian alike.[2] This included the dismissal of non-white Island writers and writing in favor of portrayals of native and immigrant people and their cultures by outsiders like James Michener and Jack London, who were somehow seen as more credible. In a 1990 speech to local educators in Hawaii, Lum asserted that "local literature has been systematically and deliberately suppressed over these 150 years [of public education]. Voices have been silenced and we have been duped into believing that we have no literature, that we have no literary history, that we have no literary traditions" (2).

The renaissance in Hawaiian culture and the multiethnic culture of Hawaii that emerged during the 1960s and 1970s as a part of the nation wide Civil Rights Movement has produced a corresponding pride in the vernacular among Islanders across ethnic lines. According to Romaine, the U.S. Department of Education's Office of Bilingual Education and Minority Languages Affairs now "recognizes Hawaii Creole English as a language qualifying for bilingual education funding" (42), and the State of Hawaii's Department of Education, after much debate, has recognized HCE "as a language in its own right" (42). At the same time, little has been done "to address seriously the crucial issues necessary for success of any special educational programs aimed at creole-speaking children" (Romaine 42), and visitors or new arrivals from the mainland, who fail to understand the regional solidarity represented by pidgin English, continue to label the dialect and, by extension its speakers, as "garbage," "a version of English useful only in slums and gang meetings" (Hall).

The Author and the Form

Lum developed as a writer in the face of such oppressive attitudes towards Island people, language, and culture. Like many children and grandchildren of immigrants, he internalized this colonialism. In a conversation with me in summer 1995[3], Lum explained that he took writing courses in college and found himself "writing awful stories"— in standard English with Midwest settings. Having no knowledge of the people in the Midwest, he focused on writing as a craft until a teacher called him on it: "This is shit," he said. "Have you ever been in Chicago?" To which Lum had to answer "no." "So don't write about it," the instructor chided, encouraging him to write from his own experience. Lum admitted that this was a hard lesson to learn: confronting "the fear of writing what you know" when "what you know" has historically been degraded (and you've internalized the degradation on some level) and of exposing your experience and language to possible public scrutiny.

But narrative was in his experience and family tradition. In our conversation, Lum related how integral storytelling and stories are to the cohesiveness of the family and community in Hawaii. He remembered the 1950s—at family gatherings, "sitting on the beer cooler in the garage, telling stories," sometimes greatly animated performances. Such images of "talking story" were and still are common to many growing up in the Islands. To him today, these experiences "challenge the notion that local people are inarticulate, lack language or a linguistic/literary tradition or practice." Instead, they affirm "a tradition of storytelling, of story-making, of retelling stories, of playing with language—a tremendous verbal fluency and expressiveness." Talking story for Lum is a cross-ethnic, multilingual discourse form associated specifically with local culture in Hawaii. In contemporary practice, it invokes an acknowledgment of place and historical context—the plantations, immigrants, their varied backgrounds and languages—and layers of linguistic and cultural mixing among immigrants and Native Hawaiians alike.[4]

Lum's use of the short story form emerges from this social context. When I asked what other factors—particularly cultural factors—influenced him in his choice of the short story, he playfully broke into pidgin, saying "no can write poetry and novels. . . ." Then seriously, "from my talk story experiences, I have enjoyed the idea of a good story . . . [and have] a sense of feeling fulfilled in a short story." This feeling is actualized by subscribing to conventions not of the traditional Western short story form, but of talk story experiences and discourse; by writing more and more through the personae of a first-person narrator (as opposed to a third-person, omniscient narrator, for example), he can thereby create a sense of the personal authority of the storyteller and the immediacy of the storytelling experience for the audience. Stories are vignettes, shorter pieces that come to some resolution or sometimes are not resolved at all.

First Try: "Primo" (1972) and Pidgin

Using pidgin English was another issue. "Primo Doesn't Take Back Bottles Anymore," the story of Rosa, once the bully of Central Intermediate School (Honolulu's equivalent to a tough inner-city school), was Lum's first attempt at using pidgin English in a short story in response to his teacher's challenge. "I was too chicken to use it in the entire piece," he told me. "Fear" made him conservative so that in this story he used the vernacular mainly in italicized passages, alternating the third-person narrator with Rosa's first-person recollections and reflections.

Although the storyline quite simply sketches Rosa's visits to the "Receiving Bottle Empties" section of Hawaii's only local Primo Brewery, now defunct, and his subsequent discovery that the company's new management has discontinued receiving empties, the pidgin sections reveal the heart of Rosa and are at the heart of the story and Lum's themes. By name, Rosario Kamahele is of Hawaiian or part-Hawaiian origins. His first statement, "We used to have kick haole ass day in school" (34), reflects the deep-seated historical antagonism between mainland haoles and locals, invaders and invaded, colonialist and colonized, also echoed in a later recollection: "I used to think all the haoles look at me funny so I kick their asses and they still look at me funny" (35). It is not just their disdain that Rosa feels but the arrogance of those in power that enrages him, that violates his sense of fairness:

> One time this one kid, little ass buggah with one big mouth, his father was one manager of someplace or something. He went come inside the bathroom, cocky and smart mouth, went push Willy so I went kick the shit out of him. (34)

Rosa's relationship with his brother reflects his unconditional acceptance of Willy as a *mahu* ("transvestite") as well as his desire to protect the weak and marginalized. In the passage opening this essay, he appeals to the social worker to let him continue to care for Willy only to find that bureaucratic policy does not support his views of kinship and loyalty. Lum uses Rosa's straightforward depiction of the social worker's response as an understated critique of a system that is based on ignorance or indifference to individual cultural values.

In his own way, Rosa recognizes that his brute strength was not and still is not enough for success in society: "Yeah, we used to think we was big stuff. Go smoke in front the teacher for see what she do" (34). His reflections on the "one time that I was scared for beef one haole" (36) depicts not only his fear of the bigger boy, but his despair over his real helplessness in the face not only of academic and economic power but of racial prejudice as well. His frustration causes him to momentarily violate a trust that bonds him to his brother:

> He was in the smart class. . . . He was one show off too, that guy. He had his driver's permit and drove one car to school everyday. . . . I thought of all the haoles in the whole world and I went punch the wall somemore. Willy, he come scared and say something about Mama and I say to him, "Fucking mahu!" and Willy come real quiet. That make me more piss off and I punch the wall somemore until my hand it start for bleed and I no can feel no sore but I still punch the wall and then the teacher come and tell me for stop and I no can stop and my hand it keep making one fist and keep going

and then I cry and Willy, he cry too, but Willy cry easy. I no
cry, I no supposed to cry, but I cry. (37)

It is this same despair that Rosa must contend with as an adult at
the close of the story: he learns that the receiving empties section is
shut down and Harry is gone, depriving him of his only source of
income and a personal relationship where, as Stephen Sumida describes,
reciprocity is the local watchword. Lum creates increased pathos by
using pidgin English in the concluding paragraphs of the story proper.
As Rosa watches the "Receiving Bottle Empties" sign being painted
over as though it never existed, he asks helplessly, "Why you paint
over the sign, why you no want my bottles, why you do that, I bring
something for Harry today, and you do that, where Harry my fren',
Harry my fren' he no do that . . . " (38). The "you" is no one in
particular but a corporate structure which has historically controlled the
economy of the Islands. Using an abandoned can of paint, Rosa paints
"F-O-C-K" in silent, unheard protest, his word blending into the newly
painted wall. Lum's use of the nonstandard pidgin dialect even here in
this spelling evokes the past relationships of oppression as well as
present feelings of solidarity and empathy between character and reader.

In this writing, Lum follows in the footsteps of writers like Philip
Ige and Milton Murayama, who had used pidgin in dialogue but were
given relatively scant attention in a literary culture dominated by
Anglocentric values (see Lum, Sumida) and a history of linguistic
chauvinism that yielded the English Standard School system discussed
earlier. Prior to the seventies, pidgin English had primarily served as a
spoken dialect that had been adapted more readily to the theater and
performance than to prose. As Maxine Hong Kingston points out in her
foreword to *Talk Story: An Anthology of Hawaii's Local Writers*, the
stage was "an excellent solution . . . to the problem of how to use
pidgin, which must be spoken for full beauty and power" (6). But
Kingston notes the difficulties of recording the language in writing:
"We are still experimenting with how to render pidgin—the language
used at home, the language of childhood and the subconscious, the
language used in emotion—into writing, figuring out its spellings and
phonics" (6). "Primo" finally emerged after numerous revisions.[5]

Second Try: "Da Beer Can Hat" (1980)

Years later, in a college playwriting class that Lum was taking, a
classmate questioned writing in pidgin English by saying, "It's okay,
but it can never express the depth and breadth of human emotion."
Highly irritated by this condescending skepticism, Lum was motivated

to write completely in pidgin despite any past fears that may have inhibited him. "He really pissed me off!" he said, still feeling the insult, still remembering the challenge (Personal Interview).

"Da Beer Can Hat," published in the collection titled *Sun*, was the first story that Lum wrote completely in the vernacular. In fact, Sumida, in his extensive study of Hawaii's literary traditions, refers to this story as "what may very well be the first narrative, beyond a mere sketch and dialogue, delivered entirely in the vernacular as it is actually spoken" (102). It was an unnerving experience, Lum admitted to me, requiring many, many rewritings: he worried not only about the mechanics of representing pidgin, but its understandability to pidgin-speaking and nonpidgin-speaking audiences. For all of this uncertainty, Sumida explicates Lum's accomplishment:

> . . . Lum crafted his pidgin narrative without having to translate terms for the benefit of audiences initially unfamiliar with the lingo or the current slang. The unbroken pidgin narration implies that the language can be taken [on] its own terms—that is, Lum's story assumes that the vernacular is understandable, not gibberish. . . . Until recently it has been rare that pidgin was used with such respect and integrity in Hawaii's writing, outside of linguistic studies. (102)

In his book *And the View from the Shore: Literary Traditions of Hawaii,* Sumida pursues the idea of the pastoral and heroic forms being central to the development of Hawaii's literature in his analysis of the story. In an alternative reading of "Da Beer Can Hat," I suggest an exploration of Lum's themes in terms of "the depth and breadth of human emotion" that the author explores through the local language, characters, and setting.

The narrator is Junior, a newspaper boy, who sells his papers on the city streets after school. He begins by introducing his friend Bobo in talk story fashion with the winsome naiveté of a Huckleberry Finn:

> You know, Bobo stay lolo in da head. Mental, you know. But he good fun sell newspaper and he smart fo' go by da cars when get stop light and sell to ladies, old ladies . . . and to da mokes who tell stink kine stuff about he belong in Kaneohe Hospital la' dat but in da end dey buy newspaypah and tip too! . . . Bobo he smart fo' time 'em good, him. He take long time get change fo' quartah at red light, bumbye da light change green and da guy tell, "Ay, ass okay, keep 'em," and

step da gas. Bobo smile big and tell, "Tanks, eh." He time 'em
real good. (10)

In these opening lines, Junior reflects an acceptance of those on the
margins like Bobo, together with a respect for Bobo's prowess at his
job—his natural instinct for survival.
The relationship between the two boys unfolds as Junior explains,
"I go after school sell papers wit' Bobo," but admits that he dawdles
"little while" at school "'cuz Bobo always stay dere and watch my
papers fo' me" (10). As in the less personal relationship between Rosa
and Harry in "Primo," this friendship is based on reciprocity between
the two boys: Bobo watches out for Junior's newspapers; Junior
watches out for Bobo, especially in relation to others:

> So me and Bobo, we stay together pretty good. Plenny
> guys tell, why I stay wit' Bobo. Dey tell he talk crooked, his
> mouth funny kine and sometimes drool lil' bit. I tell, "Watch
> out bra—he know kung fu and make like da wrestlah, da
> Missing Link, 'Whoaaa . . . yeah!'" (11)

Through his naive and forthright narrator, Lum explores compassion
and a real sense of decency developing in Junior:

> But I went show him how fo' wipe his mout' before he sell
> newspaper to da custamah. I went buy him hanka-chief too I
> wanted da kine wit' initials on top, "B.B." for Bobo. But I
> couldn't find, so I went buy one with "W" I tink, at sidewalk
> sale. Make 'em feel good, boy—I feel good, too, though. He
> learn good, wipe his mouth first before he go to da customer.
> He no talk too good. Everytime guys tell, "Hah? What you
> talking, stupid." He only can try his best but no come out
> clear. . . . (11)

Junior works out his empathy and respect for this other human
being with the aid of his parents, who help him to make sense of
Bobo's complicated life as an abused child and help him to act on his
feelings. Observing early in the narrative that Bobo's bike "stay all
junky" (p. 10), he comments, "was shetty" in reference to the bike and,
by extension, Bobo's less fortunate situation. But later Junior's sense
of moral indignation is prompted by learning why Bobo has a shaved or
"bolo-head":

> My fahdah said dat his [Bobo's] fahdah no like him already and
> like throw him out of da house but da social worker say no

can. Bobo no tell nothing about his fahdah but my fahdah tell, "Ass why he bolo-head everytime. Da fahdah no like when he bring home little bit money, he tink Bobo go spend 'em or lose 'em on da way home so he give Bobo lickins and shave his head." (11)

It is not clear if Bobo is "mental" or "lolo" (10) because of early abuse or abused because he is retarded; the ambiguity only intensifies the severity of the underlying struggle in the story and the pathos felt by the sensitive reader. Respecting Bobo's silence, however, Junior responds to this information by asking his mother to make a beer can hat for his friend, flattened beer cans crocheted together with yellow and black yarn for the McKinley Tigers, Bobo's favorite team. The boy's recognition of injustice and oppression transforms into an act of compassion and inclusion made more meaningful by his thoughtfully wrapping the hat as "one real present": "Mama, I can make 'em like one real present? No stay Christmas or befday, but can make 'em like one real present please?" (12). For Junior (and Lum), the beer can hat represents praxis[6]; social theory means nothing without action in Hawaii. "Talk" and "mouth," associated by many locals with haole culture, is not enough. Junior's mother affirms this when she not only helps him make the hat but hugs him and tells Junior "I good boy and how she proud I tink of Bobo" (12). Even though he tells her "nah" he "feel[s] good"—both responses being typical of the understatement in local Island culture. Bobo's reaction to the gift is equivalent to the caring of the giver:

Bobo was so happy when he went open da box. Was little bit big but he put 'em on and went by one car and tell, "Pape?" and da guy tell, "No tanks," and Bobo stay by da car and use da mirror on da side fo' make da hat good on his head, you know, so get one beer can label straight in da front.
"Tanks, eh. Tell you mama tanks eh. You sure fo' me? Tanks eh." Ass all he say over and over. And everytime when get green light, he take 'em off and look at 'em . . . make sure no mo' dirt on top. Me, I feel so good I miss couple customers at da red light. (12)

A significant conflict in the story arises because Bobo is tormented and bullied by "mokes" (local thugs) in a "shaka van"—a kind of elaboration on Willy's being pushed around by a haole kid in the earlier "Primo." But Junior is not Rosa and cannot defend his friend, partly because of his size, partly because of his father's rules about going into the street. He feels his helplessness. After snatching Bobo's hat, now his prized possession, and passing it among themselves to taunt him, one of his tormentors throws the hat into the street as the van speeds off. Victimization by ignorant attitudes rather than colonialism operates here in this story. On impulse, Bobo starts into the traffic to retrieve his hat until he is held back by his friend. Again protective feelings produce action but Junior does not anticipate how his actions might be misunderstood:

> . . . I went hold him back and den one car went run 'em [the hat] over and Bobo he turn and look at me jes' like was on purpose dat I went hold him back for see his hat smash. Bobo tell me fucka, too. I get piss off and I call him dat back but little while more I come sorry I call him dat cause Bobo no can understand dat good. (13)

We have already seen meanness in the behavior of the men in the van, but here Lum shows it emerging out of Junior's frustration with Bobo's silence, self-punishment, and misunderstanding of his intentions:

> Bobo no tell me nothing after dat. He go by da wall and scrunch up real small into one ball, you know, and only cry. He cry so hard he begin to hit his head on da wall. . . . But I get mad 'cause jes' like my fault but not my fault, you know, and I know dat but I get mad at him anyway.
> "Shaddup already," I tell him, but he no hear nutting. "Shaddup, I tell you! You no mo ear? You lo-lo? Wassamatta wit' you? Mo' bettah send you Linekona School, da school fo' da mental guys!" And more he cry and more I get mad. (13)

Like Rosa who calls his brother a "mahu" at the height of his anger and frustration, Junior reflects the extent of his aggravation, crossing a line of trust by referring to Bobo's disability. The reality of the job stops further escalation of both boys' anger as Mr. Kim, a familiar customer, intervenes and gives Junior a way to make peace with Bobo so that they can "stay fren's again" (14).

The boys continue to sell papers and have fun; Bobo continues to wear the symbolic hat. But Lum emphasizes the theme of caring and reciprocity as essential values in Island culture, especially in light of harsh social conditions, when Junior reflects on Bobo's future in the closing lines of this segment:

Sometimes I tink though, what going happen to Bobo. He been selling paypahs long time . . . before me and still going sell bumbye even after I quit. . . . I hope Bobo be all right. He gotta have somebody take care him. Maybe mama make him one 'nudda beer can hat. . . . (14)

In Part II of the story, Junior and his father take Bobo to a carnival in just such an act of caring, the adult making the tough decision for inclusion despite probable harsh consequences:

. . . we went pick up Bobo, he was waiting outside his house. He said he no like go carnaval, dat he raddah go sell newspaypah at da baseball game. "My faddah gimme da busfare. . . . " Bobo said dat and den he just stand by da car scraping da dirt with his rubber shoes. My fahdah look at Bobo den at da apartment building where his house stay. He look long time den he breathe long and sad and tell, "C'mon Bobo. You come carnaval wit' us. You help Junior wash and polish my car bumbye and I treat you to carnaval." (16)

At the fair, Junior at one point recognizes the bullies from the van at one of the games and tries again to protect Bobo from them. But to no avail. Neither Junior nor we as readers know whether Bobo himself recognizes them, but through persistence and guile, he wins the most challenging of games against one of the "mokes" and chooses a magnificent "happy tigah" (19) as his prize. It is a triumph of his ingenuity and sweet revenge for their tormenting him in the earlier story. Returning to Bobo's "home," Junior, his father, the adult reader and, most of all, Bobo know what he is likely to encounter when he confronts his father. However, with the threat of further abuse still looming, Bobo seals his relationship with Junior and his family by giving the prized tiger to Junior "fo' you mama."

Going home, Bobo was talking anykine. Real fast. . . . Only when we came by his house, he went stop. My fahdah came quiet too and went ask him, "You like me talk to your fahdah and explain dat I took you carnaval?" Bobo only went shake his head. He went get out of da car and tell, "Tanks," to my fahdah and den he went push da tiger back inside da car window.
"Fo' you mama. I win 'em fo' you mama. You give to her?"

"You sure, Bobo?" I went tell him. But he jes' keep telling, "Fo' you mama."
. . . I went say "tanks" to Bobo. Bobo was waving to us from da sidewalk, smiling up. We was smiling up too. (19)

Bobo makes his own choices and, though victimized, is no victim. The pathos is strongest at this point as Lum captures the poignancy of Bobo's life at home in language that ironically evokes for others (his readers) the feeling of home.

Maturity and "The Moiliili Bag Man" (1990)

Ten years later, stories like "The Moiliili Bag Man" in the collection titled *Pass On, No Pass Back* reflect Lum's continued commitment to portraying and documenting the characters of the local Island community with compassion and authenticity. They also reflect his increased comfort with the medium of written pidgin English as he continues to struggle with its voices. In "The Moiliili Bag Man," Lum gives us a child's view of a homeless man frequently spotted around the island of Oahu, both in the city of Honolulu and outside of it at local surfing areas. Like Junior in "Da Beer Can Hat," this narrator learns about issues of social responsibility as he begins to understand the meaning of human worth, personal relationships and feelings, his own limitations, and potential to be himself and a member of a community.[7] As Junior develops empathy for Bobo, an insider in his world, the observer of the Bag Man learns to respect and empathize with an outsider who touches his life only momentarily: "I nevah see him aftah dat time at Ala Moana park. And everyplace I go, I stay looking, looking, looking. But if I was to see him, I would make one bird fo him and den hold my hand down wit da shaka sign and make, 'Tanks, eh'" (76–77).

Pidgin English and Autoethnography

In 1971, a year before "Primo" was first published, sociolinguist Dell Hymes decried prejudicial attitudes among scholars and lay people alike toward pidgin and creole languages, how these language varieties—and by extension their speakers—had been considered "degenerations" rather than "creative adaptations" (3). These languages for Hymes at once epitomize the complex result of social processes and the extreme complexity of the relationship, the very "interdependence of language and society" (5). In Hawaii, linguists and writers have been working to rectify the distortions of linguistic chauvinism, to reclaim the losses created by it, to document instead the historical and social processes giving rise to these language varieties, to represent the creative expressiveness of their speakers.

Upholding this view during his more than twenty-year career as a writer, Lum has had to make sociolinguistic as well as rhetorical and aesthetic decisions. His choice of form, subject, and language reflects a political as well as a literary act. In choosing to redefine his short story form in keeping with the expectations of talk story tellers and listeners, he has practiced what Mary Louise Pratt terms "transculturation," a liberatory and creative process "whereby members of subordinated or marginal groups select and invent from materials transmitted by a dominant . . . culture" (36). Although he learned about the traditional Western short story form in an academic context, Lum has hesitantly but purposefully reinvented this genre in terms of oral talk story discourse where intensity may be based on feeling rather than action, and resolution may be ambiguous.

In subject, the author has focused on adults of various ages, ethnic, social, and economic backgrounds throughout his work, but he has used his stories in pidgin English to explore life especially through the views and voices of children or the adult recalling childhood. While this is true, these are not simply "childhood idylls" as Sumida claims (98). The fun and laughter of these stories are often bittersweet. The idealized view of childhood sets up the expectation of happy, carefree times, but these children do not live happy, carefree lives any more than do many children of this world. Lum's realism and political message are here in the children—the children who see more than adults often care to, who *feel* injustice, struggle, and pain before they even know how to name them. Junior remarks, "Bobo never tell nothing jes' like no sore, but must've been, yeah?" (11). His child's questions—understated analysis—cut to the quick of social and psychological oppression. Rather than giving us an "underview" of life (Sumida 104), these examples from Lum's work show that the child's view is a straight-on view, uncluttered by assumptions that blind adults from what is there. Herein lies Lum's meaning.

In an article titled "Coming of Age? The Literature of Contemporary Hawaii," Sheldon Hershinow asserts that "the new writers of Hawaii" share "a determined insistence on independence and individuality. There is a strong feeling that they must fight off the Mainland classical English education in order to find themselves as Hawaii writers" (9). However, precisely because of the linguistic chauvinism described by Hymes above and the linguistic and social conditions unique to Hawaii elucidated earlier, I would argue that Lum's

choice to use pidgin English be characterized as resistance to a history
of colonialism and continued elitism rather than the "independence"
referred to by Hershinow (9); and as an act of reclamation on behalf of
the collective, rather than an assertion of "individuality" (9). Lum's act
of choosing is not the adolescent one that Hershinow implies.

In the mid-1960s, Franz Fanon in *Toward the African Revolution*
described in incisive detail the processes by which the colonized begin
to free themselves (physically and psychologically) from the colonizer
by rediscovering and reclaiming the culture they have lost. In this
regard, bell hooks in *Talking Back*, refers to "mak[ing] the
revolutionary history" (3). Thus, as I have written elsewhere,

> In multicultural, heterogeneous societies like the U. S., in
> which some cultural groups like Latinos, African Americans,
> Asian Americans, and American Indians are subordinated
> (Ogbu, 1988) to those in power, members of those groups
> must not only consciously construct their realities and
> identities, but also maintain them in their complexity and
> uniqueness lest they be subsumed into and by the dominant
> society and its stereotypes. Through their own writings and/or
> those who would write for them within their own group
> (Mora, 1993), the people of minority cultures must create a
> body of knowledge about their individual and collective Self,
> their history, and their culture—in relation to themselves and
> to the dominant society around them. (Okawa, *Expanding
> Perspectives* 46)

This self-constructive process is an example of what Pratt refers to
as *autoethnography*, where "people undertake to describe themselves in
ways that engage with representations others have made of them" (35),
self-constructed representations by the objects of domination. Pratt tells
us that such works are often addressed to both the "dominant and
dominating world" (Hogan 237) and "the speaker's own community"
(Pratt 35).

Like "talking story," the appeal of pidgin English reaches beyond
any one ethnic group to the multiethnic community. Ethnicity blurs.
As through the smoke of ten thousand firecrackers—in some ways, we
remain distinctive and distinguishable, in other ways not. With the
coming of the second generation of immigrant family speakers, Hawaii
Pidgin English went through the process of creolization, a process that
Derek Bickerton says was not complete until the "erasure of group
differences in that generation was complete" (15), so that "even other
locally-born persons cannot determine the ethnic background of an HCE

[Hawaii Creole English] speaker by his speech alone" (15). Pidgin English thus had a kind of ethnic homogenizing effect among creole speakers. Reflecting a "pidgin culture" as a "hybrid culture" (Hershinow 9), it contains identity and maintains solidarity. Pidgin English is not simply a language of childhood, something that we grow out of as we "evolve," but a language that we continue to use and, in some cases, return to in varying degrees and circumstances to give us our identity and provide a sense of continuity with other speakers and our culture. Lum's very act of writing in pidgin English becomes "autoethnographic" in resistance to what Eric Chock referred to as the "numbing" of local sensibility and pride in Hawaii (8); the stories record and represent the experience of generations, in exploring "the depth and breadth of human emotion" through the language of his narrators. Experimenting first with the more artificial form of alternating sections of Rosa's pidgin English with the narrator's mainstream edited American English, then writing stories totally in pidgin English, Lum comes into his own as reclaimer. Perhaps he is bolder linguistically than Gloria Anzaldúa, who as a Chicana "no longer feel[s] that we need to beg entrance, that we need always to make the first overture," but who "ask[s] to be met halfway" (n.p.).

Lum has been joined in this project of cultural resistance and reclamation through short story by another generation of Island writers, including Lois-Ann Yamanaka, Gary Pak, and Rodney Morales. David K. Choo points out that for Lum and others "local literature is about feeling at home in your skin and comfortable with sharing your experiences even though they are not analogous with those of people on the Mainland" (8). The measure is in the integrity of the resistance and the depth of reclamation.[8] What is important to Lum is "seeing local people recognize themselves in literature, finding that this enhances their feelings of identity and self-esteem—students, teachers, and others—the responses of people who count" to him. Lum's stories and characters stand for me not in relation to Western models but rather as collective community reflections in a balance between talk and writing—documents of Island values and voices. Through them, those of us who are of the Islands can maintain our language and culture; those who are outside of it can gain insight into the heart and spirit of a people whose unique cultural and linguistic blending is expressed in pidgin English.

NOTES

1. "Pidgin English" is the local generic term in Hawaii for what is linguistically identified as Hawaii Creole English (HCE), the language variety spoken natively by the offspring of immigrant plantation laborers and other Island people. The term also applies to the local *lingua franca*, termed Hawaii Pidgin English (HPE) by linguists, which evolved as the immigrants themselves, native speakers of various dialects of Chinese, Japanese, Portuguese, Filipino, Spanish, etc., sought to communicate among themselves and with the white English-speaking oligarchy. In contemporary Hawaii, pidgin is spoken cross-ethnically and can be considered a regional dialect. See Reinecke, Carr, Sato, Day, Bickerton.

2. See Lum in Annette White-Parks, ed. *A Gathering of Voices on the Asian American Experience.*

3. All quotations for which citations are unspecified are derived from personal conversations with the author in Honolulu, Hawaii in July of 1995.

4. According to Sumida (1991), the "pidgin expression, 'talk story' characterizes a widespread and sociable form of oral, animated exchange. 'Shooting the breeze' or 'chewing the fat' are the term's kin, except, of course, for the important fact that 'talk story' is Hawaii's own, this verbal style being neither quaint nor 'waste time.' . . . By chance, our group's choice of the name Talk Story, Inc., preceded by one day the 1976 release of Kingston's *The Woman Warrior*, which none of us had yet read. We soon learned that Kingston, too, had chosen to use in her book the pidgin term she heard in Hawai'i, 'talk story,' thus naming a verbal style and form which the narrator learns from her Cantonese immigrant mother" (240).

5. This anthology was published in conjunction with the first Talk Story conference, a gathering of local Island and mainland writers primarily of Asian and Pacific Islander backgrounds.

6. Paolo Friere refers to praxis as the way of truly human beings. In his view, praxis consists of both reflection and action, theory and practice, is transformative, and thus revolutionary (see pp 75ff and 119ff). In Hawaii, local culture upholds a fusion of talk and action in a similar way.

7. Sylvia Watanabe discusses Lum's "idea of community" in this and other stories in the collection in terms of an "ethic of inclusiveness"—"as the dialectic between the self and the other, the insider and the outsider, the center and the margin" (166).

8. What some might characterize as a post-colonial critique of writing by Lum and others associated with Bamboo Ridge Press has led recently to heated controversy in some academic and writers' circles. Aspects of the controversy are related to new definitions of "local" *vis a vis* a growing Native Hawaiian sovereignty movement that has altered historical

oppositional relationships like Local vs. Haole and shifted to dichotomies like Hawaiians vs. Others (non-Hawaiians). As Chock, a co-editor with Lum of Bamboo Ridge Press, observes, "what was for many years seen as a common Local culture based on the predominant ethnic mixtures of the post-plantation period is now being dismantled, or perhaps relabeled and reassigned . . . " (6). An article in a local newspaper asks readers to submit their thoughts on what it means to be "local"; lists of humorous ethnic identifiers appear on email. Whatever the subsequent course of events, Lum's response to the social and historical conditions of his generation stands as a foundation of self-discovery and recovery, of cultural identification and celebration for many if not most of Hawaii's people. I heard this in the laughter of a roomful of people on the University of Hawaii campus in July 1996—from young college students to my eighty-year-old mother—all enjoying the familiarity and intimacy of experience in stories being read by Lum in pidgin English.

REFERENCES

Anzaldúa, Gloria. *Borderlands/ La Frontera: The New Mestiza.* San Francisco: Aunt Lute Book Co., 1987.

Bickerton, Derek. *Roots of Language.* Ann Arbor: Karoma Publishers, Inc., 1981.

Carr, Elizabeth. *Da Kine Talk: From Pidgin to Standard English in Hawaii.* Honolulu: The University Press of Hawaii, 1972.

Chock, Eric. Quoted in D. K. Choo.

Choo, David. "A Sense of Place." *Honolulu Weekly.* March 1980, 6–8.

Day, Richard. "The Development of Linguistic Attitudes and Preferences." *TESOL Quarterly* (1980) 14: 27–37.

___. "The Ultimate Inequality: Linguistic Genocide." *Language of Inequality.* Eds. N. Wolfson and J. Manes. New York: Mouton Publishers, 1985. 163–181.

Dillard, J. L. *Black English: Its History and Usage in the United States.* New York: Random House, 1972.

Fanon, Franz. *Toward the African Revolution: Political Essays.* New York: Grove, 1988.

Freire, Paolo. *Pedagogy of the Oppressed.* New York: Continuum, 1970.

Fuchs, Lawrence. *Hawaii Pono: A Social History.* New York: Harcourt, Brace and World, Inc., 1961.

Hall, John. Letter to Editor. *Honolulu Advertiser.* October 4, 1994.

Hershinow, Sheldon. "Coming of Age? The Literature of Contemporary Hawaii." *Bamboo Ridge: The Hawaii Writers Quarterly* (1981) 13: 5–10.

Hogan, Linda. "The Two Lives." In *I Tell You Now.* Eds. B. Swann and A. Krupat. Lincoln: University of Nebraska Press, 1987.

hooks, bell. *Talking Back: Thinking Feminist, Thinking Black.* Boston: South End Press, 1989.

Hymes, Dell. Preface. *Pidginization and Creolization of Languages.* Ed. D. Hymes. New York: Cambridge University Press, 1971.

Ige, Philip K. "The Forgotten Flea Powder." *Paradise of the Pacific* (1946) 58: 24, 25.

Kingston, Maxine Hong. Foreword. *Talk Story: An Anthology of Hawaii's Local Writers.* Ed. Eric Chock et al. Honolulu: Petronium Press/ Talk Story, Inc., 1978.

Lum, Darrell. "Primo Doesn't Take Back Bottles Anymore." *Talk Story: An Anthology of Hawaii's Local Writers.* Ed. Eric Chock, et al. Honolulu: Petronium Press/Talk Story, Inc. 1978.

___. "Da Beer Can Hat." *Sun: Short Stories and Drama by Darrell H. Y. Lum.* Honolulu: Bamboo Ridge Press, 1980.

___. "The Moiliili Bag Man." *Pass On, No Pass Back.* Honolulu: Bamboo Ridge Press, 1980.

Murayama, Milton. "I'll Crack Your Head *Kotsun.*" *Arizona Quarterly* (1959) 15: 137–49.

___. *All I Asking for Is My Body.* San Francisco: Supa Press, 1975.

Okawa, Gail. *Expanding Perspectives of Teacher Knowledge: A Descriptive Study* (unpublished).

___. "Cross Talk: Talking Cross-Difference." In *Writing in Multicultural Settings.* Eds. C.J. Severino and J.C. Guerra and J.E. Butler. New York: Modern Language Association (forthcoming).

Pratt, Mary Louise. "Arts of the Contact Zone." *Profession 91: Modern Language Association* (1991): 33–40.

Reinecke, John. *Language and Dialect in Hawaii: A Sociolinguistic History to 1935.* Honolulu: University of Hawaii Press, 1969.

Romaine, Suzanne. "Hawaii Creole English as a Literary Language" (unpublished).

Smitherman, Geneva. *Talkin' and Testifyin': The Language of Black America.* Detroit: Wayne State University Press, 1977.

Sato, Charlene. "Linguistic Inequality in Hawaii: The Post-Creole Dilemma." *Language of Inequality: The Post-Creole Dilemma.* Eds. N. Wolfson and J. Manes. New York: Mouton Publishers, 1985. 255–272.

Sumida, Stephen. *And the View from the Shore: Literary Traditions of Hawaii.* Seattle: University of Washington Press, 1991.

Watanabe, Sylvia. Review. *Mid-Atlantic Review* 14 (1993): 166–168.

White-Park, Annette. *A Gathering of Voices on the Asian American Experience.* Fort Atkinson: Highsmith Press, 1994.

Yamanaka, Lois-Ann. *Wild Meat and the Bully Burgers.* New York: Farrar, Straus, and Giroux, 1996.

12. Conflict over Privacy in Indo-American Short Fiction

Laurie Leach

The corpus of Indo-American writing, like the Indo-American ethnic community itself, is relatively new and small compared to other American ethnic groups and literatures. Changes in immigration laws taking effect after 1965 brought a surge in professional immigrants from the Indian subcontinent (Agarwal; Suran) including writers of and subjects for Indo-American literature, which as yet remains focused on the experiences of the first generation. Bharati Mukherjee, one of the few Indo-American writers to be included in recent surveys and bibliographies of Asian American literature, remarked in 1986 in the introduction to a special issue of *The Literary Review* devoted to the writings of "the literary commonwealth of Indian-origin authors" that "it will take another ten years for Indo-American writers to start making their mark" ("Writers" 410). A few years later, Craig Tapping noted that Indo-American literature was mostly to be found in special issues of journals, or in scattered magazines and literary reviews, with the writers otherwise unpublished (286). That situation is changing as we see signs of what Mukherjee foretold: Indo-American writers distinguishing themselves, particularly in the genre of the short story.

Mukherjee's first collection of short fiction, *Darkness* (1985), marked her emergence as an American writer after living and writing for many years in Canada and was followed in 1988 by the award-winning *"The Middleman" and Other Stories.* In an interview with Alison Carb, Mukherjee discusses shifting her focus from novels to short stories after moving to the United States, observing that writing short stories poses a particular challenge for novelists in that the "form requires us to express our thoughts concisely and not waste a single sentence or detail" (649). The details, in turn, become charged with symbolic significance, enabling the story to take a glimpse of everyday life for its theme. The author of a short story is free to linger over, indeed to focus exclusively on, those seemingly insignificant incidents in our lives and relationships that reveal the hidden tensions in even our most intimate bonds: husband and wife, parent and child. Furthermore, the short story writer need not resolve those tensions and move on like the novelist but can leave the characters at a moment of crisis or insight without specifying how it will be played out. In "Doors," "Grace," and "Paths upon Water," Chitra Divakaruni, Robbie Clipper Sethi, and Tahira Naqvi use these aspects of the genre to good effect as they skillfully explore the tensions created in Indo-American families by the differing concepts of privacy in Indian and American cultures.[1]

Chitra Banerjee Divakaruni was born in India in 1956 and now lives in California, where she teaches creative writing at Foothill College. She is the author of two volumes of poetry as well as a collection of short stories, *Arranged Marriage,* which was published in July 1995. Robbie Clipper Sethi was born in New Jersey in 1951 and now teaches at Rider University. Of European ancestry, she married "into a large, diasporic Sikh Punjabi family.[2] She has regularly published short fiction, poetry, and book reviews since 1987, and a collection of her stories, *The Bride Wore Red*, was published in June 1996. She is currently working on a novel. Tahira Naqvi, born in Pakistan, immigrated in 1971 and now lives in Connecticut. Her stories have been anthologized in various collections of multi-cultural American writing. She is also a translator of Urdu fiction and has published several anthologies of her translations, most recently *Attar of Roses: Stories from Pakistan* in 1996.

Both "Doors" and "Grace" are about how an extended visit from his relatives or friends threatens the marriage of a recent immigrant from India and his American wife. In the first case the wife is herself from India but has lived in the United States since she was twelve, while in the second she is a white woman. In "Paths upon Water," the conflict is between a Pakistani woman and her son who has settled in America upon completion of his degree. Though their conflict is far less acrimonious—indeed it is never openly expressed and may even go unnoticed by the son, it is nevertheless overwhelming to the woman because it threatens her with emotional estrangement from the most important person in her life.[3]

In each story the author foreshadows the conflict that unsettles the relationship by a small but symbolic difference of opinion or misunderstanding that reveals the differing attitudes or values of the characters. In "Doors," Asha guards her privacy by closing doors behind her whenever possible, while Deepak likes to leave them open. In "Grace," on a visit to India to announce their marriage, Grace complains that Inder's family never leaves her alone with him, and he casually dismisses her concern by pointing out that they will be alone in America for the rest of their lives. Finally, in "Paths upon Water," the son assumes his mother will be delighted to visit the ocean for the first time in her life, and she hides the fact that the prospect rather frightens her and that she would rather stay in his apartment. Furthermore, each story concludes with a symbolic gesture that hints at the resolution of the conflict yet does not finally resolve it. Several possible futures remain for these characters, and it is clear that the fundamental differences between American and Indian concepts of privacy are likely to continue to cause tensions even if the most favorable resolution is reached.

Chitra Divakaruni's "Doors" is the story of newlyweds, Deepak and Asha, who are viewed by their friends as a "well-adjusted couple," compatible in everything but "the matter of doors. Deepak liked to leave them open and Asha liked them closed" (147). While Asha closes the study door when she works on her dissertation, the gate when she weeds the garden, and even locks the bedroom door at night, Deepak leaves even the bathroom door open when he showers. Deepak attributes this difference to her American upbringing; she immigrated with her parents at the age of twelve while Deepak is "straight out of India" (147). Yet he feels somewhat troubled by it as it seems to indicate a lack of openness or warmth in Asha. Deepak's family was large and "had never observed boundaries. They had constantly spilled into each other's rooms, doors always left open for a chance remark or joke" (148). He is puzzled by Asha's tendency to close herself away.

Asha tries to reassure him: "It's not like I'm shutting you out or anything. I've just always done it this way" (148). Asha, whose mother had warned her that she did not know what Indian men "expect from their women," may fear losing her individuality in her role as Deepak's wife. Closing the doors is her way of preserving her independence, creating time for herself, and asserting control over things that are important to her. Because Deepak good naturedly stops pressing the issue, no strain develops in the relationship until Deepak's childhood friend Raj comes to visit.

Raj announces his impending arrival by aerogram just one day before his plane is due. Deepak is excited, seeing nothing untoward in Raj's assumption that he is welcome to come when he likes and stay as long as he wants, while Asha is "distraught" over the preparations required for this unexpected houseguest, preparations that will take time away from completing "the second chapter of the dissertation, which wasn't going well" (148). Nevertheless, she tidies the guest room, and prepares a special dinner only to be horrified by Raj's insistence that he will sleep on the dining room floor:

> I'm not a guest Bhavi [sister-in-law]! I'm going to be with you for quite a while. You'd better save the guest bedroom for real guests. About six square feet of space—right here between the dining table and the sofa—is all I need. (149)

As Deepak helps Raj make himself comfortable in the dining room, Asha retreats to her bedroom without saying goodnight. She is upset not only at the prospect of "trying to enjoy her quiet morning tea with him sprawled on the floor nearby" but at Raj's casual remark that his visit would be an extended one (149–50). She confronts Deepak when he comes to bed, and he confirms that his friend is planning to live with them for a year and a half while he completes a master's degree. Asha is furious that Deepak has not consulted her, but Deepak responds that if she is not willing for Raj to live with them indefinitely, she should wake him immediately and tell him he must go. To Deepak, the one act of inhospitality is as bad as the other. Although it seems clear that Deepak did not ask Asha because the idea that his wife could want to say no to a close friend's request for hospitality is simply inconceivable to him, Asha reacts as if he did not ask her because he did not think her opinion mattered. She fears that the matter of Raj has revealed Deepak's expectations that she assume the traditional subordinate role of the Indian wife, whose responsibility is to entertain her husband's friends and relatives even if she also has a job.

As a compromise, Raj continues to live with them but moves to the guest room, yet inwardly Asha is not appeased. The privacy she so carefully guarded in the first years of her marriage to Deepak is utterly lost, "for the concept of doors did not exist in Raj's universe" (150). Oblivious to her feelings, Raj is constantly interrupting her, particularly when she is trying to do her research. Asha is also jealous of the bond between Raj and her husband that seems to exclude her. "Asha took to locking herself up in the bedroom with her work in the evenings, while downstairs Deepak and Raj talked over the old days" (151). Thus, by becoming part of the household, Asha feels, Raj has intruded on every aspect of her life: her home, where she can no longer pursue any leisure activity or even housework without Raj joining her; her work, on which she now finds it difficult to concentrate; her marriage, which has been undermined by the loss of intimacy with Deepak.

Finally one day after her dissertation advisor scolds her for neglecting her students and "produc[ing] second-rate work," Asha retreats to the sanctuary of her bedroom, forgetting, in her depression, to lock the door. Raj returns home eager to boast of his success in his exams and in his enthusiasm ignores her plea to be left alone with her headache. Instead, he enters, offering her a bottle of tiger balm which she impulsively dashes against the wall, screaming at Raj to get out. Whether she is frightened by her own involuntary breech of decorum or whether Raj's invasion of "her last sanctuary" is itself the final straw, Asha packs her bags (152). But when she informs Deepak of her decision, he insists that she stay and asks Raj to move out. Asha makes no response, any relief at Raj's departure muted by the knowledge that Deepak feels she has betrayed him.

> Much later she listened as Deepak told her Raj would be staying in a hotel until he found a room on campus, listened as he stated that he would sleep in the guestroom tonight, . . . She listened as a part of herself cried out to her to go to him, to apologize and offer to have Raj back. . . . (153)

Though Asha has won back her privacy, she has sacrificed what remained of her intimacy with Deepak. "For the first time she lay down alone in the big bed. . . . And when the door finally clicked shut, she did not know whether it was in the guest room or deep inside her own being" (153). In fact, it is both. It is now Deepak who shuts himself away from Asha, but Asha also closes off the part of herself that is willing to compromise. She does not go to her husband but lies on the bed, "let[ting] the night cover her slowly, layer by cold layer" (153).

Robbie Clipper Sethi's "Grace" is another story in which an American woman married to an Indian man complains that "she can't live the way she wants to in her own house" because of the intrusive presence of semi-permanent houseguests from India. Ironically, though Inder is more sympathetic than Deepak to his wife's distress, Deepak asks Raj to leave rather than have his wife leave his house, while Inder suffers his wife to move out rather than find his parents another apartment.

Grace Madison, an American whose "ancestors, a hundred years ago had each come over from Europe alone, forgetting even the countries they came from," (620) marries Inder Singh, a Sikh who had come to Pennsylvania from Punjab to earn an MBA. Grace, an artist, is attracted to Inder because he allows her the privacy and gives her the financial support she needs to pursue her painting full-time. "He was the only man who had ever let her paint. Other men had interfered, tried to finish paintings for her, tried to out paint her" (615). But when his relatives join their household, first his mother for a four-month visit that stretches into eight months, then both parents and finally his sister for indefinite visits that lead to their applying for permanent residency, Grace finds it increasingly difficult to work at home. "The smell of cooking oil seeped into Grace's paints" (615); her mother-in-law interrupts her painting to call her attention to house cleaning or offer her a drink; the sounds of her father-in-law's favorite television programs are a distraction. Once the sister-in-law, Behanji, joins the household, Grace has no place to paint but the basement, where "her colors came out wrong" and "the dampness warped the canvasses" (619).

Grace feels that her in-laws do not appreciate that painting is her career or grant her the right to attend to work rather than focusing on their needs. When she suggests that her father-in-law learn to drive so she will not have to take them shopping, he explodes: "How much trouble can it be to take your Bibiji and Darji to the shopping center so we will have some time outside of our stinking, paint-smelling house?" (618). Furthermore, they begin pressing for grandchildren and monopolize Inder so that the only place she can talk to him alone is in the bathroom. While Inder sympathizes with Grace, he is unwilling to ask his parents to leave. "In India a parent is always welcome" (615), he tells her. Grace's view is that "in America you give up your family to take a wife" (620). Inder tries to avoid choosing between Grace and his family by waiting for them to decide to return to India of their own accord, but eventually he realizes this will not happen and begs Grace to adjust to the situation.

Instead Grace finds a full-time teaching job and rents a combination studio and apartment "in the city they had moved away from when they needed the extra room that Inder's family had filled" (620). When Inder refuses to join her, they begin living separately. Grace throws herself into her work and soon "had almost grown to like missing Inder" (623). One of her first paintings after the separation appears to portray Inder as "a gray faced man, abstractly outlined with a skeletal jaw, a hanging startled mouth and big uncomprehending eyes" (624). Her next painting, which she entitles *Grace*, portrays "two gray-white faces" which "wore the same wide-eyed stare . . . but she'd managed to work a touch of comprehension into their eyes" as if they were "reconcil[ed] to fate" (624).

Grace is putting the finishing touches on this self-portrait when she is interrupted by the arrival of Behanji, accompanied by two large suitcases. To Grace's astonishment, Behanji makes herself at home— "her big haunches spread out on the mattress" (624)—and explains, "Just because you are divorcing my brother does not mean you are not still my sister. I think of you that way. And my sister's home is my home. See?" (625).

But Grace cannot see things that way, nor can she bring Behanji to understand that her "problem was never with Inder. It was with [Behanji and her parents]" (625). The irony for Grace is that having relinquished Inder to his family, she should be invited to maintain an on-going relationship with them. In other words, she can have Inder's family without Inder, but not what she really wants, Inder without his family. As she complains to Inder on the telephone after getting rid of Behanji, "If your sister can stop by, I don't see why you can't" (626).

Why she finally telephones Inder after months of silence is not clear, even to Grace. Behanji's visit is clearly the catalyst, and Grace seems to call partly to complain about the further intrusion and partly out of compassion for her sister-in-law and to assuage feelings of compunction at rejecting her. Grace asks Inder why his family does not hate her for abandoning their son and encourages him to try to make amends to Behanji for his parents having spent her dowry on his education. "It wouldn't take much: her own apartment, driving lessons, and if you're feeling generous, a car, some employment counseling" (626), she says. This attempt to help Behanji adopt American values and establish an independent life for herself is an indication of the real purpose of Grace's call. If his sister can change, can break free of Indian traditions to establish her own independent existence, can't Inder do so as well? And if her in-laws still regard her as a daughter or sister, mustn't Inder still see her as his wife? Had she been too hasty in assuming that "she'd never again live with Inder" (624)? Grace's call is an attempt to reopen the lines of communication.

Their conversation, however, does not hold out much hope for reconciliation. Inder is impatient and distant. Furthermore, he still views "home" for Grace and himself as one shared with his family, while she believes that she is at "home" in her studio, and the only question is whether he will join her there. He refuses:

"If I stop by," he said, "I'll be caught in the middle again."
"You are in the middle."
"I've got to go."
"Good-bye." (626)

Inder's answer and the months of silence that preceded the telephone call imply that he has made his decision. If Grace cannot live with his parents, the relationship is over. But Grace knows the emotional price of this decision and reflects it in her art: the last time they were together, just after Grace had rented the studio, she had noticed his blank expression. "Turning himself off was the only way he'd managed to accept the situation" (623). Now, though she insists that Inder is "in the middle," so long as he tries to escape the conflict, there is little hope of reconciliation.

In contrast to "Doors," which ends with a door clicking shut, "Grace" does not end with the click of a receiver. After she hangs up the phone, Grace turns back to her painting and is frustrated when "the lines of the portrait blurred in front of her" (626). This seems another instance of how Inder's family distracts her from her work, of proof of Grace's dramatic claim that "the marriage would have killed her work" (623), with which she justified her abandonment of Inder. Yet it is also possible that the portrait is blurred by Grace's tears. In fact, her dissatisfaction with the painting begins not after the phone call, but before it, and perhaps even prompts it: "Grace kept staring at the painting after Behanji left. She didn't like it nearly as much. She dialed Inder's office" (626). Sethi's juxtaposition of Behanji's visit, Grace's more critical appraisal of the painting, and her call to Inder's office suggests that Grace seeks something from Inder that will help her complete her painting and that Behanji's visit has caused her to question the self-sufficient life with which she imagined herself content.

Grace determinedly focuses on her painting and after working all evening has an inspiration. "The painting needed something. She opened a tube of primary red, put a dab of paint on the tip of her finger, and touched a dot above each figure's eyes" (626). The red dots represent more than Grace's appropriation of Indian imagery and culture in her art, like the "evil eyes of peacock feathers, the stripes of the Bengal tiger" (615) that she painted after her visit to India as Inder's bride. The dots imply Grace's realization that she cannot escape the tangled situation anymore than Inder can deny being "in the middle" despite his attempts to stand aloof. For the portrait is a self-portrait, and the red *bindi* "above each figure's eyes" indicates that on some level she thinks of herself as a married Indian woman.[4] Certainly this ending complicates the bittersweet situation Grace thought she had found for herself. She is still unwilling to sacrifice her painting and her privacy for Inder and his family, but perhaps she sees that she has been too ready to sacrifice the rest of her life for her painting. The "touch of comprehension" Grace tells herself she has painted in the eyes of the figures in the painting is revealed as wishful thinking. She has not understood the depth of her loss or realized that she was sacrificing herself even as she moved out to escape the sacrifice she felt Inder demanded of her (621).

While in "Doors" and "Grace" it is the American characters who complain that Indians have no respect for privacy, in Tahira Naqvi's "Paths upon Water," it is a Pakistani woman, Sakina Bano, who feels assaulted by Americans' failure to keep their bodies private. This is a story of culture shock, and the symbol of all that is frightening, overwhelming, and yet alluring about *Amreeka* for Sakina Bano is the sea. "Sakina Bano had never seen the sea. . . . Her experience of the sea was limited to what she had chanced to observe in pictures" (207). The picture that lingers in her mind is a romantic sequence from "a silly Urdu film" that features a young couple on a beach: "The two frolicked by an expanse of water that extended to the horizon and which, even though it was only in a film, had seemed to Sakina Bano frightening in its immensity" (207). But Sakina Bano is clearly more disturbed by the sensuality of the scene than by the ocean itself. Mentally, she censures the woman for impropriety. "Small foam-crested waves lapped up to her, making her *shalwar* stick to her skinny legs, exposing the outline of her thin calves. Why it was just as bad as baring her legs . . . " (207). Little can Sakina Bano imagine what will be bared at an American beach.

Now her son Raza, who has immigrated to America and whom she is visiting there for the first time, informs her that he will take her to see the ocean. Sakina Bano's reaction is ambivalent. On the one hand "she smiled happily and thought, I've only been here a week and already he wants to show me the sea" (207). But the story's opening words suggest that she feels some uncertainty about the outing: "There had been little warning, actually none at all to prepare her for her first encounter with the sea" (207). The implication that a warning was desirable suggests some trepidation. Raza tells his mother of his plans while she is cooking his breakfast, and while she continues to fry his *parathas* she reflects to herself that "if she had had anything to do with it, she would avoid long trips and spend most of her time in Raza's apartment cooking his meals and watching him eat. . . . The most she would want to do would be to go out on the lawn once in a while and examine her surroundings" (208).

This comment hints at an unstated source of her reluctance to go on the outing : it is an intrusion on the time spent alone with her son. The mother-son bond is often the tie of greatest emotional closeness in Indian families. Separation from her son threatens to deprive her of that closeness. Throughout the story, she continually reassures herself that Raza is a good son and is gratified by any sign of his love and solicitude, yet she still worries that "one's son can become a stranger too, even a good son like Raza" (216). While it is not absolutely clear

that Sakina Bano is only visiting rather than permanently moving in
with Raza, the absence of any explicit reference to her settling in the
United States coupled with her references to the country as "his new
world" and "his new environment" suggest that she will eventually
return to Pakistan and that Raza will remain (209). Thus facing the
prospect of a long separation, she wants as much time alone with her
son as possible, preferably in a non-threatening environment that she
can make more familiar with the smells of Indian cooking. The outing
to the seashore means not only that she will have to share Raza's
company with his friends, but also that she will have to watch him in a
disturbingly foreign setting. Insofar as he feels comfortable there, and
she feels awkward, the distance between them will be emphasized.

Nevertheless her instinctive habit of deferring to her son enables
her to accept his plans calmly:

> "Is the sea far from here?" she asked casually. . . . Raza must
> never feel she didn't value his eagerness to show off his new
> environment. This was his new world after all. If he wanted to
> take her to the seaside, then the seaside it would be. Certainly
> she was not about to be fussy and upset him. (209)

Soon Raza's friend Jamal and his bride Hameeda arrive and Sakina Bano
serves them tea. She is discomfited by Hameeda, a "newcomer" to
America who resembles the girl Sakina Bano is considering for an
arranged marriage with her son but who strikes the older woman as
having "wanderlust in her eyes already." Sakina Bano notices Hameeda's
"lips, dark and fleshy with lipstick" and is reminded of the actress in the
Urdu film (209). In the car on the way to the sea, Sakina Bano rides in
the back with Hameeda, "an unfortunate arrangement," she reflects. "It
wasn't Hameeda's persistent prattle that vexed her, . . . it was her
perfume. So pungent she could feel it wafting into her nostrils . . . "
(210).

Ironically, given that Hameeda has spent less time in America than
the other people, it is she who seems to symbolize the dangerous allure
of the country that Sakina Bano fears will engulf her son and estrange
him from her. Although Hameeda wears traditional Indian dress,
behaves respectfully to Sakina Bano, and displays a childish innocence,
Sakina Bano is uncomfortably aware of her sexuality and unwillingly
dwells on the shape of her legs and lips, the scent of her perfume, and
her open eagerness to see the ocean. When Sakina Bano muses about
the wanderlust she "already" sees in Hameeda's eyes, she may mean
"after such a short time in America" as well as "at such a young age."
Sakina Bano's reflections on Hameeda are the more disturbing to her

because of her faint resemblance to the Pakistani girl who is her son's prospective bride. Such a marriage would theoretically strengthen Raza's ties to his homeland and protect him from being corrupted by the loose morality of his adopted country. But what if the bride embraces those values as Hameeda embraces "the prospect of a visit to the seaside" (209)?

Sakina Bano's discomfort with Hameeda's lipstick and perfume pales in comparison to her amazement, embarrassment, and disapproval upon arriving at the beach and getting her first view of American bathing attire. Her discomfort increases as she realizes that her son is not affected by the near-nudity around them and that the Americans regard her own clothing as inappropriate. As they pull into the beach parking lot, Sakina Bano sees a woman in a bikini bending over her car so that "her breasts stood in imminent danger of spilling out of their meager coverage" (211). Hurriedly turning her head, "she stole a glance at her son from the corners of her eyes, anxiously wondering if her too were experiencing something of what she was going through; no, she noted with mixture of surprise and relief, he . . . did not show any signs of discomfort" (211). Her relief that her son is not suffering from embarrassment brings her a new anxiety; it seems a measure of how much he has changed, how much he has moved away from her. Watching him splash in the water and chat comfortably with the bikini-clad wife of another friend of his, "she felt she was distanced from him" (216). She is also hurt by his apparent lack of consideration for her feelings. She

> wondered why her son had chosen to bring her to this place. Did he not know his mother? She was an old woman and the mother of a son, but she would not surrender to anger or derision and make her son uncomfortable. . . . She must not appear ungrateful or intolerant. (211)

Out of the desire to please her son and avoid embarrassing him, she hides her feelings about "the perturbing nakedness around her" and sits uncomplaining on the beach with Hameeda while the men swim (211). Her discomfort quickly becomes physical as well as internal, given the glare of the sun, "the sand in her mouth, and the hot-water-bottle effect of the sand beneath her thighs" (214).

At first, to avoid looking at the bodies, Sakina Bano stares at the sea. She finds it more overwhelming than the cinema image yet somehow sacred. "The immensity of the sea on film was reduced to a mere splash of color, its place usurped by a vastness she could scarce hold within the frame of her vision; a window opened in her head, she drew in the wonder of the sea as it touched the hem of the heavens" (212–13). Gazing into its depths, Sakina Bano reflects, "God's touch is upon the world" (213). She turns disapprovingly back to the sunbathers around her and notes that they "seemed unmindful of what the ocean might have to say about God's touch upon the world" (213). She finds their deliberate attempt "to be fried in the sun" incomprehensible, but she is also disturbed to realize that "from the vantage point of those stretched out on the sand," it is she and Hameeda who appear "ridiculous" (214).

It is just at this moment that Sakina Bano spots a woman in a sari, accompanied by her son and daughter-in-law who wear American bathing suits and who quickly leave her alone on the beach while they go swimming:

> Clutching the front folds of her *sari* as if afraid a sudden wind from the ocean might pull them out unfurling the *sari*, leaving her exposed, she tread on the sand with a fiercely precarious step, looking only ahead, eyes shielded with one small flat palm.
>
> This is how I must appear to the others, Sakina Bano ruminated. Suddenly she felt a great sadness . . . as she watched the woman . . . make herself comfortable on a . . . towel thrown on the sand by her son and his wife; those two hurriedly dashed off in the direction of the water. Why are they in such haste? Sakina Bano wondered. (214–15)

Sakina Bano's pained identification with the woman is reinforced by the discovery that the young people are her son's friends and her sudden suspicion that if she had not come along Hameeda might be swimming with the men. Her sadness reflects her fear that she appears timid, old fashioned, and out of place, not only to the American sunbathers but to her son and his friends. The abrupt departure of the young couple for the ocean appears to symbolize the abandonment of traditional mores, including a lack of respect for elders. Hadn't Raza treated her in much the same way? "Will Raza's wife also wear a scant swimming suit and bare her body in the presence of strange men? The question disturbed her. . . . It wouldn't go away" (215).

After the other four young people have returned to the water, Hameeda startles Sakina Bano by suggesting they go wading. Sakina Bano agrees but hesitates when she sees Hameeda roll up the legs of her *shalwar.* "She must do the same, [Sakina Bano] realized. Otherwise Hameeda would think she was afraid" (217). With Hameeda's encouragement, Sakina Bano bares her legs and "strode toward the water. As she went past the other woman in the sari she smiled at her" (217). Though the woman's face shows her surprise, she eventually smiles back as Sakina Bano happily wades into the sea after Hameeda. We can contrast Sakina Bano's sighting of the woman in the sari with the encounter with the "racial shadow" that Sau-ling Cynthia Wong has identified as a recurrent theme in Asian American literature. According to Wong, in many Asian American literary works "a highly assimilated American-born Asian is troubled by a version of himself/herself that serves as a reminder of disowned Asian descent" (92). The protagonist responds to this racial shadow with both "sympathy and revulsion" (96) and often responds with violence (92), for the figure is an unwelcome reminder of the impossibility of full acceptance by white American society (96). Although Sakina Bano is obviously neither American born nor highly assimilated, the Indian woman's presence heightens Sakina Bano's anxiety about the way she appears to Americans in general and to her son in particular. Her wading in the water could be seen as an attempt to prove them wrong. But unlike the desperate and violent encounters with the racial shadow that Wong describes, Sakina Bano seems by her smile to invite the woman to join her. Furthermore Sakina Bano is not trying to deny identity with the racial other in order to gain acceptance by white America but rather is seeking a compromise between the absurdity of sitting on the beach fully clothed on the one hand and gratuitously exposing nearly all of one's body to public view on the other. In this way she succeeds in having a new experience and sharing some of her son's pleasure in his new life while still holding on to the values that she hopes he, too, will continue to cherish.

Noting that, as a group, immigrants from South Asia to the United States are both highly successful in American society and subjected to prejudice and discrimination, Feroza Jussawalla describes them as leading a "chiffon sari existence," that is "at once holding onto the culture and beliefs of the homeland and adopting Western ways in order to be 'forward,' 'modern,' above all 'mainstreamed'" (585). When Western ways and those of the homeland are incompatible, as over concepts of privacy, conflict is inevitable and compromise is essential. Jussawalla's metaphor of the chiffon sari is a symbol of compromise, one that Sakina Bano celebrates as she wades in the ocean, one that Grace seems on the verge of embracing as she adds the red dots to her painting, one that eludes Asha as she lies alone on her marriage bed.

NOTES

1. I will be discussing the initial published versions of "Door" and "Grace." The versions that appear in the author's short story collections have been revised, "Doors" quite extensively and "Grace" slightly less so.
2. Letter to the author 28 November 1995. My inclusion of Sethi in an essay on Indo-American writers has a precedent in both Mukherjee's inclusion of Clark Blaise and Ruth Prawer Jhabvala in the issue of "Writers of the Indian Commonwealth" and in Sylvia Watanabe's inclusion of "non-Asian women who have experienced close contact with Asian cultures" in *Home to Stay* (xi).
3. The traditional structure of Indian families encourages greater emotional closeness between parents and children than between husbands and wives. While a woman may be close to her daughter, when she grows up she will marry and live with her husband's family, after which, time spent with her own mother may be quite limited. Filial responsibilities continue but are viewed as subordinate to those she bears toward her in-laws. On the other hand, "a grown man's relationships with his wife and children are subordinate to those with his parents." As a result, "a woman's relationship with her son is probably the most satisfying and emotionally enduring of her life" (Nyrop 246–47, 249). Since in American culture a married couple's duty is first to each other and then to their children, this cultural difference is also why Grace and Inder are at such an impasse.
4. Grace's painting of two figures rather than one also suggests that she views her decision to abandon the marriage as a painful tearing apart of her self.

REFERENCES

Agarwal, Priya. *Passage from India: Post-1965 Indian Immigrants and Their Children*. Palos Verdes, CA: Yuvati, 1991.

Divakaruni, Chitra Banerjee. *Arranged Marriage*. New York: Anchor Doubleday, 1995.

___. "Doors." Watanabe and Bruchac. 146–53.

Jussawalla, Feroza. "Chiffon Saris: The Plight of South Asian Immigrants in the New World." Katrak and Radhakrishnan 583–95.

Katrak, Ketu H. and R. Radhakrishnan, eds. *Desh/Videsh: South Asian Expatriate Writers and Artists*. Special Issue. *Massachusetts Review* 29 (1988–89): 573–772.

Mukherjee, Bharati. *Darkness*. New York: Fawcett, 1985.

___. Interview with Alison B. Carb. Katrak and Radhakrishnan 645–54.

___. *"The Middleman" and Other Stories*. New York: Fawcett, 1988.

___. "Writers of the Indian Literary Commonwealth." *Literary Review* 29 (1986): 400–10.

Naqvi, Tahira, tr. *Attar of Roses: Stories from Pakistan.* Colorado Springs: Three Continents, 1996.

___. "Paths upon Water." *The Forbidden Stitch: An Asian American Women's Anthology.* Eds. Shirley Geok-lin Lim, Mayumi Tsutakawa, and Margarita Donnelly. Corvalis, OR: Calyx, 1989. 207–17.

Nyrop, Richard F., ed. *India: A Country Study.* American University Foreign Area Studies. Washington: American University Press, 1985.

Sethi, Robbie Clipper. *The Bride Wore Red: Tales of a Cross-Cultural Family.* Bridgehampton, NY: Bridgeworks, 1996.

___. "Grace." *Atlantic* August 1991: 56–58+. Rpt. in *New Worlds of Literature: Writings from America's Many Cultures.* Eds. Jerome Beaty and J. Paul Hunter. 2nd ed. New York: Norton, 1994. 612–26.

Suran, Parmatma. *The Asian Indian Experience in the United States.* Cambridge: Schenkman, 1985.

Tapping, Craig. "South Asia Writes North America: Prose Fictions and Autobiographies from the Indian Diaspora." *Reading the Literatures of Asian America.* Eds. Shirley Geok-lin Lim and Amy Ling. Philadelphia: Temple, 1992. 285–301.

Watanabe, Sylvia. Introduction. Eds. Watanabe, Sylvia, and Carol Bruchac. *Home to Stay: Asian American Women's Fiction.* Greenfield Center, NY: Greenfield, 1990. xi.

Wong, Sau-ling Cynthia. *Reading Asian American Literature: From Necessity to Extravagance.* Princeton: Princeton University Press, 1993.

13. Re-Orienting the Subject: Arab American Ethnicity in Ramzi M. Salti's *The Native Informant: Six Tales of Defiance from the Arab World*

Chris Wise

"Oriental students (and Oriental professors) still want to come and sit at the feet of American Orientalists, and later to repeat to their local audiences the cliches [of] Orientalist dogmas. Such a system of reproduction makes it inevitable that the Oriental scholar will use his American training to feel superior to his own people because he is able to 'manage' the Orientalist system; in his relations with his superiors, the European or American Orientalists, he will remain only a 'native informant.' And indeed this is his role in the West, should he be fortunate enough to remain there after his advanced training."

—Edward Said, *Orientalism*

Introduction

The *fatwa* against Salman Rushdie has irrevocably clarified for the West the very real dangers that authors from within the Muslim world confront when they dare to address socially taboo topics, especially topics challenging the religious orthodoxy and its doctrines. In *The Satanic Verses*, this predicament is ironically foretold when the businessman/prophet "Mahound"—an irreverent and, for some, highly offensive caricature of the Prophet Mohammed—vengefully executes the poet Baal for creating satirical verses at the prophet's expense. More recently, the stabbing of Nobel laureate Naguib Maufouz in Egypt (which was, fortunately, not fatal) has further illustrated just how much courage is required of contemporary Middle Eastern writers who dare to tackle forbidden subjects. The publication of Ramzi M. Salti's collection of short stories, *The Native Informant: Six Tales of Defiance from the Arab World*, breaks silence on yet another highly taboo subject in the Arab world: male homosexuality. Long dismissed as a corrupting influence from the West, the topic of male homosexuality in the Middle East has rarely been explored by authors from within the Arab and Islamic world.[1] For this reason, Salti's book has received significant notice in several gay periodicals in the United States and in the Middle East. As a Jordanian transplant to the United States, Salti writes of the conflict between traditional (i.e., Muslim) notions of homosexuality and more liberating but anti-traditional perspectives on homosexuality within the United States. With great sensitivity and skill, Salti reveals the process by which a variety of gay male characters learn to claim an authentic sense of personal identity in spite of overwhelming obstacles. More importantly, his book demonstrates the complex nature of the psychological changes and traumas undergone by Arabs during their repatriation as Arab American citizens. In fact, the theme of homosexuality is actually subordinated in *The Native Informant* to this more crucial and general question.

In the United States and elsewhere, there are few Anglophone writers from the Arab world who have gained visibility in the West (unlike Francophone Arab writers of fiction such as Elias Khoury and Tahar Ben Jelloun). Hence, Salti has few literary precedents. Some notable exceptions are Diana Abu-Jabar, an Arab American author and professor of English at the University of Oregon, Ahdaf Soueif, Egyptian-born author of *In the Eye of the Sun* (presently residing in England), and the late Lebanese author Rima Almuddin, all of whom Salti has cited as important influences.[2] Additionally, Salti has been influenced by established Arab American scholars such as Issa J. Boullata and Edward W. Said, the latter from whom Salti draws the title of his story collection. If Arab American influences are scant, the proliferation of novels, short stories, and essays by Indo-Muslim and other Indian authors has provided much inspiration for Salti and countless others in transit between "first" and "third" worlds. In particular, Salti has observed that he "relate[s] very well to works by such authors as Salman Rushdie (*Midnight's Children*), Bharati Mukherjee (*"The Middleman" and Other Stories*), and R. K. Narayan (*The Painter of Signs*)." Finally, numerous writers who are Arab and write in Arabic have impacted Salti's writing in many far-reaching ways. Among these are Naguib Mafouz, Nawal el-Saadawi, Alifa Rifaat, and Salwa Baker. Not surprisingly, Salti has written that he "feel[s] a natural affinity with writers who have found themselves

attacked and threatened for writing about subjects that the Arab mainstream would like to ignore."
Presently, Salti resides in Los Angeles, California, where he writes and teaches. He is completing a Ph.D. in Comparative Literature at the University of California, Riverside. Salti has also published articles in numerous literary journals such as *World Literature Today, The International Fiction Review, Christianity and Literature,* and *The Journal of Arabic Literature,* and he is working on a study of marginalized sexualities in Arabic literature.

The *Native Informant* and the Subject in Transit

In the context of the United States, to write a short story is often to write one's self *out* of a now defunct ethnic identity and into an "absolutely modern" or newly American one[3]: it is literally a death and rebirth experience, an often deliberate (though sometimes unconscious) attempt to interpellate one's self into an utterly different symbolic order that is predicated upon the demise of a no-longer-desirable form of ethnic identity. For this reason, Ramzi M. Salti's collection of short stories, *The Native Informant,* begins with a literal death, which is also the symbolic death of the writer's identity as an ethnic subject. In "Vivian and Her Son," a Jordanian mother, Vivian, is besieged by fellow mourners during the traditional forty-day period, following the death (a possible suicide) of her writer-son Omar. Vivian differs from the other mourners in many ways, especially in her acceptance of Western ideas, resulting in her condemnation by relatives and other acquaintances. Vivian, who is university educated, has the audacity to drive her own car, and to wear French dresses and expensive foreign jewelry (2–3). "Better the dung of your own country than the jewels of the foreigner" (4), one of the mourners reflects, a folk aphorism that encapsulates the stifling traditional attitudes from which nearly all the principal characters of *The Native Informant* flee. "*This had been her story in this country,*" Salti writes, "a life of constant struggling against what most others had understood and accepted. This was the only way she knew to rebel against oppression [my emphasis]" (3). The principal themes of the other stories in Salti's collection also reiterate the writer's insistence that Vivian's story should not be *anyone's* story, that one must steadfastly refuse one's pre-cast role in a suffocating, traditional society. Perhaps the strongest example of this occurs in Salti's story "Wedding Song," in which a long-battered Muslim housewife is driven to kill her husband in self-defense. In "Vivian and Her Son," however, Omar is able to identify with his mother largely on the basis of their parallel status as oppressed, sexed subjectivities: that is, Vivian is oppressed as a gendered female subject in a repressive patriarchal society, whereas Omar, like other characters in *The Native Informant,* suffers oppression as a homosexual male subject in an intolerant and hypocritically religious society.

At the conclusion of "Vivian and Her Son," Vivian symbolically burns the pages of Omar's diary, in which her son has attempted to articulate his sexual identity. If Jordanian society provides no suitable place for Omar as a homosexual man to inhabit, his diary nevertheless provides a kind of utopian space, the only place where he can truly "live." Of course Omar's life within the pages of his diary is actually a form of death, since, as Walter J. Ong puts it, "death unavoidably inhabits texts" (238). "The kind of life [that] writing enjoys remains bizarre," Ong states, "for it is achieved at the price of death" (234). Indeed, Omar's life in Jordan can only be described as "bizarre": he is unable or unwilling to leave his bedroom, save occasional trips to the bookstore. When his mother attempts to coax him out, Omar tells her, "you just don't understand. I am happy here. I am happiest reading a book" (6). Following Omar's death, Vivian's act of burning his diary (only partly in fear that other mourners will find it, and hence Omar's "secret"), actually represents a symbolic mercy-killing of her son's bizarre life-in-death, that is his life within the pages of the diary itself, and, conversely, his death-in-life, or the death that life in Jordanian society offered him. The true hero(ine) of the story is Vivian. If she herself is trapped, she nevertheless creates an "opening" that makes Omar's rebirth possible. Though she allows the unwanted house guests to have their way throughout the forty-day mourning period, she zealously refuses them access into her son's private life and possessions. Omar's room is the one room that remains entirely "off-limits" to the mourners: on this point, Vivian will not yield (5). "I had to protect you from those bastards, those emotionless fools who had turned my life to hell," she reflects, after her son's death. "What mother can stand still and watch her son being devoured?" (8). Vivian's ritual burning of the diaries actually frees Omar from his prior and more devastating death, before his less tragic and "real" one, hence allowing for the possibility of his rebirth in a different world, if not literally for Omar then at least symbolically for the author himself.

At this point, the character Omar may be said to stand in as an allegorical marker for the author's own abandoned subjectivity as a Jordanian national. In other words, as a symbolic mediation upon a very real historical problem,[4] the story "Vivian and Her Son" allows Salti himself to symbolically immolate his former identity as a Jordanian (and oppressed) subject, facilitating his own rebirth within a new signifying system. The utter impossibility of living with any dignity or true happiness as a homosexual man in present-day Jordanian society therefore compels Salti to destroy the preordained role assigned to him, the intolerable and marginal subject position that would consign him to live in books and fantasies alone. This point is illustrated, for example, at the beginning of the following story in *The Native Informant,* entitled "Checkpoint," in which the main character, also a homosexual Jordanian man, undergoes the painful process of forging a new identity in the United States. Salti informs us, for example, that "[f]our years of university education [in Southern California] succeeded in separating and disconnecting him [the main character] from the scared and unsure boy who had reluctantly left Jordan in 1983, never to return" (11). If Sami, the protagonist of "Checkpoint," resembled Omar, we may not doubt the autobiographical dimensions of both literary characters, or their clearly allegorical meaning for the author himself. From an American New Critical perspective, it may seem a "fallacy" of sorts to conflate Salti's literary creations with his own identity as an Arab American man, but such "fallacies" are common to "resistance" literature as well as to its criticism. Postcolonial literary critic Georg M. Gugelberger refers to this aspect of third world and minority literature when he states that such texts are commonly more "realistic" than mainstream literature in the United States: "By 'realistic' I mean more *ad hominem*" Gugelberger states, "more radical in the root sense of the term . . . This implies talking about men and women not in the abstract but in the here and now" (515). For Gugelberger, the term *ad hominem* implies getting back to the beginning of things or, perhaps, getting to the real core of the problem: that is, getting back to the historical.[5] Salti affirms the *ad hominem* dimensions of his own writing in his third story, "'Antara and Juliet," when the narrator Raja reflects upon his future as a writer, musing that he "would rely on [his own] experiences to convey the injustice of [his]society without having to resort to invention" (28). We are further told that he "would probably change the names of the main characters [in his stories], but [he] might retain the first initials." In "Checkpoint," the autobiographical nature of the tale is evident in the name of the main character Sami, a play on the author's own first name, Ramzi, merged with the first initial "s" in his last name, Salti.

Salti's effort to construct a new identity is a deliberately and self-consciously *literary* one, an attempt to emphasize "the problematic aspects of writing in English" (vii), rather than Arabic. In this sense, *The Native Informant* stands in opposition to efforts of non-Western writers like Ngugi wa Thiong'o, the renowned Kenyan author, who rejected the English language in favor of Gikuyu, the language of his childhood. In *Decolonizing the Mind* (1986), Ngugi famously criticized the writings of postcolonial authors like Chinua Achebe, Sembene Ousmane, and even himself, who have chosen in the past to enrich the languages of their Euro-American colonizers, often at the expense of their own languages. Such writers, Ngugi complains, inject fresh "'blood' into the rusty joints" of European languages (*Decolonizing the Mind* 7). Repeatedly, Ngugi claims that, by writing in a European language, the very minds of oppressed peoples of the third world are recolonized in the neocolonial era. While Salti's relation to the English language is equally ambiguous, Ngugi's radical (if not draconian) solution, that is, Ngugi's wholesale rejection of the colonizer's linguistic universe, is simply not available to Salti nor to the various writer-protagonists of Salti's stories. In fact, in his "Introduction," Salti tells us that "[a]lthough these stories have been written in English, a deliberate attempt has been made to create an *Arabicized* style of English" [Salti's emphasis] (vii). In spite of the linguistic wealth of Arabic, a language that boasts one of the richest literary traditions in the world, Salti finds it inadequate for his needs as a writer in the United States. In "Checkpoint," Sami complains, for example, that Arabic grammar is simply too "complex" to maintain once he has arrived in the United States (14). Salti's contrasting of the "simplicity" of writing in English with the "difficulty" of writing in Arabic reveals subtle yet wide-ranging differences between daily life in Arabic-speaking Islamic nations and the United States, especially the widely-differing relations of Arabic-speaking peoples to their language and English-speaking peoples in the United States to their language. If Arabic's beauty and complexity is at least in part related to its historical status as a sacred language for Muslims across the globe, including its communal, oral, and ritual functions (zealously preserved by millions), this same heritage for Arabic speakers who are not Muslim is much more ambiguous. In other words, because of Arabic's centrality to Islam, Salti, who comes from a Christian background (like the narrator of "'Antara and Juliet"), may be said to experience Arabic as a form of linguistic oppression, an extrinsic imposition of an alien world upon his innermost being. The relationship between non-Muslim Arabs in Jordan, Palestine, Egypt, etc., and the Arabic language is a complex one: hence, it must suffice to observe here that Salti himself would not necessarily experience the religious devotion to his native language, that Ngugi would for Gikuyu or an Arab Muslim would for Arabic.

While seeking to remain loyal to Arabic, non-Muslim writers in Salti's position are often more ambivalent about their language. The relative simplicity of the English language and, hence, its attractiveness to Salti parallel the simplicity of the short story as a distinctively American form. In both cases, the complexity of traditional linguistic practices is experienced as a burden to be left behind along with other undesirable aspects of ethnic culture: Salti here, in fact, exhibits a quintessentially *American* sensibility. From the time of the so-called founding fathers to the present, the old world with its stifling traditions and complications has gladly been thrown off in favor of a supposedly non-sectarian, democratic, and simpler lifestyle. Hence, in "'Antara and Juliet," the narrator reflects upon a future work of fiction, stating "it would have to be written in English, of course, since I could express myself more easily in that language, but I was sure that someone would eventually translate it into Arabic" (28).[6] Whether or not the text is translated into Arabic does not concern the narrator Raja too deeply, however, since it is clear by the story's conclusion that his true interests lie outside Arabic culture altogether: in the final paragraphs, for example, while Raja is left cold by the muezzin's call, he nevertheless dreams of Shakespeare, American movies, and French restaurants (33). In fact, the Christian Raja imagines his relationship to his Muslim girlfriend Ranya in terms of Shakespeare's "Romeo and Juliet," which causes Ranya to state with some irritation, "Romantic, unromantic, it's all Western crap in the long run" (32). Similarly, Raja's mother tells him that he's been "watching too much American TV" (31). The story's epiphany occurs when Raja is able to realize that he has in fact been betrayed by Shakespeare, that Shakespeare was "only concerned with Romeos and Juliets—even Johns and Janes—but never Rajas and Ranyas" (27). However, this realization does not drive the narrator away from Western culture but nearer to it.

In "The Taxi Driver," Salti more explicitly develops the theme of the Arabic language's limitations for him though in this case his protagonist is, ironically, a Muslim. In a chance encounter in metropolitan Amman, the main character, a young man named 'Ala,' initially refuses the sexual advances of a taxi driver, Hassan, but later he comes to regret the missed opportunity. Like the character Sami in "Checkpoint," 'Ala' eventually realizes that Hassan's homosexuality (and hence his own), if stigmatized by Jordanian culture, is not really evil or sinful but an ordinary expression of human sexuality. Before his meeting with Hassan, we are told, "['Ala'] had grown to accept [the rules of his society], like everything else around him, as the way things have always been and will always be" (57). This passivity to traditional culture, however, gives way to a desire to seek alternatives (68). Following Hassan's arrest for his homosexuality, which is written up in a Jordanian newspaper, 'Ala' reflects that there exist no adequate words in the Arabic language to describe homosexuality in non-derogatory and secular terms. In thinking about alternatives to the vulgar and colloquial term *Khawal*, as well as the word *Luwat*, a term from the Qur'an referring to Lut (also to the Biblical figure Lot), 'Ala' realizes that both terms, and others, are inadequate. "He suddenly realized that he was looking for a word with neither a religious undertone nor a pejorative meaning" (68), Salti states. 'Ala' further wonders, "Why can't I find one word in the Arabic language to express what I want to say?" 'Ala's despair at the "inadequacy" of the Arabic language to articulate an affirmative personal identity for him, given the integral nature of sexuality to human subjectivity, turns to happiness when he grasps the potential to liberate himself and possibly those who are imprisoned like Hassan, through the act of writing short stories.[7] "For the first time in his life," we are told, "['Ala'] was sure of what he wanted to do [i.e., write short stories]. Whether he succeeded or not seemed to him to be secondary. All that mattered is that for now, he was truly happy" (68).

Orientalism and Arab-American Ethnicity

Inevitably, the attempt to divest oneself of ethnic roots will be complicated by the fact that the relative success of such revisionary acts will always be limited, since one cannot finally escape one's primal scene of instruction; hence, such efforts are often accompanied by profound feelings of guilt, anxiety, and remorse. Even when oppression is severe or actually life-threatening, it is difficult to avoid feeling like a traitor or "sell-out" to one's people. This anxiety is voiced by the character Sami, in the story "Checkpoint," who determines not to become a *fasahun* after his arrival in the United States. A *fasahun*, we are told, is one of those "know-it-alls who got their university degrees in America" and who, upon their return home, do nothing but complain about the backwardness of Jordanian life (12). Sami finds such *fasahin* "revolting," and he determines not to become one himself. During his first year in America, he assures everyone in his letters back home that the United States is "overrated" and "nothing special"; he deliberately reads only Arabic books and befriends only fellow Arabs. "[Sami] repeatedly told himself that he would not be a sell-out," Salti writes, "and he felt that by holding on to the culture of his birth, he would always be able to live with himself." As time passes, however, Sami stops writing (and reading) in Arabic altogether; he drops out of the Arab club and makes a few American friends. In his second year, however, Salti writes, "[t]he thought of *turning western* still worried him, but he reasoned that there was a difference between becoming western and borrowing from the west for the sake of his own people" [Salti's emphasis] (14). At this point, Sami rationalizes his own westernization by borrowing from the vocabulary of third-world resistance writers (i.e., Frantz Fanon, Amilcar Cabral, Elias Khouri), seeking to convince himself that one may legitimately "use the tools of the colonizer *against* the colonizer" [Salti's emphasis]. By the end of the story, however, it is clear that Sami (and Salti by extension) intends to use "the tools of the colonizer" for purposes distinct from those of Arab resistance writers like Mahmoud Darwish, Ghassan Kanafani, and others: namely, to resist *his own* cultural traditions and ethnic heritage. As Sami goes through the airport checkpoint upon his return to Jordan, he resolutely vows that he "won't turn into another useless grain in the desert sand" (22).

This threat is embodied for Sami by his cousin Walid, who was once an exchange student like Sami. Upon returning from four years at a university in England, Walid seems a shattered and different man, unable to fit back into Jordanian society but unwilling to immigrate due to feelings of loyalty towards his native land. Walid is left with "zero choices": he can't bring himself to leave the country, but he can't accept it the way that it is (19). Like Sami after him, Walid vows to resist oppressive traditional customs, but after his brief rebellion he eventually resigns himself to a job in a factory, a traditional marriage, and life under his father's roof. However, Sami cannot quite forget Walid's warning: "If you ever get a chance to go abroad, Sami, plan on never returning. If you ever get a job outside this country, don't hesitate for a second" (19). When Sami returns to Jordan, he brings with him the false assurance that he, unlike Walid, will be successful in his fight against traditional culture, that he will "eventually win the uphill battle" (21–22).

Far from being an anti-Western or anti-imperialist form of resistance then, Sami's "defiance" is in fact directed against oppressive, traditional values, especially the homophobia he has divested himself of during his four years abroad. In other stories, as we have seen, Salti suggests that gender oppression similarly must be resisted, even if this means using the "tools of the colonizer." Here, Salti dramatically differs from Egyptian author Alifa Rifaat, from whom he draws in his story "Checkpoint" (especially Rifaat's story "My World of the Unknown"), who also seeks to combat the oppression of women but *not* by borrowing from the West. Denys Johnson-Davies, Rifaat's English-language translator, makes this point in his foreword to Rifaat's *Distant View of a Minaret*, stating that "[Rifaat's] revolt, despite the frank terms in which it is expressed, remains within a strictly religious, even orthodox [Muslim] framework. . . . [T]he last place [Rifaat] would look for inspiration for any change would be the Christian West" (vii-viii).[8] Salti, on the other hand, finds in the West the needed tools to resist or defy oppressive patriarchal customs.

This is not to say that Salti himself becomes a *fasahun* but simply that his defiance comes at a high price, as he himself is aware. The title of his story collection, *The Native Informant*, which is drawn from Edward Said's *Orientalism*, emphasizes the problematic and ambiguous nature of Salti's resistance and subsequent repatriation as an Arab American (rather than a strictly Arab) author. This is so because for Salti, and for others like him, a "convenient" identity always already waits him, specifically as "native informant" or "manager" (i.e., *comprador* exploiter) of his own people; that is, a symbolic order pre-exists for the "oriental" (Arab) subject, a prefabricated identity within an elaborate and nearly totalizing discursive system, waiting to give him/her a name. The unavoidable fact of Orientalism's existence as a massively pre-encoded, symbolic system of representations, specifically of Arab Islamic peoples, obviously complicates Salti's Western-based defiance of repressive ethnic, Arab, or Islamic traditions. In this sense, the rejection of the complications of the Old World towards a simpler future, what I referred to earlier as a quintessentially American gesture, turns into a nightmare of complexities hitherto undreamed of by the ethnic subject in transit. To put it more simply, one set of problems gives way to a still more complicated set, and the "freedom" that is the promise of the United States turns out to be what it always was—an illusion. This is so not only because we can never finally escape the cultural traditions that define us but also because the Arab/Oriental inevitably discovers that his/her newly adopted and "nontraditional" culture has already defined him/her in many superficial and oppressive ways. For this reason, Arab Americans face distinct problems, biases, and paradoxes that are unrelated to those experienced by any other ethnic group in the United States. If such an experience engenders a specific, even privileged, epistemological vantage point, to quote Fredric Jameson,[9] the social difficulties encountered on a daily basis by Arab Americans are not exactly calculated to inspire envy.

Inescapably, Salti's "mainstream" readers in the United States are also caught in these same power relations since we inevitably mediate books like *The Native Informant* through the interpretive lenses of our own biases, cliches, and *ideés reçues* about "oriental" peoples. To put it another way, for the character Sami *not* to turn into a revolting *fasahun* (or smug "know-it-all") and for readers in the United States *not* to assume a patronizing and superior posture when confronting the "backwardness" of Arab culture may be a tremendously difficult task, not because Westerners are innately superior to Arabs (or "orientals"), which is, of course, absurd, but because our own culture has fostered such deeply racist and imperialistic attitudes within us.

Salti dramatizes this situation in his final story, "The Native Informant," which demonstrates the deeply ambivalent nature of the Arab American writer's relation to his newly forged identity as "manager" of his own people. In "The Native Informant," a young man, Majid, is ordered by his firm in Amman to escort a British writer-journalist, Ms. Penn, around Jordan to see "the real" people. Because the journalist is an attractive blond woman, Majid initially feels elated at the opportunity to spend a few days driving around with Ms. Penn, confident that he will inspire the envy and respect of all. Upon visiting the Wihdat, a Palestinian refugee camp in Jordan, however, where he is instructed to translate for Ms. Penn, Majid soon realizes that the British woman's desire to see the "real" Jordan actually means the Jordan that has already been constructed for her through the *ideés reçues* of Western orientalism.

Seeing her frustration at the responses of the inhabitants of the Wihdat and the crassness of Ms. Penn's questions themselves, Majid eventually changes her questions and the Palestinians' answers in an effort to please both parties, and because he himself grows bored and hungry. At this point, Majid symbolizes the postcolonial *comprador* intellectual who traffics in ideas or moderates the exchange between East and West:

> Majid worried that the best way to please the woman, and the only way for him to get food in his stomach soon, lay in altering the answers to suit her questions. He thus began to feel around for what response the woman wanted, then he tailored the answers accordingly. The method must have worked, because conversation flowed quickly and by the time they had left the camp half an hour later, the woman's notebook was half full. (86)

If Majid symbolizes Salti's own role as mediator or "native informant" of his own people, Ms. Penn similarly represents the Western reader of *The Native Informant,* who already knows all the answers before asking any questions, the reader who is unable to hear or listen because of what

Said calls "a learned ignorance." Like Ms. Penn, we already "know" all
there is to know about the oppression of Islamic women, the
"backwardness" of Arab civilization, and the problem of Palestine.
In reality, however, as Salti shows, we actually know nothing at
all; rather, we know *worse* than nothing. Furthermore, this state of
affairs is not simply unfortunate or comic but lethal, for the
misunderstandings that arise between Majid and Ms. Penn finally lead
to disaster: that is, Majid's unjust arrest as her alleged rapist. Both Ms.
Penn and Majid are responsible because they have failed to
communicate with one another. This failure results from laziness,
ignorance, and boredom: it is as tragic as it is unnecessary.

Finally, Salti's emphasizing of the unresolved problem of the
Palestinians in "The Native Informant" dramatizes how the on-going
oppression of Palestinians, including their lack of civil rights in the
state of Israel, their lack of sovereignty in their own homeland, and the
question of disposed Palestinians across the globe, shows how any
newly emergent Arab American identity will be complicated by the
United States' historically supportive role in the formation of Israeli
policies that are directed against Arabs; that is, the United States'
financial support for the state of Israel itself, the most powerful "ethnic
democracy" in the world,[10] remains the central obstacle for Arabs today
in forming a new identity as Arab Americans. In other words, even
Arab Americans who are utterly exhausted and bored by the problem of
Palestine cannot feel indifferent to U.S. policy that blatantly supports
current Israeli efforts to erase Arab identity.

Conclusion

The often-repeated truism that the short story is a truly "American"
literary genre, born of Washington Irving's creative genius, may be
untenable in any global sense, but the problem of ethnicity itself, the
dilemma of its proper role in a "democratic" and multi-ethnic society, is
nevertheless intrinsic to the rise of the short story as a popular form in
United States culture. The ideology imbedded within the short story
form, that is the sedimented layers of transmitted codes, reading
prejudices, and socio-political attitudes that control the reception (as
well as the production) of the American short story form, suggests the
disturbingly anti-traditional nature of the short story as a genre.
Whatever the particular "content" then, or regardless of reassuring
claims of loyalty to one's abandoned culture, the short story as a form,
at least in the context of the United States, often signifies a rejection of

ethnic identity and a dramatic movement towards a modern and traditionless future. Inevitably lost in this gesture, especially in contemporary U.S. society, is the homogeneity of American culture itself, the deeply traditional nature of life in the new, anti-traditional dispensation: this insight does not seem available to those caught in transit, to those submerged in the process of forging a new, ethnic-free identity. Not coincidentally, the over-riding imperative of the short story form, from Irving's "Rip Van Winkle" to the present, centers on the often-painful insight that ethnicity unavoidably retards modernization.

In this sense, the short story as a form suggests that, unlike Rip Van Winkle, postcolonial Americans must *not* drink too deeply from the draught of the folk—be they Dutch, Irish, or Arab. Not least among the virtues of *The Native Informant* is Ramzi Salti's ability to creatively appropriate the American short story form and thereby demonstrate its on-going resiliency and vitality, two hundred years after the time of Irving. The dialectical movement away from one's ethnic past towards a modern future as a newly inscribed U.S. subject, including often-paradoxical longings for the source, in fact motors the American short story as a form. Salti's short story collection successfully reinvigorates the age-old dialectic between ethnicity and modernization in many surprising and satisfying ways. In the process, he teaches us many valuable lessons about Arab, American, and Arab American culture.[11]

NOTES

1. Notable exceptions include Mafouz's *Midog Alley* and Youssef Idris' short story "A Leader of Men."
2. Salti mentions these authors in a personal letter (18 December 1995) responding to my questions.
3. My use of the word "modern" in this context is neither pejorative nor celebratory but descriptive. I also mean it in the sense implied by Theodor W. Adorno in his *Aesthetic Theory*, that "no work of art in the last hundred years or so has been able to dodge the concept of the modern" (30).
4. I rely here upon Fredric Jameson's definition of narrative as a "socially symbolic act" in *The Political Unconscious* (19–20). Also, see Claude Levi-Strauss's *Tristes Tropiques* (196–197) and Theodor W. Adorno's "Reconciliation Under Duress" (160).
5. The title of Gugelberger's latest book, *The Real Thing: Testimonial Discourse and Latin America* (1996), illustrates his on-going interest in the historical (rather than the purely textual) dimensions of

literature. Also, see Jameson's *The Prison-House of Language*, especially Jameson's critique of Derrida (174–187).

6. The name 'Antara from the title of this story refers to the well-known poet and figure from ancient Arabic literature, with whom the narrator feels a strong affiliation.

7. This is not to say, of course, that Arabic is "inadequate" but only that 'Ala' experiences it as such.

8. It should be noted that while some feminist writers within the Islamic world (like Fatima Mernassi, for example) adopt a similar approach, other feminists, like Salti, Ghada Samman, Hanan Shaykh, and others deliberately draw upon Western feminism.

9. See Jameson's *"History and Class Consciousness* as an Unfinished Project."

10. Following the demise of apartheid in South Africa, the nation-state of Israel remains one of the few countries globally that bases its rights of citizenship and representation upon one's ethnic heritage. Hence, while Israel defines itself as a "democratic" society, it is nevertheless a democracy wherein full civil rights are restricted to people of Jewish descent. The situation of indigenous Arabs living within Israel, both Christian and Muslim, is in some sense analogous to the situation of non-whites living under South African apartheid or African Americans living under Jim Crow laws in the American South.

11. Special thanks to Julie Brown, Georg M. Gugelberger, and Ramzi M. Salti for their helpful comments on previous drafts of this essay.

REFERENCES

Adorno, Theodor W. *Aesthetic Theory.* London: Routledge and Kegan Paul, 1984.

___. "Reconciliation Under Duress." *Aesthetics and Politics.* Ed. Ernst Bloch, et al. London: NLB, 1977: 151–176.

Gugelberger, Georg M. "Decolonizing the Canon: Considerations of Third World Literature." *New Literary History.* Volume 22, Number 3. Summer 1991: 505–524.

___. *The Real Thing: Testimonial Discourse and Latin America.* Durham, North Carolina: Duke University Press, 1996.

Jameson, Fredric. *"History and Class Consciousness* as an Unfinished Project." *Rethinking Marxism,* Volume 1, Number 1, Spring 1988: 49–72.

___. *The Political Unconscious.* Ithaca, New York: Cornell University Press, 1981.

___. *The Prison-House of Language.* Princeton, New Jersey: Princeton University Press, 1972.

Johnson-Davies, Denys. "Translator's Foreword," *Distant View of a Minaret* by Alifa Rifaat. London: Heinemann, 1989.

Levi-Strauss, Claude. *Tristes Tropiques.* New York: Penguin, 1992.

Ngugi wa Thiong'o. *Decolonizing the Mind: The Politics of Language in African Literature.* London: James Curry and Heinemann, 1986.

Ong, Walter J. *Interfaces of the Word: Studies in the Evolution of Consciousness and Culture.* Ithaca: Cornell University Press, 1977.

Said, Edward W. *Orientalism.* New York, NY: Vintage Books, 1979.

Salti, Ramzi M. *The Native Informant: Six Tales of Defiance from the Arab World.* Colorado Springs, Colorado: Three Continents Press, 1994.

14. The Naming of Katz:[1] Who Am I? Who Am I Supposed to Be? Who Can I Be? Passing, Assimilation, and Embodiment in Short Fiction by Fannie Hurst and Thyra Samter Winslow with a Few Jokes Thrown in and Various References to Other Others

Susan Koppelman

I

In a *cri de coeur*, a *geshrei*, echoed by millions of immigrants, Tevye the Dairyman, creation of Sholom Alecheim and central character in *Fiddler on the Roof*, asks "Without our traditions, who are we?" *Fiddler* is a musical catalogue of the bending, overturning, and abandoning of "our traditions," and when finally the Jews of Anitevka are expelled from their homes after the pogrom (staged always in stylized, sanitized, minimized fashion), understanding that they must leave or die, they have the flexibility to fulfill the commandment to "Choose life." They leave behind many of their possessions and many of their traditions, some already eroded and some just being challenged, but they take with them what they can. Off they go, to be strangers, in strange new lands. Off they go to learn who, without their traditions, they will be. And in these strange new lands, many of them will come to be known by strange new names.

Whether the old life was lived in another country, another culture, or a more marginalized identity, all emigrants must make hard choices about what to keep from the old life and what to take with them, what to adopt or attempt to incorporate into one's "self" in the New World. Once the journey has been negotiated and the New World engaged, what, if any, of the original self must be sacrificed (and why) to ensure survival in the New World? If an immigrant trades too much of the inherited, traditional, or early identity for the new, who survives? And what are the ethical, political, cultural, and psychological consequences to every one of these changes? And what about using the exigencies of life in a new world as an excuse to abandon onerous or despised traditional obligations and community-imposed definitions of the self? These questions and the individual and historical consequences of how individuals answer them haunt those who live in *galut*, in exile, those who wander in the Diaspora, all their lives—and their children and their children's children. The wrestling matches with these haunting questions have become a major theme in U.S. literature.

For immigrants to the United States, the courage to leave home forever, abandoning the known environment with its understood orders and disorders, risking life and limb in the actual physical trial—one which endangered all, damaged many, and destroyed some—of crossing an ocean in steerage or trekking across dangerous borders to what is, in fact, an unknown world, is often bolstered on the one hand by the death dogs of oppression, starvation, poverty, enforced servitude and separations, etc. at "home" and on the other hand by the allure of the *goldeneh medina*[2], with its promises of life, liberty, and the pursuit of happiness, with the conflicting rumors of both a classless society and class mobility, with stories of a genuine meritocracy, equal opportunity, and unlimited horizons, and, for Jews, most important of all, the hope that here, in America, there would be no prejudice, no persecution, no pogroms, no anti-Semitism.

Is it any wonder that survivors of a painful past might wish to become like those who have given them safety? Is it so awful for immigrants to want to become real Americans? Many will want, for various reasons, to become "real" Americans—whatever that means— and that "whatever it means" is the real heart(break) of the matter. Because who is to say, to decide, what and who is a "real American?"

Are the reasons the American-born children of immigrants want to shed the accoutrements of their parents' past as easy to understand (i.e., perhaps forgive, perhaps sympathize with, perhaps excuse?) as the reasons their parents might wish or might not wish to assimilate? The parents either hang onto or can't shed their cultural/linguistic past, but that past provided a context for all the accoutrements. For the American-born children, the past context has never existed: they came into a world of remnants. If they can't have whole cloth, are they to be blamed for wanting to refashion the remnants into something else?

II

The multimedia culture of the United States includes a distinguished multigeneric body of writing (and films based on this writing) exploring how other people have answered these questions. Portrayals and portraits of aspects of assimilation, passing, accommodation, and cultural invention abound in the writing of Jewish and other marginalized writers. Fictional explorations of assimilation, passing, of honoring the traditions and the past, and of choosing among the opportunities of the present characterize much American-Jewish writing.

Sometimes the issues are explored in the context of the life of a woman weighing competing marriage proposals, each suitor representing a particular life style or ethic of immigration. The woman considers her future identity, not just as a wife but as a Jew, and the future of the children: the preservation or abandonment of Old Ways and the accommodation of or resistance to New Ways. In Viola Brothers Shore's 1921 short story "Heritage," a young woman is caught in that struggle between assimilation and keeping faith with tradition. She considers her suitors in very personal, Western-style romantic terms, wavering until she realizes that in choosing which man she will marry, she is making an ethical life style choice with historical consequences not only for herself and her children but for her people.

Stories like this[3] taught young Jewish women that the choice of a mate, a life-partner, a co-parent, involves choosing a set of ethics or principles about how to choose. Will she choose with her fluttering heart and the hankering of her loins, as the American mythos and popular culture with their individualist, romantic love ethic encourage? Will she choose with an eye to his bank account as so many mothers in so much British fiction and Anglo-U. S. fiction encourage?[4] Or will she make a choice rooted in the tradition of her people? If she chooses the traditional ethic—responsibility to the continuity of her people, the preservation of their faith, and honor to their history—will she heed the advice of community elders, perhaps even allow them to make a choice for her? Is there a role for Yenta the matchmaker?

As often as the questions about traditional community survival are explored in the context of marriage choices, they are also explored in terms of the relationship between the generations. For instance, in Grace Paley's 1959 short story "The Loudest Voice," a young Jewish girl is thrilled to be offered the prominent speaking role in the up-coming public school Christmas pageant but can accept the offer only with the consent of her parents. The story dramatizes the debate: should she or shouldn't she? And who is to decide? We hear conflicting responses from her parents; the Jewish immigrant adults, the whole neighborhood, chime in to offer opinions. And isn't this how it should be? Because the decision, and those thousands, millions, of other decisions in the same vein reflect on not only the family, not only the whole neighborhood, but reverberate *dor l'or* from generation to generation.

III

Two of the most significant arenas for immigrant family conflicts about adaptation to the New World turn on two public manifestations of the self: one's name and one's appearance. Individual choices on these matters were complicated by differences among family members about which were right or wrong, acceptable and unacceptable, possible and impossible choices for them as individuals.

The problems with choosing both first and last names in any diasporic community are painfully familiar to members of the U.S. population of immigrants and their descendants who wrestle with ethnic and racial marginalization. For example, late in his life, Isaac Asimov still pondered, albeit ironically, how the question of naming had arisen in his own life:

In "Seven Steps to Grand Master" Asimov remembered:

> I was born in Russia. The land had just gone through World War I, a revolution, a civil war, and foreign intervention. . . . In late 1922, my parents decided it might be a good idea to emigrate to the United States . . . we arrived in Brooklyn in February of 1923, a little past my third birthday (19).
> . . . in the United States, my parents realized that they had gained a new status—that of being "greenhorns." Everyone was eager to advise us and to guide our faltering steps down the pathway to American citizenship, especially those old settlers who had gotten off the ship five years earlier.
> One neighbor woman said to my mother, in my hearing (I was four or five by then and so small for my age that no one noticed me . . .), "Why do you call him Isaac, Mrs. Asimov? With a name like that, he will always have a stigma on him." (Translation: "Everyone will know he is Jewish.")
> My mother said, "So what should I call him, Mrs. Bindler?"

> And Mrs. Bindler . . . said, "Call him Oiving."
> (Translation: Irving. This is a grand old aristocratic English
> family name.)
>   My mother was very impressed and would undoubtedly
> have accepted the suggestion, but, as I said, I was listening
> with each ear. I was not yet old enough to understand the
> semantic fact that the name of a thing was not the thing itself.
> I didn't understand that I was merely *called* Isaac and that I
> could be me whatever I was called. (Or as I once put it—rather
> neatly, I think—"That which we call a rose by any other name
> would smell as sweet.")
>   What I thought was that I *was* Isaac and if I were called
> anything else, I wouldn't be me. Whereupon I raised what we
> called in those days "a holler," absolutely refusing, under any
> conditions, to allow myself to be called Oiving. I was Isaac
> and I intended to stay Isaac. My mother simply wilted under
> the force of my indignation.
>   . . . . Had I accepted Oiving, it would have proved every
> bit as stigmatic as Isaac, for so many Jewish mothers had
> sought escape for their young hopefuls in that direction that
> Oiving became as Jewish as Isaac and without the biblical
> cachet of the latter name. (20–21)

Some immigrants whose names mark them as outside of the
dominant culture change all or part of their names. This name-changing
is undertaken for many reasons. The newcomers may "just" want to "fit
in," to accommodate themselves to their new environment. They may
be embarrassed or feel accosted by—rather than or in addition to
disgusted by or contemptuous of—the (usually unapologetic) self-proclaimed
inability of people whose names are rooted in different
linguistic traditions to pronounce the names of the immigrants. They
may good-naturedly wish to disassemble any barriers that separate them
from what they want to be able to consider their new community of
fellow Americans. They may want to seem or to become as assimilated
as possible in order to take advantage of the greater opportunities of all
kinds available to those who are most "like" the members of the
dominant culture, i.e., white[5] Christians. They may think little about
changing their names to become "Americanized" because they think
their history as a wandering people has been a history of successive
assimilations and know full well that there have been successive name
changes. They may, in fact, see the overarching "fact" of their tradition
as change, adaptation for the sake of survival.

In the early stories of Fannie Hurst (1885–1968), the U.S.-born Jewish daughter of the U.S.-born Jewish children of Ashkenazi Jewish immigrants, it is taken for granted that this turbulence is appropriate subject matter for literature. Fannie Hurst's early writing career was almost entirely centered on "reports" of the variety of ways that Jewish women and their natal families struggled with assimilation issues, the confusingly semi-rigid social class structure they encountered in the New World, and sexual harassment and the exploitation of their labor in the work world. Many of her stories focus on the problems of living in and embracing a new culture while trying to establish and maintain personal integrity and trying to preserve the multi-generational family connections that characterized lives in the Old Country. Hurst explores these dynamics in the context of family life from the points of view of each family members in different stories.

Many of her stories depict the intergenerational tumult and confusion that arises when parents become the pupils of their children in "how to be American"—or when their children think their parents should become their pupils. The children of immigrants sometimes disrespectfully and condescendingly assume authority over their parents based on their quick metamorphoses into "natives" at ease with local customs and the new language or by virtue of their birth in the new country. Conflicts between the generations reflect varying degrees of insistence by parents on loyalty to old ways and old values and the varying degrees of ease with which the Americanized children are able to and do insist on the Americanization of their families.

Fannie Hurst's story "The Gold in Fish"[6] is perhaps the most important fictional presentation of the struggle over names in an immigrant family in American literature. The change of the family name from "Goldfish" to "Fish" is urged on the family by the financially successful and social-status-seeking son, Morris, once peddlar of second-hand furniture who has become a high-ticket art and estate appraiser and auctioneer. He explains his decision:

> . . . I have changed our name legally because it was a liability and not an asset. No man named Morris Goldfish can hope to achieve the position in life that I have mapped out for myself. For us. . . . Morris Goldfish and Maurice Fish are two different human beings. . . . Certain walks of life are closed to Morris Goldfish that I, as Maurice Fish, propose to enter (p. 63).

By insisting on this change, he makes clear his understanding that there is a class system in America, that there is anti-Semitism here, that although economic opportunity may be great, it doesn't go hand in hand with social opportunity, and that he doesn't intend to suffer, or for his family to suffer, the cost of those realities if they can escape them by changing their name.

His sister Birdie, perhaps disgusted by what she thinks of as his pretensions, or perhaps convinced by what she knows of the history of her people—the impossibility of escaping Jewish identity—and thinking him ridiculously naive, or, perhaps aware of *his* unsheddable ethnic "markers" (Hurst refers to the quality of a certain kind of Jewish ethnicity that is recognizable in the voice and mannerisms of Morris\Maurice as "Oriental"-ness), roars with laughter and exclaims:

> You poor fish . . . how's gefuldte[7] fish? Morris Gefuldte Fish. At least when you were amputating why didn't you cut off the tail, you poor Fish, and leave the Gold?

Her brother answers:

> Because Gold is a common and obviously modified name. Everybody has done it that way. Look in the telephone book and you'll see fifty Golds to one Fish. There is distinction to the name Fish. If it is good enough for Stuyvesant Fish and Hamilton Fish, it is good enough for Maurice[8] Fish. . . . (71)

In other words, "Gold" is no longer a secure cover for being a Jew. And he wants a cover. A "cover" has often been a Jew's only chance for survival. Morris/ Maurice thinks at some level that here in America, as in previous countries where Jewish survival has seemed relatively assured, the dangers have not disappeared.

IV

Survival is nothing to belittle or dismiss lightly as it often is by those whose lives have never been in danger. And survival is at least temporarily assured by immigration. "Survivalist" immigration is often accompanied by the wish to consolidate apparent safety either by assimilation (actively seeking absorption by and transforming the self into the other) or passing (appearing to be like the other in public only). With each new wave of immigrants, the naming conundrum begins anew. For Jews, a diasporic people since the Babylonian Exile in 586 BCE, the destruction of the second temple in 70 C.E., and the Expulsion from Spain in 1492, the naming issue reemerges with each eviction and flight resulting in relocation. Morris/ Maurice's wife Irma née Striker, with the straightened nose and her ten "finger-nails, flaming ruby cabochons which hung from her hands in flowing convex surfaces," refers to this past as she defends her complicity with her husband's decision to his parents:

> You don't understand. . . . Goldfish, as it has been translated from whatever your forebears chose to call themselves, is a comedy name. Nobody bearing it can help being just a little ridiculous all of the time. It isn't the name that an important art connoisseur . . . should bear. (65–66)

Irma, of course, is not without some justification in her complaint against her husband's father's name, although she is probably wrong that the name "Goldfish" was ever chosen by the family. Where did the family get the name? Is it a ridiculous name? Jews and other oppressed people were often forced to answer to names that had about them an air of the ridiculous. All over the world people answer to first and last names not their own, not chosen for them by those who bear and rear them, names that signify their and their family's vulnerability.[9]

There is also a multi-cultural tradition of people choosing to change their names to mark or celebrate major transformations in their lives. In the 1960 film adaptation of Leon Uris's novel *Exodus*, Paul Newman's character Ari ben Canaan explains that in Russia his father was called Yaakov Rabinowitz, but after walking all the way from Russia to the Holy Land, he changed his name to Barach ben Canaan. In his review of the 1992 Israeli Film Academy Award-winning film '66 *Was a Good Year for Tourism*, Robert A. Cohn writes: "Victor Gormanzao was Haim Goren's name when he was born in Alexandria, Egypt. . . . After Israel was reborn as an independent state in 1948, Victor and his family moved to. . . . Tel Aviv. . . . As was the custom in Israel in those days, he changed his name to Haim Goren so as to be 'more Israeli'" (20). Malcolm Little changed his name to Malcolm X and changed the meaning and direction of his life when he did so. He did so again, to mark another transformation in his consciousness, when he became Shabazz just months before his murder. Cassius Clay defied the government and risked the loss of his career and the ridicule and censure of the press when he insisted on his right to choose his own name, one that represented his newly reforged sense of identity; he became Muhammad Ali and most of the people in the world now who know him by that name never knew him by any other.

If the Goldfish name represents the enforced, demeaning nomenclature of a prior oppression, i.e., if Goldfish really is comedic[10]—then why should the family continue to live with it? Isn't taking control of one's destiny by choosing one's own name an empowering act? If it is courageous for Clay to become Ali, isn't it equally admirable that Morris Goldfish should become Maurice Fish? On the other hand, if "Goldfish" is neither comedic nor demeaning to the people who claim the name as their own because they see nothing about themselves as demeaned or ridiculous, and Goldfish is only ridiculous to the current dominant culture, is it an act of self-assertion to change Goldfish to Fish? Or is it an act of surrender: I defer to you by imitating you; I will change my name.

V

Literary treatments of this naming theme appear in every form from the most recent "elite" fiction to genre fiction to autobiography to humor to history. An earlier example of this literature is Thyra Samter Winslow's 1923 story, "A Cycle of Manhattan," which follows the family Rosenheimer from their 1894 disembarkation from steerage through a quarter-century of Americanization. The story was reprinted a number of times[11], although (or perhaps because) the author takes an unsympathetic, or disdainful, attitude towards the Rosenheimers. There isn't a single member of the Rosenheimer family (which eventually numbers nine as they proudly add two "American" babies to their number) for whom a reader can feel genuine affection.

Abraham (or Abe, as he was known in Lithuania) Rosenheimer drops two letters to become Rosenheim on the advice of his children despite his initial objections: "Change my name, as if I was a criminal or something" (Winslow 112). A change of address coincides with the name A. G. Rosen appearing on the family mail box. Next he becomes Abraham Lincoln Rose. And then A. Lincoln Ross. The final family name change follows son Mannie (Emanuel)'s complaint:

> Rose is so—so peculiar. . . . Any one could tell it had been something else, Rosen or worse. I . . . go to College this fall. I'm not going to have a name so—so ordinary. Let's change it to Ross. That's not distinctive but it isn't queer or foreign. I'm changing my first name just a little, too. . . . I'm going to register . . . as Manning Ross. (149–150)
> "Ordinary." "Queer." "Foreign." Code words for "gentile," "Jewish," and "immigrant."

Each name change urged by the growing children parallels increased economic family status in Winslow's story. By the time the

Rosenheimers become the Rosses, they have moved from the fourth-floor two-room walk-up apartment on New York's Lower East Side to a five-story house on East Sixty-Fifth, just off Fifth Avenue plus a "little" country place on Long Island. As their last name changes, so, too, do their children's first names. The "progress" of the children's self-naming reflects what happens not only with this family but with several other families whose lives intertwine with theirs (among them the Abramsons whose son Sam enters adulthood as McDougal Adams). Son Isaac Rosenheimer, six years old when he first stepped onto the pavements of the New World, becomes first Irving and later Irwin; Yetta becomes Yvette; and Mannie Rosenheimer emerges finally as Manning Cuyler Ross.

The difficulty Winslow's story raises for contemporary readers several generations removed from the immigrant experience—and this difficulty is exposed in sharp detail by comparing it to "The Gold in Fish"—is that the story is told as if nothing motivates these people other than petty snobberies, decadent frivolity, and senseless pretension.

VI

The two stories are similar: we watch two sets of recent Eastern European Jewish immigrants to the *goldeneh medina* become Americanized and, in an almost feverish process, shed their old selves in favor of what seem to be possible new selves. We watch them learn to enjoy more and better material possessions; we accompany them as they adopt the customs and values of their new home both in gratitude for and in an effort to consolidate and capitalize on the economic opportunities that enable them to achieve satiety of their physical appetites for what may be the first time in generations—they aren't hungry, they aren't cold, they aren't threadbare, they don't end every day in total exhaustion from the struggle to survive. They aren't in fear for their lives from pogroms. For these things the parents are, understandably, grateful. But the children, who have never known the horrors of the past, want only to "fit in," to be "regular people," to be "ordinary," to run with their peers on equal terms. But when the desire to adapt, pass, assimilate, leave behind a painful past, etc. is presented to the reader as a desire without an historical context, when it is seen from the perspective of an unsympathetic outsider, as it is in Winslow's story, the characters devolve into little more than caricatures and the story stinks of anti-Semitism—in Winslow's case, internalized anti-Semitism. It is an outsider's story and the conflicts surrounding the issues of passing, etc., are not worked out as genuine ethical problems but rather presented as capricious, social-climbing buffoonery.

VII

A few other examples suffice to identify the longevity and continuing fascination of this particularly American literary theme. (I refer henceforth only to "insider" stories.)

In Jamaica Kincaid's story, "In Rouseau," her central character, Xuela Claudette Desvarieus, despairing about her own name because of what it reveals to her about her history, muses that " . . . the name of any one person is at once their history recapitulated and abbreviated, and on declaring it that person holds himself high or low, the person hearing it holds the declarer high or low."

In Alice Walker's "Everyday Use" one of the narrator's two daughters has changed her name from Dee to Wangero Leewanika Kemanjo. Dee\Wangero explains that she is shedding her slave name and reclaiming her heritage by assuming an African name. Her mother insists that she is disparaging her heritage—that is, the heritage from the women in their family. The mother can trace the name Dee to her aunt, her grandmother, and all the way back to the Civil War. But just as Morris\Maurice insists that his mother and father can't understand, Dee insists that her mother doesn't understand.

And probably those parents can't understand.

Just as their children don't understand their parents' perspectives on this issue of naming.

Winslow wrote "A Cycle of Manhattan" as if none of the characters had any dignity or depth. Walker tells the story as if those who espouse at least one perspective on the "problem" might have moral authority. Kincaid writes the story as if the powerlessness of women and children over their own names is one more way of the patriarchy imposing its will on its victims.

Can this story ever be told without making those on one side of the argument or the other seem insensitive? Arrogant? Shallow? Opportunistic? Narrow-minded? Usually the name-changer is made to seem morally, even aesthetically, in the wrong, as in the case with both Dee\Wangero and Morris\Maurice. But historically, at least for the few generations we can trace it in this country, the choices of the Maurices outnumber the choices of the Birdies, the siblings, who remain faithful to the old ways.

On the other hand, there are those who assert that most of the time escaped identity is, indeed, lost identity. Peoples have disappeared time and again via intermarriage and assimilation. In "The Gold in Fish" we see the beginning of the process. And even though it seems that Morris\Maurice and Irma are in the wrong, and even though, as his father lies dying and his mother urges her husband to revive and receive the gifts of his son Morris, and we hear no objection from Morris, we know that following his father's death, the son's name for the rest of his life will be Maurice, and his children will be Fish.

Can this story be written another way, in another voice, in a way that, despite the pain of those on opposite sides of the argument, forces the reader to feel uncomfortable agreeing with either side?

In addition to the meaning of names and naming in our community of origin, the issue of what and how and why we name ourselves is further complicated by the ways in which a name is (readily or not) perceived by those in the dominant culture as being self-chosen rather than given or inherited. Those who are willing to change their names, to adopt more "American," i.e., gentile, sounding names, gamble that their changed names will lead to changed circumstances and more benevolent perceptions of them by the members of the dominant culture. But anti-Semites are fairly quick to detect Jews who try to pass by obvious, or even subtle, means. And often, rather than feeling less "offended" by "Jewishness," anti-Semites are contemptuous of people who compromise their integrity by changing their names to gain the acceptance of people who don't want to have anything to do with them. Groucho Marx's twist on this issue has entered comedic history: "I don't want to be a member of any club that would have me."

When Morris\Maurice complains:

> . . . Gold is a common and obviously modified name.
> Everybody has done it that way.

he is evoking an entire ethos of assimilation. Who is the "everybody" to whom he refers? All the other Jews who change their names to escape the stigma of Jewishness, all those people who called their sons "Oiving" instead of "Isaac."

VIII

"Foreignness" in short stories sold well and widely in the early twentieth century similar to the way "regionalism" has sold in the last quarter of the nineteenth century. The literary tradition of regionalism, in terms of plots, characterization, relationships, and problems to be solved, provided the literary basics for ethnic writing. Writers had already devised the literary devices to explore a socio-geographical context unfamiliar to the majority of their readers that would invite in those stranger-readers and help them learn to be familiar with the differences, or at least to recognize them. The Gullah Blacks who populate the stories of Julia Peterkin (1880–1961) must have seemed as strange, as exotic, and were as vulnerable to caricature and stereotyping as the Ukrainian Jewish immigrants of Sholom Aleichem[12] were to the Yankee fisherfolk of Elizabeth Stuart Phelps' (1844–1911) stories. One set of the roots of ethnic stories undoubtedly grew deep in the soil of the literary regionalism of Mary E. Wilkins Freeman, Kate Chopin, Samuel Clemens, and others. There was a hunger in the United States for stories about "others," stories in which the common humanity of "us" and "them" was affirmed, thereby reducing some of the terror "natives" had of "strangers." Before WWI, ethnic stories were as popular as regional stories had been after the Civil War.

To "hear" the resonances of "The Gold in Fish," this family, this debate, not only is it important to understand the story's "general" history and context, but the story's "Jewish moment" in both the United States and in Eastern Europe, the most recent previous homeland of these characters.

In his 1994 book *Anti-Semitism in America*, Leonard Dinnerstein details the growth of anti-Semitism in the United States after World War I. The world into which the characters who had peopled ethnic stories moved when they left the ghettos is described in his chapter "Erecting Barriers and Narrowing Opportunities (1919–1933)":

> The aftermath of the first World War left Americans disillusioned with internationalism, fearful of Bolshevik subversion, and frightened that foreigners would corrupt the nation's values and traditions. . . . The Secretary of the Chamber of Commerce of one community in Florida captured an extreme expression of this feeling in 1924 when he advocated expelling all Jews and foreigners from St. Petersburg to make the community a "100% American Gentile City."[13]
>
> This intensified desire to keep America for . . . Americans coincided with the coming of age of . . . children of turn-of-the-century immigrants who sought to escape the ghetto. In the 1920s. . . . (e)fforts to acculturate . . . were met with strong resistance from members of the middle and upper classes who had little inclination to associate with Jews.

On August 17, 1915, an Atlanta, Georgia, mob kidnapped from prison and, chanting anti-Semitic slogans, lynched Leo Frank, a New

York Jewish engineer who had moved to Atlanta to manage the pencil factory of his uncle. He was posthumously exonerated in March 1986 of the murder of the thirteen-year-old girl who had been an employee at the factory. The Frank case was a cause célèbre, with much the same impact in the United States as the Dreyfus case had in France. The fabricated *Protocols of the Elders of Zion* touted the myth of an international Jewish plot to undermine Christian civilization. Invented and written by a Russian fanatic, and distributed at the turn of the century by the czar's secret police to deflect Russian peasants from understanding the mechanics of their misery and to undermine growing revolutionary fervor in czarist Russia by providing a scapegoat, the infamous libel was published in a new English translation in London in 1920; within weeks the pamphlet found enthusiastic distributors in the United States. In 1919 Henry Ford's newspaper *The Dearborn Independent* began a seven-year attack on Jews based on *The Protocols of the Elders of Zion* that resulted in increasing circulation from 22,000 in 1919 to 700,000 in 1924.[14] In approximately the same period, the membership of the Ku Klux Klan rose from 5,000 in 1920 to four and a half million in 1924. The second decade of the twentieth century in the United States was a time of economic disaster for many. Almost 5 million were unemployed in 1920, and in 1920–21, 20,000 businesses went into bankruptcy. "Under this economic pressure, and with the growth of the Jewish population, discrimination against Jews in employment, housing and higher education sharpened alarmingly" (*Not the Work* 27).

Harvard University reduced the number of Jewish students on its campus during this period. Sentiment for restricting immigration and organizations to support it swept the nation. Laura Z. Hobson, whose award-winning novel *Gentlemen's Agreement* later dealt with these anti-Semitic issues, was excluded from Phi Beta Kappa at Cornell University because she was Jewish. "All told, fewer than 100 Jews were on the liberal arts and sciences faculties of American universities in the mid-1920s. . . . " (Dinnerstein 88). Referring to the question of names, Dinnerstein writes:

> English departments generally considered themselves the bastions of Anglo-Saxon culture and not until 1939 did Lionel Trilling become the first Jew appointed to a tenure-track position in that field at Columbia University. Diana Trilling later wrote that "it is highly questionable whether the offer would have been made" had her husband borne the surname of his maternal grandfather, Cohen. (87)

While Ford was playing the demagogue in the United States, what was happening in Eastern Europe? Simon Wiesenthal records 40 pogroms in the Ukraine[15] alone, resulting in the murders of 5,602 Jews, untold wounded and mutilated, and uncountable numbers of Jewish women and girls raped in just one year—1919.[16]

Fannie Hurst was completely familiar with this complex and painful socio-political milieu with which she as a Jew also contended. That Fannie Hurst was completely aware of the horrors of the pogroms is clear not only from her social justice activism but from some of her stories. In two stories in particular, both of which received considerable public attention, one as a result of multiple reprintings and the other as a film, she details the cruelty and brutality of the pogroms and the traumas suffered by Jews in Eastern Europe during these years; although the pogroms are background to subsequent dilemmas of the U. S. immigrant characters in the 1917 "Get Ready The Wreaths"[17] and the 1921 "Roulette,"[18] the stories are still chilling, heart-rending reading.

During these years, Hurst was so involved with civil rights and human rights groups that it is hard to figure out when she had time to write. But then, one of the most frequently noted of her personal attributes was her almost unbelievably abundant energy. She slept little and lived intensely, with passion and conviction: she believed her public life as important as her literary life and her private life. She lived all three to the hilt. Her literary and public lives reinforced each other— she wove into her fiction the concerns that she supported in her public life. She committed her time, energy, money, and the power of her name to organizations that fought for open immigration, for resettlement and the general welfare of new Americans, and for protection of those who were liable to be victimized for their "differences."[19]

IX

In his book *Jewish Humor: What the Best Jewish Jokes Say About the Jews*, Rabbi Joseph Telushkin reminds contemporary Jews about traditional Jewish attitudes toward the changing of names to avoid participating in the common fate of the Jewish people: "Jewish humor consistently argues that a Jew can never really assimilate, and Judaism agrees. According to a medieval dictum, based on the Talmud, 'a Jew, even if he [sic] sins (by converting to another religion), remains a Jew.'" And Telushkin tells this joke to make his point:

American banker Otto Kahn was Jewish by birth but had
converted to Christianity. He was once walking with a
hunchbacked friend when they passed a synagogue.
"You know I used to be a Jew," Kahn said.
"And I used to be a hunchback," his companion replied.

Jokes, which are, as much as they are anything else, short-short
stories, serve many functions. Among these are exposing pretensions,
teaching about reality, and reenforcing community standards as in the
one above; jokes can also humiliate, demean, ridicule, and
disempower— all of which may feel to the butt like being
disemboweled. The same joke can do all of these things and more. Like
the short story, their "purpose" is to inspire revelation, a satori, a
moment of perfect understanding.

I think Winslow's story, an extended exploration of a bad joke, is a
bad story and that it shames the people it purports to represent.
Winslow provides no context for the feelings and choices of the
characters and she perpetrates stereotypes. In Hurst's "The Gold in Fish"
Birdie Goldfish is the sympathetic moral center of the story. Because
Hurst's story has a moral center and is grounded more firmly in an
historical context, it becomes an insider's story and the conflicts
surrounding the issues of passing, etc. are worked out as genuine ethical
problems rather than capricious, social-climbing buffoonery.

X

The issues probed in relationship to passing and assimilation have
as much to do with characters' varying physical individuality and the
unalterability of their embodiment as they do with values. Americans
are most familiar with the issues raised by different embodiments
within families as those issues have been conceptualized within the
African American community among whose families are often members
with a wide range of skin colors. From Nella Larsen's novels *Passing*
and *Quicksand* to Gayl Jones' short story collection *White Rat* we have
learned to think about the issue of passing, the internalization of the
values of the dominant culture, and the ways families can be conflicted
and torn by the differences among their members, in terms of color.

In much Jewish fiction about these issues and in Hurst's "The Gold
in Fish" in particular, the possibility of passing revolves around not
shades of skin color but corporeal configurations. Only certain kinds of
bodies can be controlled. Noses can be reshaped, hair can be straightened
(at least temporarily), accents can usually be trained away (see *How the
Garcia Girls Lost Their Accents*), but unmarried fat women in ethnic

stories like Birdie in "The Gold in Fish" represent those women whose bodies are assumed by many to reflect and embody the "peasant" ethnic history of their people; their bodies cannot be assimilated or converted; their bodies cannot be reshaped or disguised, despite the best efforts of personal trainers, corsetieres, make-up artists, fashion consultants, and plastic surgeons.[20] In this story as in many others, Fannie Hurst associates female body pampering with three kinds of women: those who are the legal consorts of wealthy men, as is Irma, the wife of Morris/Maurice; those who are their paid companions[21]; and those who earn their living as performers. Painted fingernails, "fixed" noses, diet-controlled bodies, wrinkle-creamed moisturized skin. The issue of the "controlled" body, or the body whose ontological reality is chosen, shaped, controlled by the owner of the body (or the owner of the owner of the body), occupied Fannie Hurst in her own life as well as in much of her fiction.[22]

Although Birdie is loyal to her parents' choices for themselves, honoring their independence, although she is loyal to the love of her youth and enables his transformation (he "got in with the wrong crowd" for a while but now, having paid his "debt to society," he is "saved by the love of a good woman"), although she is brave and strong, determined and hard-working, benevolent and caring, she is demeaned, her opinions are dismissed, and her values are ridiculed by her brother and condescended to by her sister-in-law because she is fat. Her sister-in-law Irma's slenderness, and her obsession with the money, time, and effort she spends maintaining it, and her husband's pride in his ability to "conspicuously consume" a skinny gentile-looking woman are contrasted by Hurst with the emotional generosity, spiritedness, and warmth of the fat sister who cannot, because of her body type, enter into the class to which her brother aspired and which he thinks he has (or will, with his new name) attained.

Because Birdie cannot disguise her basic body type, she cannot pass; her choices are limited to what attitude she will adopt toward her undisguisable, inescapable natal identity. She chooses the attitude that in our present time is usually called "Pride" (Gay and Lesbian Pride, Black Pride) and embraces the identity despised by others. In fact, Fannie Hurst's Birdie might be seen as a pre-post-modern example of ethnic and somatype pride.

XI

What is the difference between passing from the underworld to the respectable world, and passing from an ethnic lower class to the gentile upper class? Why does Birdie approve of one but think the other one is contemptible? And what is the difference between changing one's name from one representing one's ethnic history to one representing one's chosen nationality or from one representing one's previous patriarchal "ownership" to one's present patriarchal "ownership," i.e., changing one's last name from a woman's father's name to a woman's husband's name?

Slupsky, Birdie's ex-convict beloved, wants to "pass" as much as her brother Morris does, but his desired passage from the underworld into the respectable world is presented by Hurst and Birdie as a worthy desire. Morris, with his easy contempt, makes it clear that he considers Slupsky's "passage" no more possible than we know his own (Morris') passage to be. But Birdie, who is completely opposed to her brother's pretensions to pass as classier and less ethnic than his background, has no qualms about Slupsky's desire to pass as a respectable person when he is, in fact, a reformed crook. Additionally, this woman who criticizes her brother for wishing to change his name from Goldfish to Gold is delighted to change her own—from Goldfish to Slupsky.

XII

All of the questions about the relationship between identity and the self-in-exile are raised in "The Gold in Fish." Assimilation, passing, accommodation, betrayal, selling out, blending in, integrating, abdicating—what's going on here? The literature portraying the recurrent struggle with these issues by new Americans not only teaches us much about the relative and simultaneous fluidity and immutability of personal identity, it also reminds us of the cost, the confusion, and the implications of the process of Americanization. As in life, in literature there are no answers—only consequences. Nothing is ever finally settled.[23]

NOTES

1. With apologies to T. S. Eliot, who, like Fannie Hurst, Thyra Samter Winslow, and Josephine Baker, relative contemporaries and fellow St. Louisans, also moved east, although much further east than Hurst and Winslow, and tried to assimilate into an old culture. And with thanks to Martha Baker, another St. Louisan and my contemporary, for this title.
2. "... *goldeneh* is from German for 'golden'; *medina* is Hebrew for 'country, land, province.' (1) Literally, 'golden country.' *Goldeneh medina* meant America: land of freedom, justice, opportunity—and

protection against pogroms. Rarely did I hear such overtones of gratitude as went into the utterance of this compound noun. (2) A fool's paradise. In irony or sarcasm, *goldeneh medina* is used to mean a miraculous hope that ends in disappointment." *The Joys of Yiddish* by Leo Rosten. New York: McGraw-Hill, 1968. 136.

3. Stories similar to this one, although I haven't found any as well written, and they tend to be more undisguisedly didactic, appeared regularly in the publications of various Jewish women's organizations.

4. See especially the prototypical story of this type in Anglo-American literature, the 1857 "A Marriage of Persuasion" by Susan Pettigru King Bowen reprinted in *Between Mothers and Daughters: Stories Across a Generation,* ed. Susan Koppelman. New York: The Feminist Press, 1985.

5. The best exploration of this subject of "becoming white" that I have discovered is "Jews in the U.S.: The Rising Costs of Whiteness" by Melanie Kaye/Kantrowitz in *Names We Call Home: Essays in Racial Identity,* eds. Becky Thompson and Tyagi Sangesta. New York: Routledge, 1995. She begins her essay with a quotation from an essay by James Baldwin's "On Being 'White' . . . and Other Lies," from *Essence* (April 1984). His paragraph and her subsequent one follow:

> It took generations, and a vast amount of coercion, before this became a white country. It is probable that it is the Jewish community—or more accurately, perhaps, its remnants—that in America has paid the highest and most extraordinary price for becoming white. For the Jews came here from countries where they were not white, and they came here in part because they were not white; and incontestably—in the eyes of Black Americans (and not only in those eyes)—American Jews have opted to become white. . . .

> Kaye/Kantrowitz continues, "Everything I think about Jews, whiteness, racism and contemporary U. S. society begins with this passage. What does it mean: *Jews opted to become white.* Did we opt? Did it work? Was it an illusion? Could we have opted otherwise? Can we still?"

6. "The Gold in Fish," *Cosmopolitan,* August 1925. Collected in Fannie Hurst's sixth volume of short stories: *Song of Life.* New York: A. A. Knopf, 1927. Reprinted in the fund-raising collection *More Aces; A Collection of Short Stories Compiled by the Community Workers of the New York Guild for the Jewish Blind.* New York: G. P. Putnam's Sons, 1925. The story was filmed as *The Younger Generation* in 1929 in 8 reels, black and white, 75 minutes long, directed by Frank Capra, by Columbia Pictures and was premiered March 4, 1929. The

screenplay was by Sonya Levien and the cast included Jean Hersholt, Rosa Rosanova, Lina Basquette, and Ricardo Cortez. See Patricia Erens, *The Jew in American Cinema* (p. 87–89) for extensive commentary on this film; her commentary begins: "Since Fannie Hurst's *Humoresque* opened the decade, it is most fitting that her story *The Younger Generation* bring the Ghetto Film to a close."

7. When I quote Yiddish words from Hurst's writing, I retain her spelling of those words whether or not they conform to the standardized transliterations established by the YIVO Institute. *Gefilte* fish is a traditional eastern European Jewish dish made from fish (often carp, sometimes two or more kinds of fish), bread crumbs or matzo meal, onions, celery, seasoning, and an egg if it's available and the cook thinks it's appropriate.

8. It is interesting to note that even back then, in 1925, it was more soigné to slip in a Frenchism now and then than a Yiddishism, or godforbid, a Polishism. Morris has chosen a French version of his first name, "Morris," which was probably an English version of the Yiddish "Moshe," which is a Yiddish version of the Hebrew "Moses." Alice Childress' comment on this whole Francophilia in language snobbery in the United States is instructive here:

> Consider *Black English* and the furor it causes. "Zis and zat" when uttered by the French is considered charming, but "dis and dat" as an Africanism is ridiculed as gross and ugly. The echo of European accents and linguistic spillovers in American "English" fall easily upon our ear. Africanisms cause a shudder. Many Blacks now say hail and farewell with the Italian *ciao*. So What? Maybe I shoulda stood in bed and not sperl ya day awready. Okay? Like enough with the jabber and the bla, bla, bla. Got it? See what I Mean?

This is taken from "A Candle in a Gale Wind: Alice Childress" in *Black Women Writers (1950–1980): A Critical Evaluation,* ed. Mari Evans. Garden City, New York: Anchor Press/Doubleday, 1984.

9. Another "source" of new names was the immigration officer gatekeeping the final steps into the New World at Ellis Island or other points of entry. Often, the official couldn't or pretended to be unable to understand and/or spell the name of the would-be immigrant and imposed a name with this message, "This will be your name in the United States." Sometimes the new name was imposed under the guise of benevolence: "You won't want *that* name in *this* country!"

10. One Jewish immigrant who seems to have agreed with Morris and Irma about the deficiencies of the name "Goldfish" changed his name to "Goldwyn." A story that circulated in Hollywood during the time when the film based on "The Gold in Fish" was made as "The Younger Generation" is that the name "Goldfish" was chosen by the film's

producer Jack Cohn as a not-so-subtle dig at another Hollywood mogul, Samuel Goldwyn. The rumor was based on the misunderstanding that the name "Goldfish" was the movie-maker's invention and not Fannie Hurst's.

11. I can find no indication of a periodical publication of this story. It was evidently first published in Winslow's first collection of short stories: *Picture Frames* by Thyra Samter Winslow. New York: Knopf, 1923. The book was widely and, for the most part, favorably reviewed, with a number of the reviewers mentioning that Winslow was a protégée of Edna Ferber. The story was subsequently reprinted eight times between 1934 and 1958, three times by the editorial duo of Burrell and Cerf and twice by Harold U. Ribelow. Three of the eight publications were in Jewish anthologies: *Jewish Caravan: Great Stories of Twenty-Five Centuries* (1935) edited by Leo Schwartz and in the two Ribelow collections: *These Are Your Children* (1952) and *Treasury of American Jewish Stories* (1958).

12. "A little over a century ago, in 1883, an aspiring writer of comic talents named Sholem Rabinowich ... published a satirical account of local politics in the St. Petersburg *Yiddishe Folkblat* and playfully signed it 'Sholom Aleichem.' ... [T]he ancient Hebrew salutation ... (its Arabic cognate *salaam aleykum* can be heard today through the Middle East) was a prescient choice. Meaning literally 'peace be upon you,' the phrase is used in Yiddish not as an everyday greeting but as a more emphatic one that is reserved for either old acquaintances long unmet or new ones just introduced. ... " Page 1 of "Introduction" by Hillel Halkin from *Tevye the Dairyman and The Railroad Stories by Sholom Aleichem.* Translated from the Yiddish and with an Introduction by Hillel Halkin. New York: Schocken Books, 1987. Mr. Halkin gives us two more terms to think about in our consideration of name-changing: 'alias' and 'pseudonym.'

13. The town of Noble, Oklahoma, adjacent to Norman, Oklahoma, home of the University of Oklahoma, has a huge sign at the city limits: "This city belongs to Jesus Christ." Personal communication from Drs. Barbara Hillyer and Constance Lindemann, 4 January 1996.

14. The use of hatred to increase circulation, reading, viewing, and listening audiences is a phenomenon that is as familiar to readers and listeners in the United States of the 1990s as it was to Americans during WWII. Hate continues to sell.

15. I chose this part of the world and this particular year because we have such good documentation. However, other places and other times were not necessarily safer for Jews. In *How We lived: A Documentary History of Immigrant Jews in America, 1880–1930* by Irving Howe and Kenneth Libo (New York: Richard Marek Publishers, 1979), the editors quote a letter sent to a Yiddish newspaper in New York in November 1905 by Sholom Aleichem:

Together with a number of families, my wife and
children and I are cowering under a storm of bullets over
our heads. . . . On the seventeenth. . . . a rumor was
spread abroad that orders had been given to attack the
Jews—and   the   attack   began   from   all
sides . . . soldiers . . . helped to rob, to beat, to
ravish, to despoil. Before our eyes and in the eyes of the
whole world, they helped to smash windows, break down
doors, break locks and to put booty in their pockets.
Before our eyes and the eyes of our children, they beat
Jews grievously—men, women and children—and they
shouted, "Money, give us your money." Before our eyes
women were hurled from windows and children thrown to
the cobblestones.

The local newspapers publish only one hundredth
part of the frightful details of the happenings in
Kiev. . . .

What shall we do? No place to hide. Gentiles will
not give shelter to Jews.

Brother, do something. Publish this in English as
well as in the Jewish press.

. . . if I must die, I am ready. . . . My people
are being consumed. The whole of Russian Jewry is in
danger. (16)

16. Wiesenthal acknowledges Walter Bick of Toronto for the dates of the
Petlyura pogroms in the Ukraine.
17. First in *The Cosmopolitan Magazine*, September 1917, also in *The
Best Short Stories of 1917* ed. Edward J. O'Brien, and included in her
third collection *Gaslight Sonatas,* New York: Harper and Bros., 1918;
Reprinted in *Famous Story Magazine*, December 1926; Also in
Modern American Short Stories, ed. Edward J. H. O'Brien, New York:
Dodd, 1932.
18. First in *The Cosmopolitan Magazine,* May 1921, included in her fifth
collection of stories, *The Vertical City*, New York: Harper and Bros.,
1922. Reprinted in *Famous Story Magazine,* August 1926. Filmed in
1928 as *Wheel of Chance* (black and white, silent, produced and
directed by Alfred Santell, with Richard Barthelme and Warner Oland).
19. Fannie Hurst is considered to be one of the important pioneers and/or
inventors of the field of public relations, making certain that her
persona was so well known that her work would be of interest to
readers on the basis of who she was in addition to what she wrote.
Hence, her name became an important resource or commodity to fund
raisers and organizers. She lent that resource and her personal time and
energy and money as well to many more causes than I can allude to
here. The point is that she was well aware that a name can be as much a
resource, a form of capital, as money or land.

20. I recognize that I am getting into murky waters here. Many people argue against the equation of body type with ethnic, class, or geographical factors. Distinguished literary scholar and Holocaust historian Myrna Goldenberg writes, "I used to think [that body type equates with ethnicity], but I don't anymore. People come in all sizes/shapes and categories, and these two variables are not mutually exclusive." Personal correspondence, January 1, 1996. Some observers insist that the entire range of somatypes is found among all groups of people, assuming the opportunity for sufficient nutrients, but that a malevolent admixture of racism, classism, xenophobia, and other forms of perceptual distortions leads some people to make these equations.
21. Among her stories about sex workers are "Back Pay," *Cosmopolitan* November 1919 and "Sob-Sister," *Metropolitan Magazine* February 1916.
22. For further discussion of this issue, see Eileen Teper Bender's article in *Fannie Hurst: The Woman and Her Work, A Collection of Essays,* ed. Susan Koppelman, University of Illinois Press, 1996 and read Hurst's *No Food with My Meals,* her 1935 memoir of the history of her own body-hatred and long struggle with what today are called eating disorders and what she then thought of as successful dieting.
23. I want to thank and acknowledge the careful reading of various drafts of this paper and the thoughtful feedback from Betty Burnett, Barbara Hillyer, Constance Lindemann, Myrna Goldenberg, Dennis Mills, Frances Koppelman, Annette Kolodny, and Ann Brown.

REFERENCES

Alvarez, Julia. *How the Garcia Girls Lost Their Accents.* New York, NY: Penguin, 1992.

Asimov, Isaac. "Seven Steps to Grand Master." *Nebula Awards: SFWA's Choices for the Best Science Fiction and Fantasy 1986.* Ed. George Zebrowski. New York: Harcourt, Brace, Jovanovich, 1988.

Bowen, Susan Pettigru King. "A Marriage of Persuasion." *Between Mothers and Daughters: Stories Across a Generation.* Ed. Susan Koppelman. New York: The Feminist Press, 1985.

Childress, Alice. "A Candle in a Gale Wind: Alice Childress." in *Black Women Writers (1950–1980): A Critical Evaluation.* Ed. Mari Evans. Garden City, New York: Anchor Press, 1984.

Cohn, Robert A. Review of *'66 Was a Good Year for Tourism. St. Louis Jewish Light.* September 27, 1995: 20.

Dinnerstein, Leonard. *Anti-Semitism in America.* London: Oxford University Press, 1994.

Erens, Patricia. *The Jew in American Cinema.* Bloomington: Indiana University Press, 1984.

Halkin, Hillel. "Introduction." *Tevye the Dairyman and the Railroad Stories by Sholom Aleichem.* trans. Hillel Halkin. New York: Schocken Books, 1987.

Howe, Irving, and Kenneth Libo. *How We Lived: A Documentary History of Immigrant Jews in America, 1880–1930.* New York: Richard Marek Publishers, 1979.

Hurst, Fannie. "The Gold in Fish." *Song of Life.* New York: Knopf, 1927.

Kaye/Kantrowitz, Melanie. "Jews in the U.S.: The Rising Costs of Whiteness." *Names We Call Home: Essays in Racial Identity.* Eds. Becky Thompson and Tyagi Sangesta. New York: Routledge, 1995.

Kincaid, Jamaica. "In Rouseau." *The New Yorker.* April 17, 1995: 98.

Not the Work of a Day. Published by the Anti-Defamation League (no date available).

Paley, Grace. "The Loudest Voice." *"May Your Days Be Merry and Bright" and Other Christmas Stories by Women.* Detroit: Wayne State University Press, 1988.

Rosten, Leo. *The Joys of Yiddish.* New York: McGraw-Hill, 1968. 136.

Shore, Viola Brothers. "Heritage." *"The Heritage" and Other Stories.* New York: George H. Dorm Co., 1921.

Telushkin, Rabbi Joseph. *Jewish Humor: What the Best Jewish Jokes Say About the Jews.* New York: Morrow, 1992.

Walker, Alice. "Everyday Use." in *Between Mothers and Daughters: Stories Across a Generation.* Ed. Susan Koppelman. New York: The Feminist Press, 1985. 230–239.

Winslow, Thyra Samter. "A Cycle of Manhattan." *Picture Frames.* New York, NY: Knopf, 1923.